I0642356

Conversations
with Yusef Komunyakaa

Literary Conversations Series
Peggy Whitman Prenshaw
General Editor

Conversations with Yusef Komunyakaa

Edited by Shirley A. James Hanshaw

University Press of Mississippi   Jackson

www.upress.state.ms.us

The University Press of Mississippi is a member of the Association
of American University Presses.

Copyright © 2010 by University Press of Mississippi
All rights reserved

First printing 2010

∞

Library of Congress Cataloging-in-Publication Data

Komunyakaa, Yusef.
 Conversations with Yusef Komunyakaa / edited by Shirley A. James Hanshaw.
     p. cm. — (Literary conversations series)
 Includes index.
 ISBN 978-1-60473-421-8 (alk. paper) — ISBN 978-1-60473-422-5 (pbk. : alk. paper) 1.
Komunyakaa, Yusef—Interviews. 2. Poets, American—20th century—Interviews. 3. African
American poets—Interviews. I. Hanshaw, Shirley A. J. II. Title.

 PS3561.O455Z46 2010
 811.54—dc22
  [B]   2009029887

British Library Cataloging-in-Publication Data available

Books by Yusef Komunyakaa

As Author

Dedications & Other Darkhorses, Laramie, WY: Rocky Mountain Creative Arts Journal, 1977.

Lost in the Bonewheel Factory, Amherst, MA: Lynx House, 1979.

Copacetic, Middletown, CT: Wesleyan University Press, 1984.

I Apologize for the Eyes in My Head, Middletown, CT: Wesleyan University Press, 1986.

Toys in a Field, Black River Press, 1986.

Dien Cai Dau, Middletown, CT: Wesleyan University Press, 1988.

February in Sydney, Matchbooks, 1989.

Magic City, Middletown, CT: Wesleyan University Press, 1992.

Neon Vernacular: New and Selected Poems 1977–1989, Middletown, CT: Wesleyan University Press, 1993.

Thieves of Paradise, Middletown, CT: Wesleyan University Press, 1998.

Talking Dirty to the Gods, New York: Farrar, Straus and Giroux, 2000.

Pleasure Dome: New and Collected Poems, 1975–1999, Middletown, CT: Wesleyan University Press, 2001.

Taboo: The Wishbone Trilogy—Part I, Farrar, Straus & Giroux, 2004.

As Editor

Jazz Poetry Anthology, co-edited with Sascha Feinstein, Bloomington: Indiana University Press, 1991.

The Second Set: The Jazz Poetry Anthology, Vol. 2, co-edited with Sascha Feinstein, Bloomington: Indiana University Press, 1996.

Blue Notes: Essays, Interviews, and Commentaries, co-edited with Radiclani Clytus, Lansing: University of Michigan Press, 2000.

Collaborations

Slipknot. Opera commissioned by Northwestern University. A libretto based on the life and death of an enslaved man named Arthur in Massachusetts with composer T. J. Anderson, staged workshop, 2003.

Testimony. Performance piece commissioned by Australian Broadcasting Corporation. A libretto dedicated to Charlie Parker accompanied by an eighteen-song work composed and arranged by Sandy Evans, an American jazz artist living in Australia, 1999.

The Insomnia of Fire, by Nguyen Quang Thieu, co-translated with Martha Collins. Amherst: University of Massachusetts Press, 1995.

Love Notes from the Madhouse. 8th Harmonic Breakdown, 1998. A CD recording in collaboration with Dennis Gonzalez and jazz saxophonist John Tchicai and ensemble at Chopin Theater, Chicago.

Herido. Another collaboration with jazz musician Dennis Gonzalez. A live improvisational performance featuring Mark Deutsch on sitar, Susie Ibarra on percussion, and Sugar Blue on harmonica, 2002.

Thirteen Kinds of Desire. Cornucopia, 2000. A collection of Komunyakaa lyrics performed by jazz vocalist Pamela Knowles.

Shangri-La. A libretto. A chamber ensemble piece performed in 2005.

Gilgamesh. Wesleyan University Press, 2004. A dramatic adaptation of the ancient Babylonia epic in collaboration with dramaturg and theater producer Chad Gracia.

Deacons. A drama written by Komunyakaa and directed by Kemati Porter. World premiere at Passage Theater Company in New Jersey, 2007.

Covenant: Scenes from an African American Church, in collaboration with Tyagan Miller. Bloomington: Indiana University Press, 2007.

For Lost Words. An electronic sonic symphony, for which Komunyakaa wrote text and lyrics, featuring composer Vince di Mum on a multiplicity of keyboards with vocalist Julianne Chester. World premiere at Passage Theater Company in New Jersey, 2007.

Changing the Changes in Poetry and Song. A CD ranging from blues to post-fusion; collaboration with poet/singer Hermine Pinson and singer, songwriter, and guitarist Tomas Doncker with his trio. On-stage release party at Passage Theater Company, New Jersey, 2007.

Contents

Introduction

Like a wise griot or a conjure man transplanted to the Louisiana bayous from his ancestral homeland, Yusef Komunyakaa cooks up a callaloo of poetic images that excite the senses in a familiar yet enigmatic way. Indeed, he tells Fran Gordon, in an interview that followed a reception observing the twenty-fifth anniversary of the end of the Vietnam War, that language itself is "an act of conjuring." Cultural and literary critics familiar with his expansive oeuvre comment on his uncanny ability to write poetry wherein reality and imagination are constantly "fighting and reshaping each other," an observation Rebecca Carroll made when she interviewed Komunyakaa for her interview collection titled *Swing Low: Black Men Writing*.[1] "Terror and beauty" often resided side-by-side in the rural south of his youth, he maintains in a radio interview with Rebekah Presson; consequently, a writer from the south claims the oppression that existed simultaneously with moments of "severe beauty and elegance."[2] This exploration of contradictions in life creates the tension that Komunyakaa feels is necessary for good poetry. His poetic language is grounded in the African American vernacular, combined with what he tells Suzan Sherman is "an acquired literary language," transporting the reader to a realm of experience within and beyond the human psyche—from ruminations on seemingly insignificant life forms ("Ode to the Maggot") to some of the most compelling historical and life-altering events of our time, such as the Vietnam War ("Facing It") and Hurricane Katrina ("Requiem").

The nature of this compilation, covering interviews over a period of years spanning 1985 to 2007, allows for some repetitiveness. Being asked the same question by different interviewers elicits overlapping responses; however, the content of each interview offers information different from or beyond the scope of the others. Insightful and provocative questions from the interviewers, as well as audience members during live performances of Komunyakaa's work, make the collection stimulating and provide a gauge of the reading public's enduring interest in his poetry. Interview selections included focus not only on Komunyakaa's poetic career but also on his collaborations with other artists. They reveal the diversity and the magnitude of the Pulitzer Prize winner's corpus that is growing exponentially as this document is in preparation. In fact, the difficulty of documenting his output lies in his ability to produce at such an incredible rate—and, by most accounts, all of it is exceptionally good. Respectful of copyright laws and to avoid infringement, I omit passages of Komunyakaa's poetry (indicated with brackets) that either he reads or others cite in the interviews. Audio- and videotaped productions have been transcribed with as much accuracy as possible and "silently" edited for publication purposes.

Born James Willie Brown Jr. in Bogalusa, Louisiana, in 1947, Komunyakaa is the eldest of five children. His parents were James Willie Brown Sr., a carpenter, and Mildred Brown. In "Komunyakaa's Riff," he tells Lary Bloom that his father was pragmatic, while his mother, who bought the family a set of encyclopedias, encouraged him to read, thereby piquing his thirst for knowledge. An avid reader from an early age, he read the Bible from cover to cover twice and later became interested in mythology. Though his father could neither read nor write, he was a craftsman superbly skilled at carpentry. Suffice it to say that Komunyakaa is a composite of both parents: a wise wordsmith who uses the precision and craftsmanship of a carpenter with the encyclopedic knowledge of the thinker to craft some of the finest contemporary poetry of his generation.

On his sickbed, Komunyakaa's father asked him to write a poem for his birthday. This request came as a surprise, according to Komunyakaa, because his father never took an interest in his writing and eschewed it as a "real" profession. In fact, writing that poem was the most difficult assignment he has ever had, he told Jacki Lyden on National Public Radio when he was in New Jersey for the Geraldine R. Dodge Poetry Festival.[3] Despite their different interests, James Sr. during his son's childhood would occasionally demonstrate for him certain aspects of carpentry. It was not until after his father's death at age sixty-one that Komunyakaa was able to write a poignant elegy dedicated to him, titled "Songs for My Father," which is reminiscent of the relationship between father and son portrayed in "Those Winter Sundays" by Robert Hayden, a poet who, as Komunyakaa relates in an interview with Terrance Hayes, greatly influenced him.

Like his father, who would measure each piece of lumber five or six times to get it right before sawing it to the exact length, Komunyakaa tells Toi Derricotte in a videotaped interview that he meticulously revises his poetry, honing the language to produce the precision and technical excellence that have endeared him to scholars, critics, and students alike. Despite being unable to read or write, his father could measure and predict with amazing precision the amount of building material needed for carpentry jobs. In retrospect, Komunyakaa tells Radiclani Clytus, it was not until later in life that he came to appreciate his father's craftsmanship as a carpenter and to realize that he was actually a "literary" mentor because his technique for accuracy taught Komunyakaa the precision and concision that he applies in his own editing process,[4] sometimes revising a poem of 150 lines and reducing it to 40 or 50. Also during the editing process he reads his poems aloud because, as he tells David Lehman, he considers the ear to be "a great editor."[5]

Yusef Komunyakaa is a name that the poet acquired later in life as a tribute to his grandfather. Komunyakaa reveals to Tony Barnstone and Michael Garabedian that retrieval of his ancestral surname signified an act of self-naming, not in a political but rather in a personal sense. Expressing the personal liberation he felt with the name change, he says the act of "naming/renaming," that he also employs in his poetry, is "a ritual of trying to get it right." When he was a little boy, a shroud of secrecy surrounded his grandfather, a stowaway on a ship from the West Indies, who slipped into this country and was forced to relinquish his surname, Komunyakaa. He tells William Baer that he remembers as a young boy seeing a picture of his great-grandparents who were such "grand people." So one day he cornered his grandmother and urged her to tell him the grandfather's story. Family oral history tells of the stowaway grandfather getting off the ship wearing one girl's shoe and one boy's shoe, an image that the poet carried with him over the years and later captured in the poem "Mismatched Shoes," a tribute to the relative he never knew but honored by reclaiming his name.

Engaging and intense in conversation, Komunyakaa is quite humble in spite of his numerous awards and accolades, the most prominent being the Pulitzer Prize for Poetry that he won in 1994 for *Neon Vernacular: New and Selected Poems, 1977–1989*, the first African American male poet to be so honored. He also won the prestigious Kingsley Tufts Award, the Los Angeles Times Book Prize in Poetry, the William Faulkner Award (from Université de Rennes in France), the Furious Flower Award, the Hanes Poetry Prize, the Levinson Prize, the John Berryman Award, and the Ruth Lilly Poetry Award, to name a few. Referring to Komunyakaa as "understated and modest," Jeffrey Walker interviewed him in his cinder-block office at Indiana University where he was an English professor when he won the Pulitzer. Humbled by his selection for this most prestigious honor, he continued with his daily routine, telling Walker that he would teach his 4:00 P.M. class that day and later "sit down and think about it." His extended family's reaction to his being a Pulitzer recipient is the subject of a lighthearted article that Australian fiction writer and Komunyakaa's former wife Mandy Sayer wrote in 2005.[6]

Komunyakaa's humility and accessibility are two attributes that I discerned when I first met him at the University of Mississippi where he had been invited to speak in the Grisham Visiting Writers Series. Our conversation occurred at the end of a creative writing class taught by fiction writer Randall Kenan who, as Writer-in-Residence at University of Mississippi, had invited Komuyakaa to speak to his students. My interview, "Achieving Clarity through Contrasts," is published in this collection for the first time. Other interviewers, some with whom I communicated while preparing this volume, as well as collaborators on several artistic projects with Komunyakaa, also note his gracious demeanor and "quiet presence," that is often punctuated with a "mischievous smile."[7] A prolific writer, he has penned fifteen books of poetry from 1977 to 2008, turning out poetry collections nearly every other year at the beginning of his career and later publishing two in the same year (*I Apologize for the Eyes in My Head* and *Toys in a Field*, 1988). His Pulitzer Prize–winning volume was published only a year after another major collection, *Magic City* (1992).

While renovating his house on 818 Piety Street in New Orleans, the site where Rudolph Lewis conducted an interview with him in 1985, Komunyakaa suddenly began to recall his experiences in Vietnam. By this time fourteen years had elapsed since the war, but he said that the semi-tropical heat during the summer in Louisiana and the way sunlight shone through shadows in the room conjured up images of the landscape in Vietnam, where shadows lurked behind the tall grass in sweltering heat. As the images "tumbled forth," he tells Dan Webster, he began to formulate a poem in his head as he ascended and descended the ladder, the result being "Somewhere Near Phu Bai." This is one of the poems included in his award-winning collection of Vietnam War poetry titled *Dien Cai Dau* (an expression meaning "crazy" that the Vietnamese used to refer to American soldiers), the style of which he tells Kali Tal was greatly influenced by classical surrealism.[8] Tal moderated a 1998 symposium, "War, Poetry, and Ethics," at the U.S. Air Force Academy, with a panel that included Komunyakaa and four other Vietnam veteran writers—John Balalban, Dale Rittersbusch, W. D. Ehrhart, and D. F. Brown.

Poets William Matthews and Robert Hass cite *Dien Cai Dau*, which includes what is perhaps the most anthologized Vietnam War poem, "Facing It," as among the "best writing on the war."[9] Many of the poems in the collection were difficult to write, Komunyakaa tells David Houghtaling, and "Facing It" created a standard for the rest of poems in the book. His war experience, as well as that of Tim O'Brien (a fellow Vietnam War veteran and author of *The Things They Carried*) and Alex Vernon (veteran of the first

Gulf War), served as the subject of a Veteran's Day special edition of *Talk of the Nation* that Neil Conan hosted on National Public Radio in 2004.[10] Komunyakaa tells Conan that his tour of duty in Vietnam as a journalist changed him by teaching him to "critique the violence," causing an "internal dialogue" that has to do with survival of the psyche and that leads to putting oneself "on trial." Such internal interrogation caused some veterans to resort to alcoholism, homelessness, or even suicide. To cope when he returned home from the war, Komunyakaa told me that he threw himself into university studies.

Though in many of the poetry volumes he uses free verse extensively, Komunyakaa also experiments with traditional versification, such as quatrains and tercets. In *Talking Dirty to the Gods* (2000), for instance, he tells Daniel Cross Turner that he desired to achieve a kind of "compression that expands."[11] Consequently, he devised a four-stanza, four-line structure in 132 poems to give the "illusion of symmetry." In this poetry collection, Komunyakaa creates his own mythology out of the flotsam and jetsam of African American and Euro-American culture. In *Taboo: The Wishbone Trilogy, Part One* (2004), he uses three-line stanzas that allow him to create the "illusion of control" as well as command a visual presence. One commentator mentions the "elegant simplicity" with which Komunyakaa in this volume retrieves from history persons of African descent, some well-known and others obscure, placing them in the foreground while providing a "dead-on glimpse of how the fear of—and attraction to—darker races has spawned racism in lighter ones."[12]

Characterized by imagistic compression and surrealistic forays into the human psyche, rhythmically undergirded with bluesy timbres and jazzy riffs, the poetry of Yusef Komunyakaa is what some would call an "eargasmic" experience, especially when he delivers his poems orally. Like the jazz artist, he feels that a poet must "know the tradition," i.e., conventional forms such as the sonnet and sestina, before breaking the rules, then later improvising to develop a personal style. Improvisation, he tells Suzan Sherman, allows him to achieve the element of surprise in poetry, a corollary to which in jazz is the blue note, that impossible, unattainable note that all great jazzmen attempt to reach. The poet's task is to make discoveries during the creative process rather than tying things up into a nice "gift box." One jazz artist he admires, particularly for the spiritual dimension in his music is Duke Ellington, Komunyakaa says in conversation with E. Ethelbert Miller who interviewed him at the Arts Club of Washington, DC, in conjunction with the Charlin Jazz Society's Duke Ellington Centennial Commission Project.

I told Komunyakaa that when I read his poetry, I see colors. This painterly technique is one of the topics that Jeffery Dodd and Jessica Moll discussed when they interviewed Komunyakaa on April 21, 2006, the night before he gave a poetry reading for Get Lit!, the *American Poetry Review*'s twenty-fifth anniversary celebration in Spokane, Washington. In what he sees as the relationship between poetry and visual art, Komunyakaa explains how colors move on the canvas, creating a dialogue with the images, and how the spaces which equal silence between the images create tension in both the visual arts and poetry. In a videotaped interview with Tony Bolden at the Furious Flower II[13] event, Komunyakaa describes his poetry as "word paintings." His work is informed by visual experiences because as a child growing up in rural Louisiana he was keenly conscious of what was going on around him, such as the rituals of animals. The palette on which he paints his word pictures is an emotional landscape that he internalized from his rural upbringing. But he also views this internalization as a universal human trait, that wherever a person moves he carries with him an "emotional and psychological landscape" that colors everything he does. He told Ernest Suarez during an interview at Suarez's home in 1999 that at one time he considered becoming a painter, but since he did not possess that kind of artistic talent, he decided instead to use language, or images, to paint verbal pictures in his poetry.[14]

In a 1986 interview during his tenure at Indiana University, Bloomington, Komunyakaa tells Vince Gotera, whom he formerly taught and mentored, that he began to write in 1969 during his stint in the military as a journalist; however his poetry career did not begin until 1973.[15] Conscientious to a fault, Komunyakaa prefers writing every day, often jotting down notes on a pad next to his bed upon awaking. He told me that he often works on three books at a time, constantly composing in his head. In Kristen Naca's interview he discusses his five-stage poetic technique; however, as far as teaching poetry is concerned, his aim is not to influence his students with his style of poetry but rather to help them "hear their own music," as he tells Richard Mathews.[16] Furthermore, he tells David Richards that his poetry interrogates the boundary between "beauty and terror" that creates "artistic tension." Memory and forgetting play a creative tug of war in Komunyakaa's poetry. In his interview with Sally Dawidoff he expresses his definition of poetry as "celebration and confrontation." He admits that his reflections on his war experience served as a catalyst for returning to childhood memories and that if he had not written about the Vietnam War, then he would not have dealt with his childhood in the poems that comprise *Magic City*.[17]

A jazz aficionado, Komunyakaa has co-edited with Sascha Feinstein two collections of jazz poetry.[18] The tendency, consequently, has been to refer to Komunyakaa as a jazz poet, prompting one interviewer to ask if he listens to jazz while writing poetry. To the contrary, he disavows the artifice of jazz accompaniments that are a throwback to the beat poets of the fifties. Rather, he says, there is an internalization of the jazz impulse expressed in his poetry stylistically as the oscillation between short and long lines that simulate swing, alternating with silence between the lines. Rhythmically, Elizabeth Cho says in her interview with Komunyakaa, the music in his poetry is so discernible that she found herself drumming and tapping her feet with the sound of the poems as he read in the Schuerer Room at Swarthmore College in 1998. He tells her that when he was a young boy growing up in Bogalusa, he would listen to his mother's radio tuned to New Orleans stations that introduced him to the rhythms of gospel, blues, and jazz, the latter of which characterizes the tonality and rhythm of his poetic canon. She notes, further, that not only in his readings but also in his conversation is a musical quality apparent in his baritone voice.

To Komunyakaa silence is an integral part of poetry and music. On the page in poetic expression as well as in musical composition it creates tension as a space for tonal contrasts. Silence in jazz, for instance, is evidenced through modulation. Among jazz artists, Thelonious Monk holds the distinction as a "technician of silence," an appellation that Komunyakaa accords the jazz great in an interview with Kevin Bezner. Indeed, he says that language is "our first music," with the body as amplifier, an observation he makes in his interview with G. F. Mitrano.[19] Consequently, when poetry embraces sounds made by instruments, the two shouldn't collide; they should work together to produce "a whole sound" that is not harmonious but rather a "lyrical discord that creates tension and thought" about life and its implications. Such a philosophy probably led to Komunyakaa's collaborative efforts with other artists.

In addition to turning out several poetry collections in rapid succession over the years, this consummate multi-disciplinarian leaps across genre boundaries to discover common ground with other artists. Consequently, in recent years he has collaborated across a variety of genres—music, dance, drama, visual arts—to produce cutting-edge performance pieces, blending text and music in the form of song lyrics, librettos, and verse-plays that almost defy categorization. Several interviews attest to these collaborations with blues and jazz musicians, classical music composers, operatic producers, and dramaturgs.

As far as the origin of these collaborations is concerned, Komunyakaa tells Michael Collins that he does not have to seek such opportunities because "they seek me out."[20] No other poet traverses the artificial boundaries between poetry and the other arts with such adeptness while maintaining "mutual respect and trust for the talents of each artist," ingredients that, composer T. J. Anderson says in his interview, are essential to success during the creative process. For instance, in collaboration with Chad Gracia, Komunyakaa transports into the twenty-first century the ancient Sumerian epic *Gilgamesh* in a verse-play adaptation. The themes of loss, death, and grief that resonate in this primeval text Gracia finds present in Komunyakaa's work as well, prompting Gracia to ask him to pen the dramatic version which they brought to the stage.

Komunyakaa says in a 2007 interview[21] that he was concerned about his lack of experience as a playwright when Gracia approached him with the project. However, the dramaturg convinced him that the desired product would be a language-driven, as opposed to a plot-driven, play, as Gracia is a founding member of Inverse Theater (i.e., theater in verse) in Manhattan. The idea of creating a lyrical narrative for performance appealed to Komunyakaa. Therefore, his wordsmithing complemented Gracia's dramatic vision, resulting in a dramatic reading that a group of actors delivered in 2004. The completed adaptation of the five thousand-year-old epic was published in 2006.[22]

Shangri-La is another performance piece that had a lengthy gestation period. The kernel of an idea for this classical performance piece began in 1990 when Komunyakaa was on his way back to Vietnam where he would join other American veterans of the Vietnam War to meet with authors from the Vietnamese Writers' Union. His plane, unfortunately, was delayed overnight in Bangkok where he witnessed the sex trade in full swing at a club in the hotel where he found lodging. Disgusted, he returned to his room and continued to Vietnam the following day. Some eight years later he read a magazine article highlighting the problem of men from the West engaging in the so-called "pleasures" of this Eastern "paradise" then later committing suicide as a result of their inability to free themselves from the paradisiacal illusion. So he contacted jazz drummer/composer Susie Ibarra, and she readily agreed to write the musical score while Komunyakaa wrote the libretto for *Shangri-La*.

In addition to being a dramatist, Komunyakaa is a lyricist, collaborating with blues and jazz musicians. His blues CD with poet/blues singer Hermine Pinson, and producer/guitarist Tomas Doncker is titled *Changing the*

Change. He also collaborated with composer William Banfield on a blues piece titled *Free Blues Suite.* Performed by a double chamber ensemble, it is based on Komunyakaa's poem "The No Good Blues." This piece is so powerful, according to Banfield, that twice it literally "knocked me off my chair."[23] While in Sydney, Australia, Komunyakaa also penned lyrics for jazz singer Pamela Knowles. Their collaboration resulted in a CD titled *Thirteen Kinds of Desire.*

In 1999 musician, composer, arranger Dennis Gonzalez received an invitation from Tony Getsug to assemble a group of jazz musicians to collaborate with Komunyakaa on what later became known as the *Herido* Project, which was performed at St. James Cathedral in Chicago. The group included musicians Susie Ibarra (percussion), Mark Deutsch (electric bass, sitar, and sitar bass), Sugar Blue (harmonica), and Gonzalez (trumpet, keyboard, and samples), none of whom had previously performed together. Playing off each other, the musical ensemble was essentially engaging in an improvisatory performance, as Komunyakaa added the fifth "instrument" through the musicality of his voice in improvised poetic lines. Gonzalez titled the collaboration *herido*, a Spanish word meaning "wounded."

Getsug, founder and producer of 8th Harmonic Breakdown, a recording company, was involved in another collaboration. For this venture he supplied the title *Love Notes from the Madhouse* for a CD that Komunyakaa recorded with John Tchicai and his jazz ensemble. Perhaps one of the most innovative jazz collaborations is *Testimony*, a musical piece that Komunyakaa developed while on sabbatical in Australia in 1995. Christopher Williams, a radio producer at the Australian Broadcasting Corporation in Sydney, asked him, following a poetry reading on ABC Radio, if he would write a libretto that celebrates jazz and its relationship to gospel and blues. Komunyakaa accepted the challenge and decided to write a poem that pays tribute to Charlie "Bird" Parker, the legendary jazz musician who revolutionized the medium in the 1940s. The result was a lengthy, lush "tonal narrative" in fourteen movements, more like a musical composition than a poem, that bears witness to the genius as well as the humanity of the inventor of BeBop.

After he mentioned the idea of collaborating with Australian jazz saxophonist and composer Sandy Evans, she enthusiastically accepted. Having first appeared in print in *Brilliant Corners*, a literary magazine edited by Sascha Feinstein whose interview of Komunyakaa is included in this collection, "Testimony" is the centerpiece of his poetry collection *Thieves of Paradise.* Commissioned by the ABC Radio Drama, *Testimony*, featuring the Australian Art Orchestra, had its official world premiere in Sydney in 2002, marking a milestone in Australian music theater. In these musical collaborations poetry and music work complementarily.

Komunyakaa's penchant for creating performance pieces that appeal to the intellect while simultaneously satisfying the musical impulse has led to several operatic collaborations. One of these, *Slipknot*, was presented in a staged workshop at Northwestern University School of Music in 2003. African American composer T. J. Anderson wrote the musical score and Komunyakaa the libretto for this opera based on the true historical account of an enslaved man known only as Arthur who lived during the 1800s in the Massachusetts colony. Wrongfully convicted of raping a forty-year-old white woman, he receives a sentence of death by hanging. When the authorities call a clergyman to the gallows to get a confession, the twenty-one-year-old is unrepentant. Refusing to confess to a crime of rape that he did not commit, Arthur defiantly goes to the gallows singing of freedom.

Opera is also the genre for another creative production, *Ish-Scoodah*, based on historical evidence. This performance piece chronicles the story of sculptress Edmonia Lewis, of Native American and African American ancestry, who attended Oberlin College in the 1800s and later exiled herself to Italy. Lewis intrigues Komunyakaa because as early as the nineteenth century she had "the audacity to be an artist with black skin." An adaptation of Komunyakaa's poem "Hagar's Daughter," the libretto is accompanied by the musical score of William Banfield, a black composer, pianist, and guitarist and performed by dancer Aleta Hayes. Overlapping his development of *Ish-Scoodah* and *Shangri-La*, Komunyakaa had in mind yet another performance piece, *The Reincarnated Beethoven*, on which he collaborated again with composer T. J. Anderson (*Slipknot*) and The Boys Choir of Harlem. It relates the tragic story of a child prodigy from the Bronx named DeWitt White. This young musical genius, with talent comparable to that of Bach and Beethoven, lacked the funds to make his dreams of becoming a renowned composer and classical pianist a reality. When he was still a youngster, his mother died from AIDS. Orphaned, vulnerable, and living in poverty on the streets, he succumbed to a life of drug use and dealing that ended in his untimely death at age seventeen.

Dream Horses was an opera in progress at the time that Michael Collins conducted his interview in 2005. It developed, or as Komunyakaa puts it, *"Dream Horses* rode in," while he was still working on *The Reincarnated Beethoven.* Hal France, conductor of Opera Omaha, called and left a voicemail message indicating that he wanted to do an opera about the trial of Chief Standing Bear. With some reluctance, as he was already involved in two other collaborative projects, Komunyakaa finally returned the call and became fascinated with the story. Prior to 1876 Native Americans were not considered "human beings" and could not own land or appear in court on their own behalf. Consequently, the Chief had to prove that he was human before laying claim to land that was rightfully his so that he could bury his son. The collaborators, or as Komunyakaa calls them "co-conspirators," on this operatic project were Rhoda Levine and Anthony Davis. In addition to Collins's interview that discusses these collaborations, the 2005 *Callaloo* special issue on Komunyakaa[24] includes excerpts from the song lyrics, librettos, and dramatic pieces as well as selections from the various musical scores.

The special issue of *Callaloo* also published translations of several poems. As a testament to Komunyakaa's ability to capture the essence of the human experience across cultural, racial, and ethnic boundaries, his poetry has been translated into several languages, including Italian, Czech, Polish, Arabic, Spanish, Brazilian Portuguese, and Bengali. His poem "How I See Things" transcends the southern American landscape that it portrays, according to Khaleed Hegazzi,[25] who translated the poem into Arabic for a bilingual Arabic/English literary journal. Goutam Datta, a poet and playwright from India, is drawn to the improvisatory aspects of Komunyakaa's work because of the similarities between jazz and Indian classical music, both of which, he notes, "thrive on improvisation." I have included Datta's interview because it provides background for his decision to invite Komunyakaa to India for the Kolkata (Bengali for Calcutta) Book Fair and to co-edit an anthology of African American poetry, the first to be translated into Bengali and published in India.[26] The format of this interview differs from that of the others, as it includes entries in a diary that Datta kept to chronicle his and Komunyakaa's travels in India.

Of Polish descent, Katarzyna Jakubiak was a Ph.D. candidate in translation theory when she began translating some of Komunyakaa's poems for a book that would be published in her native Poland. Another Polish writer, Michal Tabaczynski, notes the "cross-cultural dialogue" that Komunyakaa's poetry expresses through a discourse of exclusion and liberation, themes to which he can relate as a member of an ethnic minority in his own country. Czechoslovakian writer Josef Jarab was overcome with emotion while reading the poems focusing on Komunyakaa's coming-of-age experiences in *Magic City*, especially "Venus's Flytraps," that caused intense memories of his own childhood in Czechoslovakia to surface. Also he says "Songs of My Father" provided glimpses into his relationship with his own father.

Komunyakaa is a very private person, seldom discussing details of his personal life; therefore, I include the following two interviews because they provide an intimate glimpse of the reticent poet. Lary Bloom's 2002 interview provides a portrait of Komunyakaa as a doting father interacting with his precocious seventeen-month-old son, Jehan, named for Shah Jehan who built the Taj Mahal. Bloom conversed with the poet in the kitchen of his hundred-year-old home in Trenton, New Jersey, just prior to his giving a reading at the Sunken Garden Poetry Festival where he had been chosen to kick off its eleventh season. Topics of discussion range from the importance of silence in the text to a book-length poem titled *The Autobiography of My Alter Ego* that was in progress, which are interspersed with the sounds of an active and inquisitive toddler. These sounds, unfortunately, would soon be silenced in 2003 with the untimely deaths of the child and his mother, Indian poet Reetika Vazirani, with whom Komunyakaa had been in a long-term relationship.

Shortly thereafter Chris Hedges writes in his interview published in the *New York Times*, appropriately titled "A Poet of Suffering, Endurance, and Healing," that throughout his life Komunyakaa has been experiencing a process of "healing through remembering," bearing witness to violence during childhood in the rural south and as a soldier in the Vietnam War. Such considerations prompt the interviewer to reflect on the funeral where a family friend read "Venus's Flytraps," one of Komunyakaa's poems that begins: "I am five . . ." an age, Hedges reflects, "his child would never reach." An article in the *Washington Post* describes Vazirani as "warm and open," "brilliant," "beautiful," and "gifted."[27] Komunyakaa and Vazirani both had been offered jobs at Emory University prior to the tragedy.

Working at his usual indefatigable rate, Komunyakaa continues to produce outstanding poetry. One of his most recent works is "Requiem," which some would call an "occasional" poem because it addresses the devastation of Hurricane Katrina. However, that categorization would be too limiting, as it addresses the entire history of the Crescent City, New Orleans, including the property on which the city is built that was "stolen" from Native Americans, as Komunyakaa attests in the interview with Tod Marshall. *Warhorses* is another recently penned work, the first section of which is titled "Love in the Time of War." He tells Marshall in a 2006 interview that the poetry in this collection only tangentially deals with the present Iraq War, while it addresses "multiple dimensions" of war as it relates to the human proclivity toward violence. From this point forward one can only speculate about the direction that Komunyakaa will take in his poetry or with whom he will collaborate to produce multi-artistic experiments that are as delightful as they are thought provoking.

With gratitude I acknowledge the contribution of Yusef Komunyakaa who graciously granted me an interview despite being pressed for time to deliver a poetry reading in the Grisham Visiting Writers Series at the University of Mississippi. His personable and humble demeanor made my job easy. I thank, also, Dan Williams, former English Department Chair, University of Mississippi, who interceded on my behalf for a spot on the poet's itinerary. In the process of researching another book focusing on African American veteran writers of the Vietnam War, I was led to choose Komunyakaa during discussions with Joan Wiley Hall, to whom I am deeply indebted for her guidance and *joie de vivre.*

Thanks are in order for all the authors and publishers who granted permission for me to use interviews. Also, I extend regrets to those who were equally accommodating of my requests but whose interviews could not be included in the final manuscript because of publication exigencies.

Brenda Hampton has been my right hand, providing publications assistance and keeping me organized throughout the publication process. Despite both of our health challenges, she stayed the course; consequently, I owe her a tremendous debt of gratitude. I also thank Janice James for her indexing expertise.

I would be remiss if I did not express my appreciation to my literary mentor, Jerry Ward, for providing expert guidance and advice as well as being a sounding board, and Jay Watson for valuable information regarding permissions. Moreover, I thank both of them for their usual encouraging words. Farah Miller (University of Mississippi) and Kristie Cole (graduate assistant, Mississippi State University) provided valuable services. Thanks, also, to the following: Richard Raymond, English Department Chair (Mississippi State University), who championed my efforts to secure an Academic Excellence Fund grant to help defray expenses related to this book project; William Person, for his help locating a graduate assistant; and Aretha Jones Cook.

Librarians and information specialists have provided invaluable assistance in bringing this project to fruition: John Cloy and Janice Smith, as well as the Interlibrary Loan Staff (University of Mississippi); Gail Peyton, Reference/Outreach, and Access Services staff (Mississippi State University); and Rose P. Marshall, who provided resource references as well as inspiration and encouragement (University of South Carolina at Aiken). I also thank the following people for moral support: David Willson, former editor, *Viet Nam*

Generation; Ousseynou Traore, William Paterson University, New Jersey; Colby Kullman (University of Mississippi), who encouraged me to publish my interview; and Linda Simone (Manhattanville College) who interceded on my behalf to get current contact information for Komunuyakaa.

I am grateful for the patience and kindness of two people who offered invaluable guidance ushering me through the publications process: Seetha Srinivasan, Director Emerita, and Walter Biggins, Acquiring Editor, University Press of Mississippi. Most importantly, I thank God for giving me strength, endurance, and stamina to see this publication to its completion, and my children, Okera and Nneka, for being my "cheerleaders" in this and all my efforts—professional and personal. I hope I did not overlook anyone; but if I did, I hope they will "charge it to my head and not my heart."

This book is dedicated, in memoriam, to my parents, Mr. T. J. and Mrs. Mary Alice Gillespie James, whose moral values shaped me and gave me the desire to learn and teach.

SAJH

1. Rebecca Carroll, *Swing Low, Black Men Writing* (New York: Crown, 1995), 131.

2. Radiclani Clytus, "Notations in Blue," in *Blue Notes: Essays, Interviews and Commentaries*, eds. Yusef Komunyakaa and Radiclani Clytus (Ann Arbor: U of Michigan P, 2000), 139.

3. "Interview: Poet Yusef Komunyakaa Reads One of His Poems and Talks of His Father's Influence on His Life." National Public Radio. *All Things Considered:* Weekend Edition, 24 September 2000.

4. Clytus, 138.

5. "Yusef Komunyakaa—Interview and Reading." *The Cortland Review Online Literary Magazine*, 10 November 1999. http://www.cortlandreview.com/features/millenium/index.html.

6. Sayer published an article in *The Weekend Australian* (NSW Country Edition, Review Section, 19 February 2005) that lightheartedly bemoans how the extended families of writers often misunderstand the significance of their work. For example, she says: "When my ex-husband, Yusef Komunyakaa, won the Pulitzer Prize for poetry in 1994 (being the first African American man to have done so), . . . my teenage brother left a note on the fridge for my mother: Yusef won the Paulette Surprise" (p. B02). In 1985 Komunyakaa married Sayer, a union that ended in divorce ten years later.

7. Chad Gracia, "Collaborating with Yusef Komunyakaa: The Creation of *Gilgamesh*," *Callaloo* 28.3 (Summer 2005): 542.

8. "War, Poetry, & Ethics," *War, Literature, and the Arts: An International Journal of the Humanities* 10.2 (Fall/Winter 1998), 6.

9. "Yusef Komunyakaa," poets.org from the Academy of American Poets, http://www.poets.org/poet.php/prmPID/22.

10. "Analysis: How the Experience of War Changes People," *Talk of the Nation*, National Public Radio, 11 November 2004, http://www.npr@newsbank.com.

11. Daniel Cross Turner, "Remaking Myth in Yusef Komunyakaa's *Talking Dirty to the Gods, Taboo*, and *Gilgamesh*: An Interview," forthcoming in The Mississippi Quarterly.

12. John Freeman. "Paint It Black" *Times Picayune*, 4 November 2004, 6.

13. The mission of the Furious Flower Center, dedicated to the memory of poet Gwendolyn Brooks, is to advance the genre of African American poetry by providing opportunities for education, research, and publication. Located at James Madison University, the Center has organized two conferences that brought together well established and emerging African American poets. Furious Flower I was held in 1994 and Furious Flower II ten years later. Komunyakaa presented his poetry at Furious Flower II where he was interviewed afterward.

14. "Yusef Komunyakaa," *Southbound: Interviews with Southern Poets*, ed. Amy Verner (Columbia: University of Missouri Press, 1999), 132.

15. "Lines of Tempered Steel: An Interview with Yusef Komunyakaa," *Callaloo* 13.2 (1990): 216.

16. "A Conversation with Yusef Komunyakaa," *Tampa Review* 23 (2002), 20.

17. "How Poetry Helps People Live Their Lives: APR's 25th Anniversary Celebration," Special Supplement. *American Poetry Review* 28.5 (1999): 21–27.

18. *The Jazz Poetry Anthology* (Bloomington: Indiana University Press, 1991) and *The Second Set: The Jazz Poetry Anthology*, Vol. 2 (Bloomington: Indiana University Press, 1996).

19. "A Conversation with Yusef Komunyakaa," *Callaloo* 28.3 (Summer 2005): 527.

20. *Callaloo* 28.3 (2005), Special Issue on Yusef Komunyakaa, 621.

21. Turner, unpublished interview. Turner interviewed Komunyakaa during his appearance at Siena College's Greyfriar Living Literature Series in Loudonville, New York, on April 12, 2007.

22. Wesleyan University Press was the publisher.

23. Michael Collins, "On the Phone with William Banfield," *Callaloo* 28.3 (2005): 638.

24. *Callaloo* 28.3 (Summer 2005), Special Issue on Yusef Komunyakaa.

25. Hegazzi is co-editor of *Meena* (with Andy Young), a bilingual journal between Egypt and the U.S. See *Callaloo* 28.3 (Summer 2005), Special Issue on Yusef Komunyakaa.

26. The anthology of African American literature translated into Bengali is titled *Ami amar miritur por sadhi nota chai na* [trans. *'I Do Not Want My Freedom When I Am Dead*].

27. In her article, "The Failing Light; Why Did a Rising Young Poet Plunge into Despair, Taking Her Own Life and the Life of Her 2-year-old Son?" Paula Span writes an extensive, detailed article describing the brilliant, gifted, though troubled, Vazirani and events leading up to and following her death. She focuses on the utter disbelief of family and friends alike and the stoic silence of attendees at the funeral, except her brother Ashish (*Washington Post*, Sunday, Final Edition, 15 February 2004), http://wwwv.lexisnexis.com/us/Inacademic/frame.do?tokenKey=rs h-20.788636.81645160.

Chronology

1947   James Willie Brown Jr., born April 29, 1947, is the eldest of five children born to (James Willie Sr., a carpenter, and Mildred Brown in Bogalusa, Louisiana. He later changes his name to Yusef Komunyakaa, a tribute to his grandfather, a stowaway on a ship from the West Indies who slipped into this country and was forced to relinquish his surname.

1965   Komunyakaa graduates from Bogalusa Central High School at eighteen years of age. Soon afterward he enlists in the U.S. Army and leaves for a tour of duty in Vietnam.

1969–70   Serves in Vietnam in the Americal Division, assigned to duty as Information Specialist. Works as correspondent and managing editor of *The Southern Cross* military newspaper. In addition to covering major actions of the war and interviewing fellow soldiers, he writes a column titled "Viet Style" on Vietnamese literature and culture. Receives the Bronze Star for his journalistic work. Feeling somewhat disoriented after his return to the U.S., Komunyakaa lives in several places and works a number of odd jobs, such as air conditioner repairman and a six-month stint as policeman.

1971–73   After moving to Colorado—with sojourns in Boulder, Fort Carson, and Colorado Springs—Komunyakaa works for Racial Harmony Council, an organization that investigated racial incidents; also he edits *HARAMBEE*, a race relations magazine.

1973   Enrolls at University of Colorado under the GI bill and pursues a double major in English and sociology. He remains in Colorado for seven and a half years.

1974   Encouraged by creative writing teacher Alex Blackburn, he enters the Rocky Mountain Writers Forum poetry contest, judged by John Edgar Wideman, and wins first place.

1975   Earns bachelor of arts degree from University of Colorado.

1976   While enrolled in the graduate program in writing at Colorado State University, Komunyakaa is instructor of English composition. Along with Adam Hammer, he initiates *GUMBO: A Maga-*

	zine of the Arts, a journal of short fiction, poetry, and translations that they publish until 1979.
1977	Komunyakaa again wins First Place Poetry Award, Rocky Mountain Writers Forum. Publication of first chapbook, *Dedications and Other Dark Horses*, a limited edition.
1978	Komunyakaa earns the Master of Arts degree in creative writing from Colorado State University.
1979	*Lost in the Bonewheel Factory*, his second chapbook published in a limited edition.
1980	Komunyakaa receives the master of fine arts degree from University of California at Irvine. His M.F.A. thesis is titled "Premonitions of the Bread Line." Lands a fellowship at Provincetown Fine Arts Work Center, a close community of artists, and spends time in semi-isolation where he methodically deals with his writing and develops his own voice.
1981	Awarded first creative writing fellowship from National Endowment for the Arts. During summer Komunyakaa returns to Bogalusa to live with grandmother for brief period.
1982	Instructor in English composition and American literature at the University of New Orleans, Lakefront, until 1984.
1984	Komunyakaa writes first Vietnam War poem, "Somewhere Near Phu Bai," while renovating a house in New Orleans. From 1984 to 1985 he serves as poet-in-schools for fourth and fifth graders in New Orleans Public Schools. *Copacetic*, book of poems inspired by a return to his hometown, Bogalusa.
1985	Awarded Louisiana Arts Fellowship. Marries novelist and short story writer Mandy Jane Sayer. They move to Bloomington, Indiana, where he assumes one-year position as visiting professor at Indiana University, Bloomington. They are married for ten years.
1986	Publication of *I Apologize for the Eyes in My Head*, a book of poetry that won the San Francisco Poetry Center Award, and *Toys in a Field*, a chapbook. Komunyakaa takes his first trip to Australia, where he stays for the entire year.
1987	His position becomes permanent at Indiana University, Bloomington, with a promotion to associate professor, Afro-American studies and English, and he remains there until 1996. Awarded a second National Endowment for the Arts Fellowship.
1988	*Dien Cai Dau*, book of Vietnam War poetry, has been cited as

being among "the best writing on the war in Vietnam." Also listed in the 1988 Young Adults/American Library Association "Best Books for Young Adults."

1989 Named winner of the Dark Room Poetry Prize for *Dien Cai Dau*. *February in Sydney*, a chapbook that reflects his admiration for aboriginal culture and his interest in jazz composition. Holds the Lilly Professorship, an endowed chair in poetry, from 1989 to 1990, during his tenure at Indiana University, Bloomington.

1990 The William Joiner Center Institute for the Study of War and Social Consequences, University of Massachusetts, Boston, invites Komunyakaa and five other veterans to return to Vietnam to meet with members of the Vietnamese Writers' Union. "Facing It" anthologized in *The Best American Poetry 1990*.

1991 Wins the Kenyon Review Award for Literary Excellence and the Thomas Forcade Award for his work toward "the healing of Vietnam and America." *The Jazz Poetry Anthology*, co-edited with poet and jazz saxophonist Sascha Feinstein. *Tenebrae*, written by Komunyakaa and performed as a tribute to Indiana University percussion professor Richard Johnson who committed suicide. Komunyakaa is visiting associate professor, University of California, Berkeley, 1991 (fall).

1992 *Magic City*, a poetry collection, is published and selected by *Village Voice* as one of twenty-five best Books. Holloway Lecturer at the University of California, Berkeley, 1992–1993.

1993 *Neon Vernacular: New and Selected Poems 1977–1989*. Nominated for the *Los Angeles Times* Book Prize in Poetry.

1994 For *Neon Venacular* wins Pulitzer Prize and the Kingsley Tufts Award for $50,000, the largest prize bestowed for a single work. This poetry collection also nets him the William Faulkner Award from Université de Rennes.

1995 While Komunyakaa is on sabbatical in Australia, Christopher Williams, of the Australian Broadcasting Corporation, approaches him with the idea of writing a libretto that celebrates the relationship of jazz with gospel and blues. This artistic effort later results in a performance piece titled *Testimony*, a collaboration with Sandy Evans, Australian jazz saxophonist. With Martha Collins, translates *The Insomnia of Fire*, a prose work by Nguyen Quang Thieu. Presented the Furious Flower Award at James Madison University.

1996   Holds visiting professorship at Washington University, St. Louis, Missouri. Poems "You and I Are Disappearing" and "Boat People" adapted to musical score in Eliot Goldenthal's Vietnam War Oratorio *Fire Paper Water*. Commissioned by the Pacific Symphony Orchestra, this piece commemorates the twentieth anniversary of the formal end to the Vietnam War. *The Second Set: Jazz Poetry Anthology*, Volume 2, co-edited with Sascha Feinstein.

1997   Edits *Ploughshares Journal* (during the spring). In September, performs a jazz/poetry collaboration, *Love Notes from the Madhouse*, with John Tchicai and his ensemble at the Chopin Theater, with 8th Harmonic Breakdown, Inc. Assumes position at Princeton University as Professor, Council of Humanities and Creative Writing. Awarded the Hanes Poetry Prize and the Levinson Prize from *Poetry Magazine.*

1998   *Thieves of Paradise*. Receives the Morton Dauwen Zabel Award from the American Academy of Arts and Letters. Records *Love Notes from the Madhouse*, a jazz collaboration with Dennis Gonzalez. African American composer T. J. Anderson presents the idea of collaborating on an opera about an enslaved man. The result was *Slipknot*. Anderson wrote the musical score and Komunyakaa the libretto for this opera based on the true historical account of Arthur, a Massachusetts slave who is wrongfully convicted of raping a white woman and sentenced to hang.

1999   Elected Chancellor of the Academy of American Poets, a position in which he served until 2005. *Testimony*, Komunyakaa's epic poetic tribute to Charlie Parker set to Sandy Evans's jazz score, is broadcast on Australian Broadcasting Company Classic FM Radio's "Soundscapes." *Herido*, a collaboration with Tony Gonzalez, performed November 5, at St. James Cathedral in Chicago.

2000   *Talking Dirty to the Gods. Blue Notes: Essays, Interviews, and Commentaries*, an exploration of the development of his blues/jazz aesthetic, co-edited with his friend Radiclani Clytus. Writes song lyrics and collaborates with Pamela Knowles, an American jazz singer based in Australia, on *Thirteen Kinds of Desire*. In Chicago, musician Susie Ibarra agrees to collaborate on a performance piece, *Shangri-La*, that has been presented in workshop at Passage Theater, Trenton, New Jersey; Union College,

Schenectady, New York; and The Kitchen, New York, New York. In Australia, Komunyakaa reads poems from *Neon Vernacular, Magic City,* and *Thieves of Paradise* accompanied by the Cathy Harley Quintet.

2001   National Book Critic's Circle Award nomination for *Talking Dirty to the Gods.* Visiting writer at the New York State Writers Institute on March 8. *Pleasure Dome: New and Collected Poems, 1975–1999.* Awarded the Ruth Lilly Poetry Prize. Records *Herido,* a collaboration with jazz musician Dennis Gonzalez, which features live improvisational performances from Mark Deutsch on sitar, Susie Ibarra on percussion, and Sugar Blue on harmonica.

2002   Official world premiere of *Testimony.* The performance, which the *Sydney Morning Herald* called "a marriage of sound and vision," featured the Australian Art Orchestra. Publishes *Scandalize My Name,* a volume of selected poems, and *Langston Hughes, 1902–1967: Langston Hughes + Poetry = the Blues. Ish-scoodah,* a chamber opera with dance, in collaboration with dancer/choreographer Aleta Hayes and dance/vocal soloist and composer/musician William Banfield, premieres at the Princeton Atelier Arts Studio Program at Princeton.

2003   Work-in-progress *Slipknot* is presented in a staged workshop at Northwestern University School of Music on April 26. Edits *The Best American Poetry 2003.* Komunyakaa is one of a group of poets who threaten to protest a White House Forum on poetry that Laura Bush was to host. The forum was called off as a result. *Shangri-La* presented in workshop at Passage Theater Company in New Jersey. Tragedy strikes when Indian poet Reetika Vazirani—Komunyakaa's long-term partner—takes her life and that of their two-year-old son Jehan. One of Komunyakaa's poems about his boyhood, "Venus's Flytraps," was read at the funeral service.

2004   *Taboo, The Wishbone Trilogy—Part One.* Featured reader at Buffalo/Williamsville Poetry, Music and Dance Celebration, April 22. As a Ghana Education Project board member, Komunyakaa leads a delegation of prominent African American poets to Ghana during March to motivate a literary and artistic response to the AIDS crisis in Africa. In collaboration with two other African American poets, Komunyakaa participates in a film, *Making Heard the Buried Cry: A Poetic Documentary on the AIDS*

Crisis in Africa. Collaborating artists are Willie Perdomo (a PEN award-winning poet, children's author, and performer on HBO's Def Poetry Jam) and Thomas Glave (O'Henry Award recipient and James Baldwin biographer).

2005   In January, travels to Kolkata (Calcutta) with Goutam Datta who edited the first collection of African American poetry translated into Bengali language. Komunyakaa is the first African American poet to visit Burdwan University where he gives a reading along with Datta and Subodh Sarkar. Komunyakaa and Sunil Ganopadhaya officially open the Kolkata Book Fair with Datta's anthology of African American poetry, *I Do Not Need My Freedom When I'm Dead.* In September, at the U.S. Embassy in Warsaw, Poland, Komunyakaa presents reading on program titled "America Presents: The Poetry of Yusef Komunyakaa."

2006   *Gilgamesh: A Verse Play*, Komunyakaa's collaboration with Chad Gracia, dramaturg and theater producer, is published. Joins the creative writing faculty at New York University as Distinguished Senior Poet and professor in the graduate creative writing program.

2007   *The Deacons*, a drama written by Komunyakaa and directed by Kemati Porter, has world premiere at Passage Theater Company in New Jersey. This performance piece explores brotherhood and love through the story of two men who served in the underground civil rights militia known as the Deacons for Defense. *Covenant: Scenes from an African American Church*, in collaboration with Tyagan Miller. Passage Theater Company in New Jersey premieres *For Lost Words*, an electronic sonic symphony, text and lyrics by Komunyakaa, featuring composer Vince di Mum on a multiplicity of keyboards, with vocalist Julianne Chester, and Jasper McGruder as "The Poet." Komunyakaa wins Robert Creely Poetry Award. *Changing the Changes in Poetry and Song*, a CD ranging from blues to post-fusion, has on-stage release party at Passage Theater Company, New Jersey. Komunyakaa collaborates with poet/singer Hermine Pinson and singer, songwriter and guitarist Tomas Doncker with his trio.

2008   Komunyakaa is one of thirty poets selected to be a part of an innovative effort to introduce new audiences to great contemporary and classic poetry. Titled *Poetry Everywhere*, this series of short poetry films featuring poets reading their own work, animated interpretations of much-loved poems, and celebrities reading personal favorites, is produced by WGBH and David Grubin Productions, as well as student filmmakers at the University of Wisconsin-Milwaukee's docUWM media center. A series of short poetry films premiered online throughout National Poetry Month at Public Broadcasting Station websites, The Poetry Foundation website, and on Transit TV, a network that runs programming on LCD screens in public transportation systems in Atlanta, Chicago, Los Angeles, Milwaukee, Orlando, and San Diego. In April *Gilgamesh* is performed at 92nd Street Y Poet's Theater in New York with Robert Scanlan as director. In October Komunyakaa judged the National Poetry Series mtvU Prize competition. The winner, Kristen Naca, had the honor of interviewing him on national television on the mtvU program titled "My Shot With . . ." and having her winning book of poetry, *Bird Eating Bird* published by HarperCollins.

Conversations
with Yusef Komunyakaa

Interview with Pulitzer Prize–Winning Poet Yusef Komunyakaa

Rudolph Lewis/1985

From *Chicken Bones: A Journal for Literary & Artistic African American Themes* (interview conducted in May 1985 and published online in 2007). Reprinted by permission.

The interview below is seventeen years old, nine years before Yusef received his Pulitzer (the first African American male to be so honored). I recently dug it out of boxes I have been lugging around from one residence to the next. It was written in longhand on lined yellow legal-sized sheets. At the time of the interview Yusef was a mentor and a friend. I am not sure what I had intended doing with the interview at the time. It was an intellectual exercise, an exploration of his methods and his thinking. As much play as anything. We worked then on a number of projects, including building a stage and a bar for a community center, Copacetic-Piety, dreamt up by Ahmose Zu-Bolton.

We spent a lot of time in Lee Grue's Poetry Forum and riding about town in my orange VW bug discussing writing, culture, and politics. We also spent a considerable amount of time at the archives at the University of New Orleans going through the papers, and especially the poems, of Marcus Bruce Christian. That exercise was intended to pull out the best ones. That project ended up finally fourteen years later as a book of fifty poems, titled *I Am New Orleans & Other Poems* by Marcus B. Christian. One might even say all those New Orleans activities with Yusef eventually led to the creation of *ChickenBones: A Journal*, as a means of fulfilling a commitment of making Christian more public and accessible.

When the community center fell and our relationship with Ahmose went sour and his relationship with Mandy had fully developed, Yusef left town with his new wife, leaving me in his house on Piety Street, which is where I think I first got to know the poet Mona Lisa Saloy, who was then staying on the West Coast. I have not seen Yusef since his marriage and his first trip to

Australia, though I spoke to him on the phone, and communicated to him by post when he reviewed my poetry manuscript and made suggestions. This interview was conducted in his house on Piety Street, probably soon after I met him in New Orleans.

They were heady days when I thought everything was still possible. I was still young enough then to be very naive.

Part 1

Rudy: You're working in the Poetry-in-the-School program now? Is this work you want to do?

Yusef: It's work I like doing. Had some doubts about it—teaching grades 3 to 6. It's, however, been exceptionally rewarding. You can see the discoveries they make—by the way they state things, by how their faces light up. They can be very brutal, in their assessment of life, and at the same time humane. At the same time you have innocence and keen observation. They don't bite their tongues. The system hasn't yet instilled the editing machines inside their heads. They are lucky that way.

Rudy: You say sometimes the kids can be "brutal." What do you mean?

Yusef: Sometimes I am forced to tell them not to use the name of fellow students.

Rudy: So you have been working with this program how long? How long do you intend to stick with this program?

Yusef: Since October '84. I'm playing it by ear as long as it is a reservoir of surprises.

Rudy: How has this teaching affected your work and life?

Yusef: It's helped to lead me back to an assessment of my own childhood, and I hope to cover that in a book called *Magic City*. It will deal with my childhood in Bogalusa with the Knights of the Camelias—to rediscover that psychological terrain that I tried to forget, to help me to piece together all aspects of my background. Many times in the faces of some of these children I feel as if I'm looking into a mirror.

I'm in the process of writing a children's book. It's about the observations of a little boy, and it's to be called *Blues Boy*. It's about a little boy who happens to be a blues singer—nine or ten years old—and how he deals with the existential aspect of what he sings.

Does he know? Yes, he does. Like Lightning Hopkins who climbed up on the wagon with Blind Lemon Jefferson. We think of him as a grown man. But he was nine years old when he began. Born in Centreville, Texas. Our observations sort of bleed into each other. That's what poetry is about.

Rudy: These are some of your future projects. What's going on now, or what are some things that have happened recently?

Yusef: A few months ago, I finished writing poems about Vietnam—an attempt to reassess, to look at things in retrospect.

Rudy: This "going back in the head," what real use does it serve you as a person? I understand that it offers a source of material.

Yusef: It's a cleansing process. You're finally able to deal with that whole stockpile of images—brutal, bloody images. It helps you take a look at the American soldier, at the Vietnamese—to look at the people as the enemy. They were "gooks" and "dinks." It helps you to take apart all the things you observed and ask why. And try to answer some of those whys in the writing. In a sense it helps to release oneself from the war, which I think is necessary.

Rudy: You seemed to have been deeply affected by the war. Your sensitivity as an ex-soldier seems to be somewhat unusual. How do you account for it?

Yusef: For me, it was different. I was a combat correspondent for the AMER-ICAL-PIO. Anytime boys were pinned down, such as Hamburger Hill, you were expected to get in the chopper to get the story, to get the picture, and to come back and write after you had time to digest the information. As a writer, you were sensitive to the images. So you internalize the image.

At this time, I was reading everything—poetry, issues of *DownBeat*, *Negro Digest*, and *Black World*. I was reading short stories, poetry—Baraka, Baldwin; magazines like *Dissent*; some political analysis of the Vietnam situation. Constantly wrestling with the conflict. One fact saying, yes. The other, no. Questioning why I had not gone to Switzerland or jail. And also by being a combat correspondent, you see numerous firefights because that's what you're expected to do—cover those things. Consequently, it becomes volumes of images.

Rudy: What did you do after the war? Were things really different for you when you returned to the States?

Yusef: My first day back I got a ticket for jaywalking. It was very strange. I didn't think about crosswalks. In a way I was still back in Vietnam. I took a number of jobs that were pits—worked as an air-conditioning mechanic in Arizona; six months as a policeman in Arizona. It was difficult. If you think you're going to change people with a gun on your hip, you're mistaken. You end up behind a desk. So I decided to go to Colorado, University of Colorado.

Rudy: Did you know people in Arizona and Colorado before you left?

Yusef: My mother lives in Arizona. And my daughter lives in Arizona.

Rudy: Why did you choose Colorado?

Yusef: I also worked for the Racial Harmony Council, an organization that dealt with investigating racial incidents. We worked out of Fort Carson, Colorado Springs. I edited *HARAMBEE* a race relations magazine. We had essays, artwork, literary works—short stories, poems; but mainly a lot of articles on race relations and some of prison writings. Some dealt with political theory. We had a hundred-odd investigators.

Rudy: So what year was this?

Yusef: 1971 to 1973. In 1973, I started University of Colorado.

Rudy: You decided to go to the University because you were not satisfied with your job?

Yusef: My idea was to go into sociology. But my orientation became English—creative writing. I took more English courses. It went back to my concern in Vietnam. I was reading. At the University, I had big blocks of time to do just that. It kept me busy. Busy so you don't have to think about what happened.

Rudy: Was there anyone at University of Colorado who took you under his wing?

Yusef: Dr. Alex Blackburn. He was teaching creative writing. He had come back from living in England. He had a lenient view of poetry. He was critical but allowed experimentation. He took an interest in my work. Young writers need support from a critical point of view. He would always read my work. Some of it was published in the *Writers Forum*, started in 1970. I took first place in the contest. John Wideman was the judge that year—1974. It was the fire I needed to help me to move on.

Rudy: Did you like Colorado?

Yusef: It was interesting. I stayed there seven and one-half years. After University of Colorado I went to Colorado State. It's where I started *GUMBO* with Adam Hammer. *GUMBO: A Magazine for the Arts.* We published short fiction, poems, translations.

Rudy: Do you consider *GUMBO* a success?

Yusef: We printed a thousand copies. We got rid of most of them. Four issues of the magazine and a chapbook came out of the venture. We took money out of our pockets to publish those things. It also served to show me exactly what people were writing throughout the country. I was surprised by the sameness. What I mean by that is if you cut the names off you'd have a single collection that could be from one author. Homogenized voices in contemporary poetry. Too often safe.

Rudy: So the poets, the artists, you published with *GUMBO* were different?

Yusef: I tried to introduce a variety. To show that everyone wasn't writing the same poems throughout the country. Some of these were very young poets who had never been heard from before. We didn't have to publish a name. Many of them still do not fit into the contemporary scene. Others are doing other things. But I think these chances with literary ventures are chances worth taking.

Rudy: Adam, the co-editor, was a good friend of yours?

Yusef: Adam was a poet who died in Birmingham in a car accident last year. We were both in the writing program at CSU. We were different in styles of poetry. Adam had been influenced by French Surrealists—Breton, Appolinaire. He wrote *Deja Vu Everything* (1970), published by Lynx House Press. That book can be obtained from Small Press Distribution in Berkeley, California. He was good, unusual. The playfulness in each line. The lack of imagistic continuity. But yet the poem would hold together by theme.

Rudy: *Lost in the Bonewheel Factory*, you consider your first book. Could you tell me how it came about?

Yusef: Consider it a chapbook. *Copacetic* was the first full-length book.

Rudy: So then you had two chapbooks published? How did they come about?

Yusef: Both *Dedication* and *Lost in the Bonewheel Factory*, Chris Howe asked me to submit them to Lynx House for publication. Chris Howe is one of the editors of Lynx House. Bob Abel and Chris Howe started Lynx House Press, published out of Amherst.

Rudy: So the publication was successful? I mean did the publication lead to something?

Yusef: Distributed by Small Press Distribution. Printed five hundred copies. The problem is distribution. The small presses take more chances, print more innovative fiction and poetry. You don't have to have published in the *New Yorker* and the *Atlantic*. The small press is the mainstay of contemporary literature. It probably has always been so. At one time the writer published himself.

Rudy: Did something special happen as a result of the publication?

Yusef: It encouraged me to continue to write. It gave me room to move away from that manuscript to something else. As far as pay, I think I received fifty copies. The only thing I received—fifty copies. The only thing received from the small press is inspiration. No dollars and cents. It's important for the young poet that someone sees something in his work. I think there should be more mimeographed/xeroxed books, which I think they did in the thirties and forties, so that you can get a book for a dollar or a couple of dollars—where publishing doesn't seem like big business.

Rudy: So *Dedication* and *Lost in the Bonewheel Factory* were all of the same fabric?

Yusef: They are pretty much the same. It covers the psychological terrain associated with Colorado. This place helped me to see things anew. It's somewhat of a multi-cultural experience. I began to read some Indian, Chicano, and the black literary experience. If I had to write the same poems today, I would write them differently. I'm in a different place.

In Colorado, I felt somewhat isolated. Maybe because of the geography of the place. I learned that I enjoyed to take long walks, walks of meditation in an attempt to work things out. Poetry tries to work the problems—one's attitude towards oneself, the world. You're able to journey through the subterranean corridors of the head. Some call them headtrips.

Part 2

Rudy: You've touched on, accidentally, a point that concerns a poem in *Lost in the Bonewheel Factory*. "Poetics" seems somewhat at the heart of the book. Could you give us a sense of what's behind the writing of this poem?

Yusef: The poem is about the two sides of everything. Behind beauty lies the ugliness of things. Ugliness can be a kind of Beauty, the old Janus head, reflecting the reality of things.

Rudy: But you also have a criticism of other poets or poetic methods— "quick draw artist/crouches among chrysanthemums."

Yusef: In the midst of the garden of lovers can lurk death, or, at least, perpetrators of death, violence, and evil. Disguises. The gift of the poet is to see behind things, to look at things in many ways and create an emotional overlay. The overlay helps to surface that which is, helps us to ask what's necessary, helps us to deal with the horror of our existence. The factory is the U.S. We're great producers. Many of the poems were written while the Vietnam War was new inside me. I hear someone crying, "Man, everything isn't a laugh, a good time." I'm not against these things.

Rudy: "Sunbather" seems to be a statement of what the imagination is capable of and your response to what the "Poetics" poem seems to suggest.

Yusef: One's poems come from a personal experience. One day when I was in Colorado Springs a nude bather, this woman lying on a white towel. My response was to wave at her and keep going. Later on the image helped me to write this poem. The poet's imagination is no different from any others. The poet takes time to put it on paper. The mind is capable of conjuring up good and bad, tangible and intangible.

Rudy: Would you consider it true to say that your poems are complete with violence and terror? Is that what you see beneath the flowers?

Yusef: I see violence and terror. I see the paths to the underworld. Once we realize that they are there, they can plot the course of the action. We come to the realism of that situation, a way of getting down to everything that humans are about. We could put together the worlds of Wordsworth and Coleridge. Coleridge's world is just as valid as Wordsworth's. When Coleridge saw the slave ships—gray spectral ships, the ghost ships. "Daffodils" of Wordsworth, less grounded in reality.

Rudy: So your assessment is that we are full of violence and terror?

Yusef: Violence and terror can help define what America is all about. Once we realize that, the healing can begin. To recognize the errors of history and not to repeat them. No cleansing can begin without recognition.

Rudy: "High on Sadness"—a paradoxical title. Imagination transforms memory.

Yusef: The imagination can lead one to the edge of terror. This surreal world is made out of the same things as dream. Reality is put beside the imaginative world and they bleed into each other and thus becomes more real than we would like to believe. The terror is within us. A condition of the flesh. We're programmed not to deal with the terror. Only by dealing with the terror can this facing up come about. A kind of revelation.

Rudy: "Light on the Subject"—wondering whether this is an allusion to Robert Johnson's song.

Yusef: Yes, we know each other. It's as if I'm as bad as you. His history is no different from ours, when it comes to bloody hands. Pontius Pilate washes his hands. We as a people—as a collective conscious—are guilty as Jack, with just as much a sense of justice. We the silent majority. We glorify our henchmen. We make them into our heroes. Look at our heroes: Wild Bill Hickok, Kit Carson—the Indian killers.

Rudy: "Punchdrunk"—there is an allusion to Randall Jarrell who "knew how to take a solid left jab."

Yusef: Jarrell walked into the traffic and was killed. Some suggest it was suicide. He was not all here at the moment. His mind was divided, distracted. Something was wrong. He wasn't completely in the world. No way that flesh can argue with metal.

Rudy: Yeah, I suppose you are right on that point. Surely, flesh will not win that argument. What is corrigenda?

Yusef: It's the taking back. You retreat, change your mind.

Rudy: Vallejo. What is his importance to you?

Yusef: His poetry opened up possibilities for me. I saw what he was doing. There was an emotional connection. It was a different world. But it was familiar to me. That's the power of the imagination. It can create bridges across cultural barriers. It helps us to get into the hearts of each other.

Rudy: Do you think your work is similar to Tolson's in that your poetry draws upon, in a very conscious manner, European and Afro-American allusions, images, folk manners while simultaneously yoking things together in a sort of "metaphysical manner"?

Yusef: I love Tolson's "Libretto" and I admire his facility with language. We're doing things differently. He seems to be conscious of the yoking of European and Afro-American sensibilities. Most of my writing is improvisational, and it just happens that those images come. Part of a total experience.

Rudy: "Reconstruction of a Crime," "Stepfather," "Stepmother," and "S & M" seem to be of the same tenor. What's that all about?

Yusef: When I was in the military, I saw too many officers were hurting for combat because it aided in their promotions. I know that many justify their activity in war to their wives and girlfriends. It's putting bread on the table. Sex, war, economics, and violence—all connect and create the overlay that helps to define what America is all about. I'll go on the range and kill Indians. I'll go to Vietnam and make the little lady comfortable. I wonder whether women want to be connected to violence this way—to make bombs so I can vacation in Hawaii. More than the active participants should be implicated. That's part of owning up.

Rudy: Who is Weldon Kees?

Yusef: His car was found on the Golden Gate Bridge. Some assumed that he drowned, others that he went to Central America or Mexico. He's a poet, painter, jazz musician.

Rudy: The section "Passions"—how did you come to include this as part of the overall work?

Yusef: The whole section was written in a single sitting. Each of these titles was given to the poems later. Each section was a stanza. Yet there is a thematic thread, tied to the pathos of loss and violence, love and sexuality and greed.

Rudy: Do you think your characters have an inordinate difficulty with their sexual lives?

Yusef: Those who are around us we visit violence upon them quick. Maybe that is the place the healing should begin. It starts with the personal first. I know that people are sexually violent with each other. Not that it should be. Sexual violence is akin to other kinds of violence.

Part 3

Rudy: From the acknowledgments in *Copacetic* and *I Apologize for the Eyes in My Head*, I see that you've published in a considerable number of literary magazines. At first did you expect such a ready response?

Yusef: No. Initially, I didn't think too much of it. Just an effort to get out on the page. I got initial help from Alex Blackburn. Mainly, encouragement. I could trust his hard criticism. There's been a multi-cultural response.

I usually feel that certain journals will be responsive to my work. Journals that will take a chance. Journals that are not concerned with safe poetry because there is a political edge to most of the poems. We don't have to worry about the censorship that Ginsburg and Burroughs had to concern themselves with. Books like *Howl* and *Naked Lunch*. If we were to write like *Tropic of Capricorn* or *Black Spring*, we don't have to go off to Europe.

Rudy: You now have little difficulty getting your poems published in journals—that is, do you still get rejection slips?

Yusef: Yes, I still get them. We all still get enough rejection slips to plaster a wall. Sometimes it makes me feel I'm doing something right.

Rudy: Do you think with *I Apologize* you have reached your mature poetic style?

Yusef: I think that book is different. There are still poems to write. Other styles to explore. I still need to surprise myself. If I couldn't I'd stop writing. There are more controversial subjects to touch upon, which I hope to do in other books.

Rudy: At this point in your writing do you think your poems are identifiable, I mean your style.

Yusef: I would hope so. The reason I say that is because I hope my voice is different, not that it has to be. But that it has a different edge to it. Maybe the whole of one's work defines one's voice.

Rudy: Okay, let's explore a little bit of your poetic process, of what you try to get into a poem. What do you think are the technical virtues of a good poem?

Yusef: The top of my list is that I have to be surprised by the language, the images, in the process of writing the poem. The poem has a certain amount of energy. It has to sound contemporary. Within the context of a poem you can have a lot of things going on side by side. You can have different senses of language. You can have the street alongside the more sophisticated colloquial. All those things that help define our individual lives. No subject is taboo. Samuel Johnson in talking about diction wants to substitute *rat* for its

Latin equivalent. Poetic diction is the language we speak. Otherwise it is an attempt to remove the poem from the people.

I have to have sometimes a certain tension going on in my poem. [John Crowe] Ransom emphasizes tension, and I am in agreement. What he meant may be entirely different from what I mean. I mean all those things that push and pull against the individual help to create a natural tension in the poem. I'm not talking about an artificial tension through technique, the tension that makes the common individual's life worth living.

Rudy: Some of your poems are improvisations on a line or theme. Did you have this ability early on?

Yusef: I think that ability was there in the early poems, but not as developed. Perhaps I didn't trust that method to the extent that I trust it now. Perhaps early on I didn't allow the poem enough freedom to exist. The early poems seem to seek a resolution, whereas the later poems are more grounded. There is breathing space inside the poem. The print could mean many things depending on what the reader brings to it.

Rudy: Would you say that you have a more relaxed self-assured voice in *I Apologize* than you have in *Lost* and *Copacetic*?

Yusef: I think maybe so. I worked on that book a long time. I started on it in '79. There are topics that I've thought about a lot. There is writing taking place inside the head before it is put to the page, shaped in more or less unconscious way. I have had time now to work those poems through without undermining the urgency.

Rudy: How many of the poems have gone through revisions in *I Apologize*?

Yusef: Many of the poems were written off the top of my head, and some have been cut to clarify, to boost the emotional connection.

Rudy: At this point, do you think you have to use a network of words and images, or are there types of words you tend to use.

Yusef: Yeah. Especially for a certain book, certain words tend to recur. There is a sort of repetition that holds things together. Phrases that you might not use ever again. But there are certain words that I could never use again, unless in an entirely different context.

Rudy: How did the writing of *Copacetic* come about? It seems to pay homage to Afro-American history and culture.

Yusef: These poems were written through the years. And it was only when I got back to Bogalusa that I realized they should be in a book. Some of them were in *I Apologize* manuscript. It was sort of natural for me. I will deal with that topic again and again. I'm working in the back of my mind on a book called *Magic City*. The whole landscape that I grew up in and of course that is Afro-American.

Rudy: The most unusual of the poems in *Copacetic*, in a way, is "Instruction for Building Straw Huts." Different from the others, it lacks the dark images of the underworld. Do you also find this poem different in its texture?

Yusef: The poem might have started when I was in Okinawa. They built many of the buildings flimsy. And they were supposed to withstand storms more easily. In the back of the mind, I thought of African straw huts. Maybe behind this very primitive architecture is a philosophy. In the context of this poem there is a celebration. It is anti-technology in an unspoken way. Here is an attempt to acknowledge wisdom in simplicity.

Rudy: There have been a few prominent writers—for instance, C. K. Williams and Clarence Major—who have made very important statements about your work. Why these two in particular?

Yusef: They were sent the manuscript by Wesleyan University Press. With C. K. Williams, there is a political edge in his poetry. Read his books. All of them political. Maybe the same kind, not to be pinned down in a category, I might relate to Clarence Major in *Swallow the Lake* (1970) and his novel *Reflex and Bone Structure* (1975). The sort of surreal quality that Majors has in many of his works is a connection.

Rudy: Many of your poems are entitled "Blues" and you have poems dedicated to jazz figures and also to the jazz poet Bob Kaufman. How did this interest come about mixing several media?

Yusef: Jazz has influenced the American cultural landscape. It has affected our speech patterns or rhythms. Even listening to cartoons as kids we were touched by jazz rhythms. Many of the movie scores are actually jazz, even though we don't like to acknowledge Monk, Coltrane, Billie Holliday. The blues is something basic to those who grew up in rural America. Whether they are listening to Sleepy John Estes or Bill Munroe. They are being affected by the pathos of the blues, a very realistic music.

Rudy: So what about Kaufman?

Yusef: Kaufman is definitely the most brilliant jazz poet in America. He influenced the Beats. But you might not find him in a case book on the Beats: *Solitudes Crowded with Loneliness* (1965) and *The Ancient Rain: Poems 1956–1978* (1981). Three early broadsides, *Abomunist Manifesto* (1959), *Second April*(1959), and *Does the Secret Mind Whisper?* (1960). [There is also now *Cranial Guitar: Selected Poems.*]

Read those books and you know that Kaufman is important to the San

Francisco Renaissance. Some might have stolen the thunder. He comes from New Orleans. Most literary people here in New Orleans have not heard of Kaufman. It is said that Kaufman coined the term "Beat."

Rudy: You have this strange combination of artists yoked together in "Villon/Leadbelly."

Yusef: When I think of Villon, I think of Leadbelly. I think of two daring men born in different times. But both have pure energy at the base of their works. When Villon says, "I will my bones to the dice maker." I can hear those words in Leadbelly's mouth. It's interesting if you look at their background. Both were jailed for murder. Both released by government decrees.

Rudy: You have a poem entitled "Vicious" in *Copacetic* which appears in part of "The Beast & Burden: Seven Improvisations" in *I Apologize*. What is the connection?

Yusef: Initially, all of the poems were written together in one setting. I thought that "Vicious" should go in *Copacetic* because of the subject of a group of poems there.

Rudy: How did "Seven Improvisations" get its start?

Yusef: One day I was thumbing through a copy of *New American Review*. And I saw seven drawings by Harold Kube. They are about oppression in South Africa. Consequently he was tried for blasphemy and exiled. That was the only thing that they could try him for.

When I saw those drawings, I just began writing. I felt a connection to his artwork. I felt the gravity of his political statement.

Rudy: The first poem in the book *I Apologize*, "Unnatural State," seems to be a statement of independence. Was it intended as such?

Yusef: The whole thing is that you're first a person before you're a poet, a writer, an artist. And that's the most important. That human connection ties all your artistic endeavors together in some way. The imaginative world has to be linked to human experience.

Rudy: You have several "Thorn Merchant" poems. What is the origin of this phrase?

Yusef: Just one of those phrases that came out of my head. When I thought of the phrase, I thought of the person who sells pain, violence. The dealer in human suffering is represented by the "thorn merchant."

Rudy: Some of the imagery of what seems natural in speaking of Hitler and South Africa spill out in poems that have an American landscape.

Yusef: There is a connection. The whole thing of the racial question can be connected. It doesn't matter whether we talk about South Africa militia, the KKK, White Citizens' Council, or the Nazis. Those groups can be thrown into one group. They deal with oppression and murder. Members of such groups are able to smile when others are suffering and crying out for help.

Rudy: The poem "Dreambook Bestiary" . . . was that written all at once?

Yusef: No, it was written at different parts and in different places. However, I do think that they go together. They were not written in the order they appear.

Rudy: Your poem "1984" seems somewhat science fiction.

Yusef: When we think of 1984, we think of Orwell. We think of Orwell's "Politics of Language." That particular poem deals with the politics of language. I don't think it's as science fiction as it sounds. In the context of the poem is a realistic center. Some of these things are around in everyday life, such as missile silos—in too many places—in Russia, in Israel.

Radio Interview
with Yusef Komunyakaa

David Houghtaling/1989

Originally broadcast on WCBU Radio (Peoria, Illinois), on 24 February 1989. Published by permission of WCBU.

Houghtaling: This is a book of poetry (*Dien Cai Dau*) focused on your experiences in and your reflections on the Vietnam War. You said it took thirteen years before you could write about it. Why did it take so long?

Komunyakaa: In a way, the brain is sort of like a reservoir. It contains all the frightening images and what have you. I finally realized that writing the book would be a sort of letting-go process. It was a way of dealing with the images inside of my head. But the reason for it taking that long is that I had been reading numerous poems about the Vietnam War by other Vietnam poets, as such, and just reading those poems kept me away from writing about Vietnam, I think to an extent. The horrific imagery that came through was also a way of reliving that kind of experience. It wasn't working for me as much as it possibly could have.

Houghtaling: Was it the letting go?

Komunyakaa: It was the letting go that was necessary.

Houghtaling: What kind of reactions have you gotten from, I guess, both from veterans and also from students? You're addressing young students that probably were in diapers when Saigon fell. They have different perceptions of the war. What kind of reactions have you been getting to your poems?

Komunyakaa: I've gotten rather positive reactions, surprisingly so.

Houghtaling: What types of people have been reading it? Are vets picking this up?

Komunyakaa: Some veterans are picking up copies of the book, of course, and they are responding in, of course, different ways to the book because one also brings one's experience to the book. It's a way of looking at the war perhaps in a different way, a way of looking at it through retrospection.

16

Houghtaling: What was the most difficult poem for you to write in this book or were they all difficult?

Komunyakaa: They were all rather difficult. The poem that came easy for me, "Facing It," came quite easy; and I was surprised by it. And I think that particular poem guided the other poems along. It created a standard for the book.

[Komunyakaa reads "Facing It"]

Houghtaling: And one of your poems is a reflection of a fairly famous picture.

Komunyakaa: Yeah.

Houghtaling: What was the picture? Why did you feel moved to write about it?

Komunyakaa: Well, the picture really, in a way, objectifies the horror of Vietnam. Of the girl running down the road aflame. Through the whole process of destruction, automatically you realize that seeing that individual on fire is also to see part of yourself on fire.

[Komunyakaa reads "You and I Are Disappearing"]

Houghtaling: Does this put the Vietnam War to rest for you or are there going to be more poems?

Komunyakaa: If there are more poems about Vietnam, it will be about vets back here in America after they came back. I've had this title I've carried around inside my head and it's called, "Debriefing Ghosts." Maybe that title will fall into a different kind of book, but I know it won't be a book of poems only. I think probably it will be a book that contains a combination of things; maybe even a play, short story, that kind of book.

Conversation with Yusef Komunyakaa

Rebekah Presson/1995

Originally broadcast on *New Letters on the Air: Contemporary Writers on Radio*, KCUR-FM
(University of Missouri, Kansas City, 1995). Reprinted by permission of *New Letters on the Air.*

It's *New Letters on the Air* and I'm Angela Elam. Today's guest is Yusef Komunyakaa, who won the Pulitzer Prize in 1994 for his book of new and selected poems called *Neon Vernacular*. Komunyakaa was born in 1947 in a small Louisiana town called Bogalusa. He left right after high school and traveled around the country working various jobs until 1969 when he joined the army and ended up serving a term in Vietnam. His travels since have taken him as far as Australia but now he's back in America living and working as a poet and professor.

Here is Yusef Komunyakaa in a 1995 interview with Rebecca Presson.

Presson: What is Bogalusa, Louisiana, like?

Komunyakaa: It's a very small town, deep South, rural. When I was growing up, I thought of it as sort of bucolic, but in retrospect it's a town that might be defined with terror and beauty side by side.

Presson: Like something out of Faulkner?

Komunyakaa: Yes, in many ways. Yes I think so.

Presson: Those Southern movies that we see.

Komunyakaa: Well, not necessarily; but there are moments, perhaps, of those images, yes.

Presson: What was your upbringing like? You said you read a lot in high school. Were you raised reading a lot?

Komunyakaa: For me, I think reading was a sort of escape. It was a meditation on the future. I thought that reading would lead me to this great expansive world out there someplace.

Presson: And it did.

Komunyakaa: And it did [laughs]. Especially poetry, but also short stories, novels.

Presson: Contemporary poetry?

Komunyakaa: Well, traditional poetry, but also some contemporary poetry if we can say that Gwendolyn Brooks and Langston Hughes are.

Presson: Oh yea, we'd consider them contemporary.

Komunyakaa: Yes, contemporary.

Presson: And why is it that so few young people can see that now? Do you have any idea on that? It was the same for me.

Komunyakaa: Well, I think maybe television is part of it. Television is such a passive activity. Reading is a lot more active because automatically it invites the reader in as a participant and as at least a co-creator of meaning.

Presson: And so, of meaning because maybe television encourages people to see life as meaningless?

Komunyakaa: Well, it's defined in thirty-minute blocks or hour-long blocks and everything is resolved.

Presson: Unlike your poems, which are unresolved, right? And also resolved with a lot of violence.

Komunyakaa: Yes, very much so. However we've always had violence with us if you look at ancient mythology—Greek mythology, Roman mythology. Gosh, you know it's quite visual, violence there. But it's a different kind of violence.

Presson: Would you read a poem that is set in Bogalusa? Maybe from *Magic City*.

Komunyakaa: "Venus's Flytraps"?

Presson: Sure, great.

[Komunyakaa reads "Venus's Flytraps"]

Presson: That's wonderful. Can you really remember being five?

Komunyakaa: Yes, of course. This incident, I say five in the poem, but I think I must have been four at that time.

Presson: And you remember playing on the train tracks?

Komunyakaa: Yes, yes, yes of course.

Presson: And Mama telling you, you made her a bad girl?

Komunyakaa: I remember hearing. It's about secrets you know. My play-house was underneath the house, I remember that. And it was a great place to hear all kinds of things. For me I think that the writer, the artist has to have a need to do what he or she does and everything that's done is pretty much influenced by that need.

Presson: Now you're saying as opposed to making a decision to write?

Komunyakaa: Yes.

Presson: Is it fun for you to write?

Komunyakaa: Yes. Sometimes I laugh out loud and I think, gosh, where did that come from? And that's a surprise. I like to be surprised.

Presson: You laugh out loud because you are so pleased, not because it's funny?

Komunyakaa: A combination. I'm pleased and also it's rather sometimes an image that's sort of satirical so there's that kind of satirical ironic spirit behind and informing everything, so yes, I find myself laughing out about the possible meaning of a given line or phrase.

Presson: Are you pretty much just able to turn the work over and let people get what they need out of it?

Komunyakaa: I hope so, yes.

Presson: Seems like that would be a hard thing, you know. I wanna be understood. When you say, "write out of need," you don't mean like write out of a need to make some social statement, necessarily?

Komunyakaa: No, no, no. I'm talking about a need that is within the center of one's being and personality.

Presson: I read somewhere that going to Vietnam is what spurred you to be a writer. But do you think that's true?

Komunyakaa: I don't necessarily think that's true. For me, Vietnam, I didn't really deal with the pathos under the Vietnam connection for a long time. It took me fourteen years to write about Vietnam so I very systematically wrote around my Vietnam experience. I think that I was pretty much influenced by classical surrealism, especially Breton, Mallarmé, and also some of the American surrealists.

Presson: And your early poems were a lot about music . . .

Komunyakaa: Well, my earlier poems I think it's really difficult to pin down what they were about because they were about any and everything. There was kind of an attempt to create, you can say, tonal, visual kinds of collages.

Presson: Do you want to read one of them just so we can have an idea of what you are talking about?

[Komunyakaa reads "More Girl Than Boy"]

Presson: This might be stretching it but in a way that poem is not that far from some other Vietnam poems. The one thing about turning the guy over . . .

Komunyakaa: Yes, yeah.

Presson: It's not that far from that you know . . . about sort of falling in love with these guys that you're in this extreme condition with.

Komunyakaa: The photographs, yes. That kind of visual connection as such.

Presson: And having a real love connection that you even compare to a connection with a woman in this poem.

Komunyakaa: Those kinds of connections are made because essentially there are emotional overlays and emotion tapestries in a way and certain things are woven through other things.

Presson: Yeah, I think it's pretty apparent that these are heterosexual poems on the whole.

Komunyakaa: Right, right, right, right.

Presson: But with an understanding of the kinds of connections that can be made.

Komunyakaa: Yes, yes. Emotional ones. Yes.

Presson: Most of these poems have a fair amount of narrative. The jazz poem.

Komunyakaa: Yes. Well, I like to think of them as sort of fractured narratives. So, yes, the narratives are there, but there is a kind of tonal narrative running underneath everything.

Presson: No, I didn't mean just a simple story at all. You know what I mean? But you can follow them. They're not so disjointed that you never know where you are. Some poems are. Some poems are so insular that it's hard for an outsider to penetrate them.

Komunyakaa: Well, one has to pretty much meditate on them.

Presson: That's true, but you have to kinda come up with what your own . . . I think it can be hard to find out what the poet is trying to say. You just have to figure out what you want to hear.

Komunyakaa: Yes, I've said before that I attempt to do that to an extent, like I try not to resolve poems if possible, because I want the listener or the reader to enter that landscape and become an active participant.

Presson: I think that's true that you don't resolve poems, but you end them beautifully. I think that's a real strength in your poetry. Maybe if you'd read your poetry, "Facing It," because that's an example of a really extraordinary ending for a poem. It's about the Vietnam Memorial.

[Komunyakaa reads "Facing It"]

Presson: She's using it as a mirror.

Komunyakaa: Well, that's the whole reflective power of the memorial, the stone. It is a mirror in a certain sense.

Presson: You talk in the poem about how the light can be used to pull yourself into it or pull yourself out of it.

Komunyakaa: Yes, yes.

Presson: It's an ominous ending.

Komunyakaa: Well, it was one of those endings I said, gosh, I can't go any farther. This is it.

Presson: As I think about, I think it's kinda like there we are standing in front of those 58,022 names, and we're not gonna learn from that. That's kinda like what it seems like to me. Is that what you're saying?

Komunyakaa: No, I don't think so. At least I think, that I hope that we're going to learn from that.

Presson: You got a bronze star. What did you get it for in Vietnam?

Komunyakaa: I was part of the Americal Division, and it was for my participation with the Americal Division. When I first went there initially, well the first six months there was a lot of activity. Anytime anything happened within the area of operation, military correspondents were sent to the field in the middle of the action. So it was that kind of participation.

Presson: Do you want read another poem from, how do you pronounce the book that the title means crazy in Vietnamese? *Dien Cai Dau.*

[Komunyakaa reads "You and I Are Disappearing—Bjorn Hakansson"]

Presson: Wow, as you read that I kept thinking of your poem, "Thanks." And I guess that's what everybody who goes to war comes back being torn about. They see sights such as this one just described and then have to constantly think, "Well, why didn't it happen to me," or "I'm glad it didn't happen to me," or "It could have happened to me."

Komunyakaa: Well, you do internalize the pathos. However, I think you find ways to deal with it.

Presson: In your case would that be writing?

Komunyakaa: In my case, I think it's a kind of meditation on life; on what it's all about and maybe writing is part of it as well.

Presson: What did finally happen after fourteen years that made you start writing poems about Vietnam?

Komunyakaa: Gosh, I just found myself writing about Vietnam. At the time, I was living in New Orleans and was in the middle of renovating a house and in the whole process of running up and down the ladder, taking off layers of plaster and paint, and I found myself writing about Vietnam.

Presson: When you got back from Vietnam, you went to writing school, got an MFA in creative writing. Were you encouraged to write about the war then?

Komunyakaa: Well, I attended the University of Colorado. Then I took my first creative workshop in 1973 as an undergraduate, and I very systematically wrote around that experience. I wanted to pursue other things in my writing, and so in 1984 I found myself writing about Vietnam. One of those things that creeps up on you.

Presson: Do you have a new volume, like ready to go, or are you taking your time on that?

Komunyakaa: The way that I work is that I work on three collections side by side. I simply go back and forth between those collections. Perhaps I'll have something coming out in '97.

Presson: How do you decide what poems belong in what collection?

Komunyakaa: Oh well, for me sometimes it's theme, sometimes it's tone, subject matter, what have you.

Presson: Could you characterize the three in any way right now?

Komunyakaa: Well, the three I'm working on now are fairly easy to distinguish the differences. One book is a very long book of short poems, sixteen-line poems, four four-line stanzas. The other *Pleasure Dome* is really a kind of excavation of Black history. It started off with just an excavation of Black American history, literature, and culture. And then it included Africa, and now it's more extensive than that. So it's a very long book, and those poems are composed of three-line stanzas, staggered three-line stanzas. So it gives a kind of symmetry to the whole book.

Presson: And a real stylistic tone to it too.

Komunyakaa: Yes, stylistic, yes.

Presson: And the third?

Komunyakaa: The third is really what is called *Thieves of Paradise*. It's in seven sections. The first poem in the book is entitled, "The Memory Cave," and it goes from that particular poem. Hopefully there is kind of a voyage taking place.

Presson: These more personal poems?

Komunyakaa: No, not necessarily more personal. I think they're probably a combination of personal, public observations, what have you.

Presson: So, the poem "Ode to the Maggot" is from the first book?

Komunyakaa: The four-line stanzas . . . When you say first book?

Presson: The first book you described. The one with short sixteen–line poems.

Komunyakaa: Yes, yes.

Presson: Do you want to read that poem? Do you mind?

Komunyakaa: Okay. This is the first poem to actually—if not the first, at least one of the first—that sort of sparked the idea of a whole collection. [Komunyakaa reads "Ode to the Maggot"]

Presson: This is *New Letters on the Air* and our guest is Yusef Komunyakaa who was just reading a new poem but who also won the Pulitzer Prize for his collection of new and collected poems, *Neon Vernacular*. I know that you change your poems even after they're published, so what incarnation do you think this poem is in?

Komunyakaa: For me, revision means to re-see. Basically, the poem can be revised if there is a kind of desolation that takes place. So I never really add to poems, I sort of subtract, extract what I think is extraneous.

Presson: So even later on, you never really, like change a word. You just remove it usually? Is that what you mean?

Komunyakaa: Very seldom do I change a word; usually it's removing a word, especially articles, for some reason.

Presson: Oh well, that would make sense. So you don't mind taking . . .

Komunyakaa: Yes, yes. It is a kind of improvisation. I think reading is an improvisation in itself but writing for me is also that kind of act.

Presson: Is that something you learn from jazz or do you think it's inherent in reading and writing as well?

Komunyakaa: I think it might be inherent, but also I listen to a lot of jazz of course.

Presson: Do you want to read a jazz poem?

Komunyakaa: Well, I don't know if I have really a jazz poem, but let me read a poem that might have been influenced by jazz.

Presson: Okay.

[Komunyakaa reads "Blue Light Lounge Sutra for the Performance Poets at Harold Park Hotel"]

Presson: How do you do it? I mean how do you come with . . . ? Do you work hard on endings? Do you sometimes come up with them first?

Komunyakaa: For me, the writing process is to write everything down, and instinctively there is a line that sort of opens up the poem and doesn't close it down in any way; and that's the ending for me. My method of composition is to just put everything down and very systematically cut back.

Presson: And rearrange the order?

Komunyakaa: Very seldom.

Presson: Very seldom? So that last line then, if you write something after it you just get rid of it?

Komunyakaa: Yes.

You've been listening to Yusef Komunyakaa. He was interviewed in late 1995 by Rebecca Presson when he visited Kansas City as a part of the Midwest

Poet Series at Rockhurst College. He read from his 1994 Pulitzer Prize winning collection, *Neon Vernacular*, and also from his recent book, *Magic City*.

New Letters on the Air is a production of *New Letters*, the quarterly magazine of new writings published by the University of Missouri at Kansas City and edited by James McKinley.

Hotbeds and Crossing over
Poetic Traditions

Kristin Naca/1996

From *Blue Notes: Essays, Interviews, and Commentaries* (University of Michigan Press, 2000, pp. 85–92). Reprinted by permission of Kristin Naca.

Kristin Naca: Let's start off talking about process. Recently, there have been collections of essays available on poets writing about their process.

Yusef Komunyakaa: Essentially, my process involves writing everything down. When I work on a poem, there's virtually, I should say, a number of brainstorms. Then there comes the organizing—what lines create certain connotations, or become the basis for another line. So it really becomes a sort of juggling act. It seldom comes out whole, complete as a poem. I write everything down and then I cut back. Furthermore, I'm able to extract words, phrases, lines, even whole stanzas, that seem rather extraneous—so I'm able to strike those. But I do think process is greatly affected by reading, for me that is. If I'm reading history, an article on science from *Scientific American*, some kind of historical or scientific information might end up in the poem—so that's all part of the process as well. Finally, what I'm trying to get at is a layering, so that everything has a full quality. The layering influences the tone, the rhythm. I think about the rhythm. Richard Hugo talks about the necessity for writing with long and short lines—influenced by Swing music. He's stated that he's able to bring Swing into his process. So I'm thinking about how the poems actually sound, and this goes back to the "oral" tradition. I come out of a tradition where people tell stories. But I'm not really reaching for a linear narrative. I prefer the lyrical narrative where there are certain leaps in the poems. So the process focuses on really drawing them out.

KN: When I think about the leaps that happen in say "Venus's Flytraps," in the narrative, where you're practically looking through the boy's eyes, walking through the field, and the images collapse or they leap onto you, is this what you mean: the images becoming very magical, very surreal?

YK: When we think of magical realism, we usually think of South American writers. But then it's also important to note that the South American writers are somewhat Faulknerian, and of course Faulkner was shaped by the cultural and social landscape—that marriage of beauty and terror side by side, especially with that tepid "dialect." There's danger and terror. So I grew up realizing that beauty is connected to terror, that it can really turn against one—life itself. It's something I learned through observation, though of course I didn't realize it at the time when I was living it—not until about twelve years ago.

KN: So when you were studying as a young man in that place, in Louisiana, you were influenced, maybe, by Southern texts, but their value has or does increase as you are able to go outside and read South American works and then come back to that idea of magical realism in your own place?

YK: Yes. I don't know why, but there comes a time of psychic closures because there's this great boom, and everything flies back together—except there's the first moment of intense disorientation when one realizes, "this is what I came out of," and then all of a sudden—"this is something I should know."

KN: It's also hard for people to recognize and accept this. And there's a great power in accepting one's culture, even when it means coming back to the elements of being from the South, its roots in the Faulknerian.

YK: Yes, it is continuously, because everything around one is attached. There are clear moments, that we accept with certain details, a reality, and we realize there are other realities attached to this one.

KN: So have your processes been different when you're writing from a loosely autobiographical perspective, striving toward the lyrical narrative, like in *Magic City* or *Dien Cai Dau*?

YK: It isn't. It still entails writing everything down and trying to make some sense out of the narrative. Everything isn't—I think, in a certain sense—conceived as a strict narrative structure. There's an internalized phonology, and it's sort of put down that way. And yet one has to realize that certain things are extraneous to the story and that they pretty much take energy away because their contexts affect the whole chemistry of the piece. The poem is a kind of organism that grows, it has natural phases of maturation.

KN: So you're saying, the poem cuts off pieces of itself until it becomes whole?

YK: Yes.

KN: On the back cover of *Magic City* the word *autobiographical* appears. *Autobiographical* is such a strange word; it appears in so many different ways and is used perhaps to catch the attention of or get more people interested in reading a book. What's your idea of an autobiographical poem?

YK: I suppose for me it's a poem that comes together, fusing a number of facts—in this way it is autobiography, though it is constantly changing. I asked my brothers about moments we experienced, and often they see them entirely differently than I do. So autobiography is also filled through with a number of hallways, like places on a map—sometimes there's a kind of clarity; rights, wrongs—that make themselves known, other times there's a more blurred reality.

KN: In some essays on process I've read, authors might refer to the word *truth.* Maybe your truths are musical truths, imagistic truths, things that attach themselves to each other for a reason? And so when I look at *Magic City*, I don't necessarily say, "Oh that happened" or "This guy's got twenty different people running through his head."

YK: Well, autobiography becomes a kind of beaded necklace of possibilities. There's evidence for that as well. Sometimes I have an idea that this is the poem I want to write, but if the poem turns into something else, it turns into something else. Say, if I might have written twenty lines and I get to the twenty-first line, and that twenty-first line becomes a line that should be a different poem altogether, though it's loosely connected to the cadence of the first twenty lines—I might go with this new direction—without taking away from the emotional makeup of the poem.

KN: When editing, then, you're not too attached to the emotional weight of say single lines?

YK: Sometimes one can put the line in a box and try to get some distance from it, so that, when editing, one can be vicious.

KN: So then as an editor, it's a different process, a different stage. Does this play over into when you're looking at other people's poems?

YK: In workshop, let's just say, I don't want to see everyone writing the same poem. I like the fact that there are different voices, styles, subject matter. At first, it seems oppositional, but then we realize they're not really oppositional to each other—that they are informing each other as well. Often, I wish I could do that in a poem or in a book where one has numerous styles. That would probably be the most ideal for me. And yet I realize that there is a tone in books, they have an almost seamless quality. But, I think, the real challenge for me would be to write a book that contains a number of styles or aesthetics with each influencing the other.

KN: Almost what *Neon Vernacular* is, but, instead, the book wouldn't take its work from different books, because you can see how the poems in *Neon Vernacular*, their styles, are so organically connected to each other within each section. So when you're writing poems, or say organizing a book of poems, do the poems that "don't fit in" not make it into the book?

YK: Many of them. When I think about it, a lot of those poems, well those poems that are actually finished, I try to hold onto. But there are some, there are hundreds of poems really, that don't arouse me any longer, and so I can abandon them. But then there are others that I keep coming back to that I'm *never* going to finish—some poems I've been working on for ten years, and there's something about them that keeps me curious, because it's not happening.

KN: Maybe if you put the poem down for ten years and then come back to it?

YK: Well, it's just an obsession really. An obsession and a determination to make it work. But at the same time, there's a certain invincible distance to them.

KN: Recently you've had eight poems in *American Poetry Review*. And these are poems that are historical/literary moments—very different than say your "autobiographical" poems, though they contain the same deep and heavy voice that guides the reader through the moment. Could you say something about these poems?

YK: There's a book I've been working on, *Remembrance of Things to Come*, it's a three-part book; maybe it's really a trilogy contained under a single title. I realized that there are so many historical facts I seem to be aware of, some things I've been reading through the years, and other people are not made aware of these facts or exposed to these points of view. For example, for years I've been reading "A Rose for Emily," and one thing that's interesting to me is that the character Tobe doesn't have a voice—it seems as if it were impossible for Faulkner to give him a voice. Maybe silence is a voice. Maybe that act of walking out at the end of the story, going into the woods, can be the only act of defiance. For me, I've always heard a verbal voice for that character. The first time I thought about it, I had my students write a monologue in Tobe's voice, with what he would have said, living and coming to that house as a servant, as a cook, as an individual, shocked—what would he have said. So finally, I got around to writing a poem called "Tobe's Blues," a poem from Tobe's point of view.

Or I might have a fact in my head and I improvise on it. For example, when we think about Russian literature, we think of Pushkin as the father of Russian literature. But I'm also drawn to Pushkin's African background, and he was very much aware of it as well. So I wanted to write a poem about Pushkin and how he served as a muse for Anna Akhmatova.

KN: I think in "Homage to a Bellboy" I was impressed to see moments, and a voice, of someone whom we're not usually made aware of, that we don't ever hear his voice, and nobody knows about these things that happen to him.

YK: It's a strange moment in *Black Boy*, that moment when we're confronted with invisibility, where the bellhop goes into a room. I think he's serving whiskey to this typical white southern man and woman, and they're nude in the bed. And he comes in, and it's as if he doesn't exist or as if he doesn't have the freedom to acknowledge what he sees. In the same way Tobe doesn't have a tongue to speak in Faulkner's story—it's this kind of severe invisibility that, think about it, also Ellison addressed, Michael Harper addresses in his poems. So many people address.

KN: It is, as well in recognizing maybe even the reason for it.

YK: Think about that Richard Wright epigram "It startled as no more than a blue vase or red rug." One has to disappear. Because if you don't, if you acknowledge, then you lose your life—that's the situation, so you don't have a freedom to acknowledge. It's almost as if some kind of strange pact has been made with the devil, that defines your invisibility, that you're participating in your own invisibility, which in this way is doubly tragic.

KN: It's difficult for people to understand how some people don't have the ability to come out and say who they are. Is this a choice, do you think people allow it to happen?

YK: I think they don't have the freedom. Especially in that particular story, at that particular time, these bellhops in a Southern city. You know, the whole idea of "looks that weren't looks."

KN: Then, as well, it's a difficult process for people who decide to go from invisibility to visibility?

YK: Yeah, it's a hell of a risk.

KN: Has your process changed at all over the years, say, maybe how you read?

YK: One way I read poems is that I try to read them over and over. It's very important to me to take them out and look at them at different times because it depends on what's happening around you, or happening to you, because it will lead you to see something else. That's what really attracted me to poetry: that I could continually come to a poem and get something different from it. Whereas in prose—I like reading short stories, novels—it's different.

KN: Maybe with prose we're perhaps influenced or directed more by plot?

YK: Yes, the whole thing about attempting not to resolve a poem. You know, where one hopes the reader can continually come into the poem and there's not a clear-cut resolution—that it's somewhat open-ended.

KN: I notice in reading either *Copacetic* or *I Apologize for the Eyes in My Head*, especially in the latter, the speaker's voice comes through from a specific moment in time. We come into that moment and we exit from that moment not very far apart in time, and so there's discreet or subtle changes. The speaker does not say, "I've made these large changes in my life, living what I have been for a number of years, or months, or days," and so we come back to those poems over and over, they have a tendency, an inherent quality to turn and change, and in that way they never end.

YK: Yes, I don't think this was ever a conscious strategy, but I realized that this is something I wanted to do in poems, that I didn't want them to end. It's the same way that I often read poems, that I don't want them to end.

KN: It's very attractive to step back into that moment, but then it's difficult to ever say what the poem's about because you come into it different each time. I think that this quality is very distinctive in your poetry, say, for instance, in "Facing It," when the speaker realizes that the woman is brushing the boy's hair, or maybe in *Magic City* too, the main speaker is obviously very full-voiced, and he as a person or character is going to keep going on. It makes you want to follow him on further.

YK: It's a strange place, going back to that landscape I realize there are so many things I didn't write about, and perhaps I'll never write about—that's alright because it's really a sort of hotbed. I was very much aware of language early on, when I say hotbed I can go back to a moment, which portrays hotbed, where you plant seeds, and you pluck the pepper seedlings or whatever out of it, or you transplant the greens. And I realize that that's a place where things begin to grow. So, in that way, Bogalusa was sort of a hotbed.

KN: And some hotbeds have seasons, and some don't.

YK: It depends on how you enclose it.

KN: I wanted to ask you a little bit about the *Jazz Poetry Anthology* (1991). You've finished collecting and editing poems for the second edition that will be published this year, *The Second Set*. Was there anything specific you were looking for when you decided which poems to use in the second collection?

YK: We, Sascha Feinstein and I, realized that there were a number of poems we wished were included in the first edition. A good example would be some of Gwendolyn Brooks's poems. And, in a way, I'm glad we didn't originally include her work. That makes the second book so much more important. A number of voices were influenced by jazz in a complete way, and so the second anthology is an attempt to go back and take a look at other jazz-related poems and poets who had written about it, a poem by Yevtushenko, an important Russian poet. And once we finalized *Second Set*, we kept thinking, "Is there a third set?" And of course there's a third set. The reason why there's a third set is that jazz has a real international scope. So, obviously, if there's an international scope, there's some other Russian poets besides Yevtushenko; there are some Japanese poets, Scandinavian poets. Impulsively I surmised that yes, and already there are so many. For instance, the popularity of jazz in Japan—why wouldn't jazz influence their poetry as well? It's very popular in Russia and at times it was forced underground—why wouldn't it influence the poetry? And what I'm finding is that, yeah jazz did, at least in the poets' individual voices. I'm thinking about Lorca's *Poet in New York*. Borges loved jazz, and now I'm wondering if he ever wrote a jazz-influenced poem.

KN: Who were the jazz poets who influenced you the most?

YK: I began to realize maybe about 1980 that there were certain poets who wrote about jazz a lot. And I think I started with Michael Harper, Jayne Cortez, and William Matthews, those were the poets who came to mind. Then I started to look around and realize that there are a lot of others. And of course Langston Hughes, writing blues-related poems, and Sterling Brown's poems. All those poets were there, and then in retrospect I realized that even some of the poems written by Gwendolyn Brooks have a jazz base or a jazz feel. But those voices didn't have an immediate influence on my work. The music itself did have an influence.

KN: I think there's a great musical allure in some poems that you're exposed to as early as high school. And you ask why is this poem so great, and at the time your teacher can't explain it to you because she or he has no clue.

YK: I think I've said that lately I've been equating language as music—and the body as an amplifier.

KN: As well, maybe the poem I was drawn to earliest was "Theme for English B," not consciously by the music but by the subject matter.

YK: Well, Hughes at the time didn't seem as close to traditional blues; he wrote "English B" because of subject matter; it's closer to traditional American/European expression.

KN: A music that attracts your ear, and then it's what leads you back to that poetry or that music. Like a kind of bridge from one tradition to another. Gwendolyn Brooks's work is another example of that.

YK: Yes. With Gwendolyn Brooks, it's also the way she reads her poems. It's the music and rhythm in her voice. And she's influenced by traditional literary pursuits, but she's very conscious of the spoken quality informed by the community.

Terror Aligned with Beauty: A Visit with Bloomington's Pulitzer Prize–Winning Poet

David R. Richards/1996

From *Arts Indiana* 18.1 (February 1996). Reprinted by permission.

When James Willie Brown Jr. was a youth in Bogalusa, Louisiana, he watched his father, a carpenter, measure a board carefully seven or eight times before cutting it with a handsaw. The board invariably slid into place in his woodwork. The fit was perfect.

"My father would include me in the ritual of carpentry. I would hold the board. The whole rhythm of cutting it would vibrate through my body," recalls Brown, now known as Pulitzer Prize–winning poet Yusef Komunyakaa. "That ritual is akin to writing poetry. I write everything down, then I systematically cut back to the essential images."

Professor Komunyakaa, a teacher of English literature and Afro-American studies at Indiana University in Bloomington since 1985, had a bumper year in 1994.

He was awarded the Pulitzer Prize for Poetry for his 1993 book *Neon Vernacular*, a composite of new poems and selections from seven of his previous collections. The same month as that $3,000 award, he received the second annual $50,000 Kingsley Tufts Poetry Award from the Claremont Graduate School in California for the same book. In addition, the University of Rennes in northwest France awarded him the William Faulkner prize for literature which included a trip to the university. Consequently, some of his poems are currently being translated into French.

Despite the accolades, worldwide recognition, and prize money that he's received, when you talk to the soft-spoken poet in his office high above the Bloomington campus, his mind quietly drifts back to his boyhood days in the deep South. Such early memories feed the rich imagery of his verses.

33

"I grew up in the deep South," he explains, "where terror is aligned with beauty, in a rural, bucolic vibrant place full of vegetation and small animals. Just fulfilling the daily rituals of life, I realized that death had a lot to do with that beauty."

His attention turns quickly to Vietnam, where he served in the U.S. Army. The poet finds many connections between the two locales—"even the physicality of Louisiana and Vietnam are linked in my psyche," he says. "It was very rainy in Vietnam, just as in Louisiana which has a semi-tropical climate. Growth of vegetation would come overnight. As a boy I wasn't afraid of snakes or spiders, and I would go exploring. This stood me in good stead in Vietnam compared with troops who grew up in urban settings. They found it difficult to handle the vegetation and the landscape."

Komunyakaa joined the army immediately after graduating from Bogalusa Central High School in 1965 and left for a tour of duty in Vietnam at the age of eighteen. Two anthologies of poetry accompanied him. He served as a correspondent and editor for the *Southern Cross*, a weekly newspaper produced for the U.S. military in Vietnam, and received the Bronze Star for heroism. "For the first six months, I was in the field every day in situations of potential conflict," he says.

Dien Cai Dau, his book of poems about Vietnam, is richly alive with these experiences: the death of Vietcong snipers; an American prisoner-of-war trying to remember TV shows to retain his sanity; U.S. soldiers having sex with sisters of Vietcong soldiers they were out to kill only the week before; soldiers watching skin flicks projected on a dirty sheet.

Komunyakaa's poetry is not concerned with the politics of the Vietnam war, rather its imagery. There are tunnels, manholes, odors of dampness, and ghostlike feelings of pitch blackness. Sights are seen through the scope of an M-16 rifle.

It took the poet eighteen long years before he wrote the first of his Vietnam poems.

"In 1984, I was renovating an old house in New Orleans," he says. "It was a hot, rainy summer and I was tearing off layers of roof and stripping off paint. I got strongly into the physical activity, which I really needed to do. As I worked, the first Vietnam poem in the book, 'Somewhere Near Phu Bai,' simply came into my head. I'd never written any poem about Vietnam before that moment. Then all the other poems followed.

"It was very surprising for me. Why? It wasn't a planned direction. It just happened. I kept on writing until the book felt complete and whole. In 1987 I submitted the manuscript of *Dien Cai Dau* and the book was published in

1988. There have been four or five editions since then, and the book is still in print.

"The title, incidentally, means 'crazy' in military Vietnamese jargon. That's what the VC thought the GIs were—crazy. Or at least that the military situation was crazy. They used the words with sarcasm."

He adds: "I never approached writing poetry from the perspective of making a living. It was simply a need. I just had to write poetry, and still do."

To understand Komunyakaa's conversation and his poetry one needs to know that he was deeply influenced by the French surrealist poets André Breton and Stéphane Mallarmé as well as by the American poet Robert Bly who stress the pull and the power of the unconscious mind.

Surrealism has to do with dreams and the unconscious landscape. Breton, one of the leaders of the surrealist movement in France in the early twentieth century, believed that surrealism aimed at eliminating the distinction between dreams and reality, and between reason and madness. Mallarmé, a leader of the French nineteenth century symbolist movement in poetry, was fascinated by the concept of escape from reality, and used language magically to do so.

"In my poetry, surrealism has led me to create a montage," says Komunyakaa. "Distinct pictures blend into each other to make one: a super-reality. This has influenced my writing.

"My real world is attached to a private dreamscape. As a result, things become more vivid, truer," he says in his slow, rhythmic voice. "Surrealism allows one to surprise oneself with images and language." Komunyakaa doesn't rely directly on his nighttime dreams to inspire his work, but "they certainly add a type of emotional coloration to my life and writing," he says.

Memories of his childhood merge with images of Vietnam in the poem "Tu Do Street."

But Komunyakaa is far from a one-note writer. Often he writes in a mysterious way, with high imagery. In the poem "The Thorn Merchant," he writes: "He knows how death waits in us like a light switch." In his 1983 book *Copacetic*, the poems hearken back to his boyhood. Settings are decidedly southern: "piney woods," and "cottonmouth country." The reader meets bloodhounds and freight train hoppers. His poetry has also been influenced by jazz.

Location has also affected his work. The poet, who has lived briefly in Australia, St. Thomas, Puerto Rico, and Japan, has taken degrees at the University of Colorado, Colorado State University, and the University of California at Irvine. After his stay at the University of Rennes, he visited St. Petersburg in Russia and then went to Prague where he performed his poetry and met young American poets and writers living in the city. Komunyakaa is now working on three new books of poetry, all with arresting titles. The first, *Chameleon Couch*, will be a dramatic monologue by a psychiatrist describing modern times in America, its divisions, sense of flux, and discontinuity. *Thieves of Paradise* will explore the rituals of early man. *Pleasure Dome* (the title is taken from Coleridge's mysterious poetic fragment "Kubla Khan") will be a composite of black history.

Komunyakaa is convinced that the United States is experiencing a vibrant time in poetry writing. "We have many major poets being published. Their work is good, and much of it will endure," he says.

"Poetry readings are held every week in major cities and in lots of small ones. Can you imagine this?" he asks with a laugh. "There has been at least one poetry reading every night in San Francisco for the past sixty years. And that's the truth."

The Body Is Our First Music

Tony Barnstone and Michael Garabedian/1997

From *Poetry Flash* 227 (June/July 1998). Reprinted by permission of Tony Barnstone.

Barnstone: The epigraph to Toni Morrison's *Song of Solomon* reads, "The fathers may soar / And the children may know their names," and the book is very much a quest for authentic naming. As one of the characters says about Malcolm X: "his point is to let white people know you don't accept your slave name." Here's a passage from the book, an internal monologue by the protagonist, Milkman Dead: "Surely, he thought, he and his sister had some ancestor, some lithe young man with onyx skin and legs straight as cane stalks, who had a name that was real. A name given to him at birth with love and seriousness. A name that was not a joke, nor a disguise, nor a brand name. But who this lithe young man was, and where his cane-stalk legs carried him from or to, could never be known. No. Nor his name. His own parents, in some mood of perverseness or resignation, had agreed to abide by a naming done to them by somebody who couldn't have cared less" (17–18). In your poetry, and in your life, naming seems to be a major issue as well. I'm thinking particularly of the poem "Mismatched Shoes," which is a poem that explains your act of self-naming—a kind of act of self-invention. Would you mind talking about that poem and about naming in your life?

Komunyakaa: Well, actually, it comes from a secret within the context of the family, my grandfather having come to Louisiana. I think first they landed in Florida, and then came to Louisiana, and they sort of slipped into the country as stowaways.

Barnstone: When was this?

Komunyakaa: This would have to have been a little after the turn of the century.

Barnstone: In that poem you talk about the name Brown and the name Komunyakaa, and changing to Komunyakaa as a connection with an elided past. Am I getting that wrong?

Komunyakaa: Well, I think in a certain sense because it was like a secret—it was a dare more than anything else, and in the context of the dare there was a kind of liberation. And I'm talking about a personal liberation as opposed to a political statement; one has to feel a certain freedom within the context of one's name.

Garabedian: I'd like to move from the subjective naming to your naming of reality. In some of the poems there is the suggestion that humans or human senses are flawed, as in "Jonestown: More Eyes of Jadwiga's Dream," where "reality bleeds into fiction." In "Audacity of the Lower Gods" the search for the truth via science is inadequate: "I'd rather let the flowers / keep doing what they do best," says the speaker, as opposed to calling the poison oak "Diversiloba," for instance. The suggestion is that categorizing tends away from the natural or the real. How is poetry as an alternative "mode of perception," more adequate? Is it more adequate?

Komunyakaa: Well, I think what happens is that the naming of a thing, things in nature being named by human beings, is a way of branding. Emotional branding. There's also a kind of claiming more than anything else. A good example would be the instances where American Indians ventured into the mountains—Pike's Peak, particularly. And yet those places such as Pike's Peak (there are a number of other places) do not really bear the early names . . . there was an attempt to claim the places by renaming them. As far as poetry goes, I think it's a naming and renaming. It's a constant ritual of trying to get it right. That is really the energy—that is really the urgency— of the poem. That's why I think refrains are interesting, because the poem becomes a motor—not of conquest as much as a motor for direction. In that process there's a kind of renewal . . . in that kind of naming, something is being observed, and in that observation, let's assume and hope that there is a connection, and that there is a naming that has to do with celebration, not the naming to dominate.

Barnstone: And for you science is more as a naming to dominate?

Komunyakaa: I think often so. It's a naming to divide and . . .

Barnstone: Categorize.

Komunyakaa: Yes.

Barnstone: It's interesting. I was recently reading William Carlos Williams's *The American Novel*, and he was talking about just this—about scientific naming and how it nails everything down and kills it, and how this is a source of suicides and trips to the North Pole . . .

Komunyakaa: Right! It is a naming that lays claims to the land and its people. In regards to the North Pole; automatically, I think of Matthew Henson, whom I would like to dedicate a poem to. Usually, we think of Admiral Peary, of course.

Maki: I'd like to know what kind of role poetry plays in talking about these things that are considered insignificant.

Komunyakaa: The things we tend to overlook—the things we see as insignificant—I don't think of them as insignificant at all, and that's the reason I attempt to embrace these things. There's a celebration in those things we tend to overlook, when, in fact, it's all part of a kind of immense unity. I was very curious, like science, how we see into things in the same way Aboriginals do paintings—we call them "X-ray drawings." They look inside of things, and look into things. I was interested in that cosmology . . . I think about the poem as layered with images (it's a composite of things that we might see as insignificant), which are there to illuminate us. Or if not illuminate us, at least force us to pose questions. And sometimes those are rather silent questions—we are posing questions without even being aware that we are posing them.

Barnstone: I have a lot of questions about *Dien Cai Dau*, but, first, could you translate the title for us?

Komunyakaa: It means crazy. That's what the Vietnamese would call the American soldiers. *Beaucoup, dien cai dau:* Very crazy. So it made perfect sense that I would use this title, because it pretty much nailed things down.

Barnstone: The other question I was going to ask returns to this issue of nature. It seems to me that nature is used in very interesting ways in this book. There's a kind of pattern of nature imagery—I'm thinking of the first poem in the book, "Camouflaging the Chimera," in which the soldiers "wove / ourselves into the terrain, / content to be a hummingbird's target." [He reads the ending of the poem.] This proliferates connections with the deep image poetry of Robert Bly and James Wright, or classical Chinese poetry, about connecting with nature—the poet as Taoist sage. And so, when I think about the world revolving "under each man's eyelid," I keep thinking of Emerson's "transparent eyeball." But it seems to me there's some kind of ironic transcendentalism going on here, where connection with nature is not to connect with the oversoul, but simply some kind of survival in a Darwinian sense.

Komunyakaa: Well, camouflage is part of it, the fact that there is a need to blend into nature—to almost become nature. But I think the reason the soldiers almost become nature at that moment has to do with a kind of severe fear more than anything else. And let's face it, if we go back to the reason why animals camouflage themselves, it is out of fear. Predator and Prey. Often, nature is a beckoning, but also a warning.

Barnstone: So it seems a kind of total connection that undermines the discourse of the connection with nature.

Komunyakaa: I think there's something else going on here as well . . . There's a certain kind of fear, and it has to do with the fact that one hasn't been initiated. So, in that situation there's a certain kind of initiation going on, even though it might not be a conscious initiation. There's an unconscious situational initiation going on.

Barnstone: To follow this up, in other poems nature is terrifying. In "Somewhere near Phu Bai" the soldier on guard is desperately trying to read the shapes of the night, trying to see which might be the Viet Cong, and in his mind "The moon cuts through / night trees like a circular saw / white hot." And in "A Greenness Taller than Gods" again a soldier is trying to read the enemy through a gorgeously unfamiliar nature, monkeys jabbering in flame trees, torch birds burning through the dark-green day. In *Paradise Lost* Milton speaks of how Adam must read God through the book of nature. It seems to me that the soldiers here are trying to read this unfamiliar book, this unfamiliar nature. But also, in some peculiar way, that makes the unseen enemy almost like a god, who is known only in the moment of death.

Komunyakaa: Yes. My feeling is that often the soldiers were more afraid of their surroundings than their so-called enemy. And I'm not just talking about vipers and tigers; I'm talking about how nature becomes part of the disguise. I think it was very difficult for the soldiers to deal with that. I think those coming out of urban—or small towns even—hadn't been fully initiated into that which we define or classify as nature. Nature not as precious or as commodity, but nature as part of oneself. In order for that to happen, there has to be a certain trust. So they had not really reached the place of trust.

Barnstone: And, of course, how could they in that circumstance?

Komunyakaa: Yes.

Barnstone: I'm also interested in the ways in which in your imagination or memory of Vietnam, nature becomes a terrain in which you have this extraordinary beauty, but it's also described in mechanical or technological terms. In "Hanoi Hannah" "Flares bloom over the trees" like flowers, while "Howitzers buck like a herd / of horses." In the next poem, "Roll Call," seagulls are a "metallic-gray squadron." So, nature is technology, and technology is blossoming—it's a very interesting connection. There's even a moment where a human being is reduced down to a rifle in that poem, in an image in which an M-16 is "propped upright / between a pair of jungle boots / a helmet on its barrel / as if it were a man" . . .

Komunyakaa: Which is ritual. When a GI was killed, often they would have ceremonies. Sometimes out of a platoon one might see five pairs of boots and five rifles, sitting there, as icons.

Barnstone: It also seems to me that it turns the man—and nature—into a kind of weapon; something that might go off at any moment in ways you can't know.

Komunyakaa: I think that's really the essence of guerrilla warfare—to turn nature into a weapon. To make nature at least an ally.

Garabedian: This seems almost contradictory: an alliance of opposites. Dr. Barnstone was reminded of Emerson, but, when I read a lot of the poems, I note a particularly Whitmanesque quality. Whitman is wholly inclusive in his poetry and writes rather graphic descriptions of death, violence, or ugliness, which, though these things seemingly contradict, attain beauty of their own. He writes, "Very well, then, I contradict myself." This idea plays out in several of your own poems. For instance, in "Praising Dark Places" the speaker finds beauty in the scorpion and the insects revealed beneath an old board. You have said in another interview with Muna Asali that you are interested in contradictions, like Whitman. Why are you interested in contradiction, particularly between the beautiful and the horrific?

Komunyakaa: A good example comes from growing up in Louisiana. Being conscious of English and what's buried within the context of the English language—I'm particularly thinking of that which is dark, that which is always defined as horrific, always mysterious—98 percent of words, phrases, prefixes about darkness would probably be regarded as negative. And yet when I looked at nature, going back to childhood experiences, I always saw those places of darkness as places of a celebration of life, an embracing of life, the making of life. In the same way of Theodore Roethke's poem "Root Cellar," you know, this down in the intense murky existence of things, going back to the basic concept of life. As a matter of fact, probably sunlight, especially immense, intense sunlight, would destroy.

Barnstone: . . . I think you can take it back to the Zoroastrians, when you begin to separate a god of light from a god of darkness, and say that the god of light is the god of good and the god of darkness evil, as compared to Taoism, where you have yin but also have yang, and they're interconnected.

Komunyakaa: But we—as writers, critics, whatever—have sort of embraced the contradictions.

Garabedian: Do you think this negativity associated with darkness is a particularly Western convention?

Komunyakaa: It seems more apparent as a Western condition. It's all woven into the language, and I think it has a lot to do with the Western psyche.

Barnstone: And not only the language but also the images. Was it *Newsweek* or *Time* where the image of O. J. Simpson was darkened to make him look more threatening?

Komunyakaa: Yes, it's amazing—the technology.

Barnstone: Or the other [image] that jumps out in my mind is Sadaam Hussein during the Gulf War. I believe it was a *New Republic* cover, where they shortened his mustache so he would look like Hitler. Talk about disinformation!

Komunyakaa: I have a sense that these individuals—beyond the airbrushing and so forth or coloration—know exactly what they're doing. And it's amazing that they would know what they're doing and we, often, as audience, are not aware. I would rather think that we are aware of all this baggage.

Barnstone: As Orwell writes, I have the quote here, "political language—and with variations this is true of all political language from conservative to anarchist—is designed to make lies sound truthful, and murder respectable, and give the appearance of solidity to pure wind. One cannot change this all in a moment, but one can at least change one's own habits, and from time to time one can, if one jeers loudly enough, send some worn-out and useless phrase into the dustbin where it belongs."

Komunyakaa: Let's hope so! This whole thing with praising darkness—why not praise darkness along with light?

Garabedian: A sort of all-inclusiveness.

Komunyakaa: Well . . . we cannot define one without the other.

Garabedian: I would think that generally violence is regarded as negative. But the representations of violence in some of the poems seem to attain a contradictory status of good, and, if not good, then neutrality in the matter-of-fact presentation. Instances of sex are often treated in a similar manner, and, in fact, they (violence and sex) are sometimes allied; for example, in "Woman, I Got the Blues," the woman lies "Half-naked on the living room floor; / the moon falling through the window / on you like a rapist." If I could go back to Whitman—he celebrates sex and violence because he is a transcendentalist; there is an all-inclusiveness where everything is good. How does the neutral exposition of violence or sex function in your poetry?

Komunyakaa: Well, first of all, I think it's not the fact that the country is so violent, or "the making of civilization" is so violent—one war after another, one army conquering the other. For me, in looking at violence, we recognize its extreme in order to go past it. We deal with it. We break it down to its elements and deal with it in that way. We take it apart. I've been fascinated recently about how we talk about mass murderers in this country. We have a profile today of such murderers: a Midwesterner looking a certain way—not exactly like James Dean, but coming pretty close. And I think it's taken us some time to recognize this image. Maybe in recognizing this image we can deal with it. Because violence is not new, as all civilizations can attest to.

Garabedian: Thinking about civilization, do you see a distinction in the type of violence related in the corpse garden in "Blasphemy" from *Copacetic* as opposed to, say, the goat's slaughter in "Happiness" from *Magic City*?

Komunyakaa: When we think of violence in this country, we think of urban violence. How about rural violence? My tendency is to think of rural violence as the most severe. And, interestingly enough, the whole thing with the ritual of the goat killing or the hog slaughter is associated with the rural violence that we take for granted. I'm particularly thinking of the child who internalizes this ritual. Getting his hands bloody as well. And this is something we accept.

Barnstone: My understanding of *Dien Cai Dau* is that it is a kind of extension of the kinds of dramatic monologues and third-person story poems that your first two books were engaged with, in which you blend together autobiography with speaking in a more general way as a universal soldier. When you move to *Magic City*, are you fully in autobiographical mode, or are you still speaking in dramatic monologues? Do you worry about the boundary between fiction and autobiography?

Komunyakaa: Not really, because when I wrote the first of those poems, "Venus's-Flytraps," I realized that here I had reintroduced myself to a certain terrain—and it was a necessary terrain to deal with. I had very systematically written around this, in the same way I had systematically written around the Vietnam experience. It became important to write about things I had dismissed from the territory of poetry.

Barnstone: That's interesting, because so many writers today feel that they can't get past their lives and their childhoods as the territory for poetry, and yet it took you a long journey to come to this point. It's an interesting journey, and in a lot of ways it mirrors a lot of the confessional poets—people like Robert Lowell, Adrienne Rich, and others who started off formally and moved toward the more personal.

Komunyakaa: Yes.

Barnstone: I have a more nuts-and-bolts question about the poems. As an aside, I should say that I love the fact that they are such visual poems, and short-line poems. Do you really see yourself as a poet of the eyes—of the visual sense—and do you think that is one thing that makes you write shorter lines, because it tends to frame those images more clearly?

Komunyakaa: I think so. It has a lot to do with growing up in a rural space. Oftentimes I found myself as a child attracted to wooded areas, attracted to the rituals of the birds and insects. If I hadn't become a poet, I'd probably be a painter. Often I wish I could paint, but that might be something I can attempt later on.

Barnstone: The follow-up to this is that John Engels, in what's otherwise a positive review of *Magic City*, complains of what he calls "obsessive simile-making." Certainly, throughout *Dien Cai Dau* simile dominates the rhetoric, and is the primary form of figurative speech. It seems to me, however, that this use of simile is quite self-conscious, particularly in one poem, "You and I Are Disappearing," which is wholly structured around a proliferation of similes. I'm wondering why this is so relentlessly a book about what war is like. Is it something about the ineffability of the violent sublime of war that you can't name it directly?

Komunyakaa: Well, I think what it is, is an attempt to name it. Because I do think it is a composite of so many things—history, culture, and so forth. So, it's always something that seems to escape naming. One reason is that we don't want to believe what we have witnessed. Some people say, "No, this can't be true—it has to be this." And then we say, "It's this—no! It can't be this, it is something else." So, it is that kind of journey—a journey into the mystery.

Barnstone: Is it also a kind of mending? I'm thinking of one moment in "A Greenness Taller than Gods" where the soldiers are breaking the landscape, as they walk they're breaking spider webs, and "the spiders mend [the] webs [the soldiers] march into." It seems like the similes are doing this mending somehow.

Komunyakaa: It's an attempt to suture that which has been disturbed, that which has been cut into and cursed by the presence of the outsider.

Garabedian: In *Dien Cai Dau*'s "Hanoi Hannah" or "Tu Do Street" (and some extent "One Legged Stool") you deal with the African American experience and Vietnam. I was interested in the presentation. You are African American and a Vietnam veteran, and both of these groups have been marginalized in many ways at various points throughout American history. Other African American poets and writers—Langston Hughes, W. E. B. Du Bois, Naomi Long Madgett, Audre Lorde—in addition to veteran poets and writers like Randall Jarrell and Amiri Baraka, tend to manifest in their works particularly angry sentiments, perhaps because of this marginalization. I find in your poems a greater objectivity. I was wondering what you hope to achieve through this objectivity.

Komunyakaa: I think it had a lot to do with the fact I waited fourteen years to write about the experience. Consequently, there is a certain kind of objectivity. I wanted the images to do the work—I wanted to avoid statement, if possible.

Barnstone: Is there an influence in your work of Chinese poetry—I know that there is the wonderful poem about Li Po: "Everyone's Reading Li Po." But the reason I say this is because there seems to be this ability in Li Po and Du Fu to blend an absolute crystal-clear objectivity of vision—of the self, the body, and the world—with quite extraordinary statements of countries destroyed in rebellion and warfare.

Komunyakaa: Well, I've read some of the classical Chinese poets, some of the classical Vietnamese poets as well, and I think it has to do with an attempt to understand—to have a sense of a place. That is, not to reap any kind of domination, but in a sense to try to cultivate celebration.

Garabedian: I was going to ask if this objective presentation called into question some of the issues that these images might suggest. For example, the absence of anger calls anger into question.

Komunyakaa: I don't know if I could say that anger has been totally erased from the canvas. I do think there's a certain kind of anger there, and it has to do with the ability to present the whole of the picture. It's not cut off in any way, and I attempt to show every little corner of the picture, if possible. And in that sense, the reader or the listener enters in as an active participant of meaning, definition.

Barnstone: In some ways it's harder to preach to people than it is to show them.

Komunyakaa: Yes. I think, automatically, because what I hope I'm doing is trying to activate participation.

Barnstone: As in "Reflections," it seems to me that what we're talking about is how you put the second person—the you, the reader—into his shoes.

Komunyakaa: Such a long-ago poem! That sort of surprises me.

Garabedian: I kind of saw a progression in the four books, sort of getting darker and darker from *Copacetic* to *I Apologize for the Eyes in My Head* to *Dien Cai Dau*, but then in *Magic City* there is a sort of rebirth. Did you perhaps need to go through the experience of writing *Dien Cai Dau* to get to the "Happiness" or "Glory" of *Magic City*?

Komunyakaa: Well, it's not so much the happiness—it's a different landscape. But it's still a part of my psychological landscape. I do think, yes, the writing of the Vietnam poems helped me to get to *Magic City*. If I hadn't written *Dien Cai Dau*, I probably wouldn't have written *Magic City*.

Barnstone: I have a follow-up to that question, about *Dien Cai Dau*. The book goes through some pretty awful places but seems to end surprisingly upbeat. It ends with poems about boat people daydreaming about "Jade Mountain," about the half-American and half-Vietnamese children who were the product of so much death, and with an extraordinary poem about memory, emotion, and loss. And also that extraordinary poem "Facing It," which ends ambiguously upbeat: "In the black mirror [of the monument] / a woman's trying to erase names: / No, she's brushing a boy's hair." It's both a kind of erasure, forgetting all this tragedy, and at the same time a gesture of either comfort or affection. It seems to me that the book is moving toward some kind of resolution through emotion, affection, maybe even forgetting. Was the writing of the book itself that kind of resolution for you, or did it help?

Komunyakaa: No, not really. It wasn't an erasure. It was more an attempt to gain a certain clarity, because I wanted to understand the experience, and I think that, in writing the book, I understood the steps through the ritual.

Barnstone: The ritual of war?

Komunyakaa: The ritual of war through reflection.

Barnstone: The Argentine writer Jorge Luis Borges was once touring the Midwest and was asked by a member of the audience, "Mr. Borges, could you tell us whether there has been one woman in your life who has been your muse, and your great love?" And Borges thought about this in silence for a minute before replying: "Yes, as a matter of fact, there was, but the strange thing about it is that she kept on changing her name." In *Dien Cai Dau* you also seem to be creating this universal woman, a kind of anima figure, who is simultaneously prostitute, betrayer, lover, mother, fighter—all these things. In a number of poems you talk about her always appearing in different wars in different places. I'm interested where the female resides in your wartime imagination, and where does sex and motherhood and generation come into this activity in which, for the most part, men kill men?

Komunyakaa: Well . . . on the boundary, on the periphery, of every war, there seems to be the spoils of war alongside an industry of sex. But it's more than that, because often there's a kind of cleansing going on as well. People are getting killed, and people are being born on the periphery. This has always been the case, and so I see it as a kind of natural presentation. Because the same men who are killing, the next day are loving. And often risking their hearts. So there is all this contradiction in their personality and perception. And I suppose we need that kind of complexity in order to make ourselves whole—you'll find all the contradictions.

Barnstone: There are also a lot of moments in the book where the men fighting with each other are described as lovers. There's that moment in "Sappers," where the sappers with dynamite wrapped around their naked bodies are throwing themselves into the arms of the GIs; there's a moment where the speaker in a poem is shooting a soldier who's swaying in the grass as if dancing with a woman at that moment, and at the end of the poem turns him over so that he's not kissing the ground, but kissing the sky like in "Purple Haze." So, there's a kind of erotics of death going on, too.

Komunyakaa: I suppose we might go back to Alexander the Great. When Thracian soldiers paired, they fought harder, they defended each other to the death, I suppose. That might at least be the background.

Barnstone: Achilles and Patrocles.

Komunyakaa: Yes.

Garabedian: You talked before about including the contradictions—presenting it all. It seems perhaps that you want to present "the truth." In fact, many of your poems are concerned with what one might call "the search for truth." Here I'm thinking of poems like "Safe Subjects" or "Gift Horse," or even "Instructions for Building Straw Huts," where it becomes imperative "to understand" and "to know." To some extent "Tunnels" from *Dien Cai Dau* might be thought upon as the tunnel rat's own search. There is also the notion that what is real has been hidden for whatever reason; again and again there are allusions within the poems to masks, which both hide the wearer and obstruct his or her view.

Komunyakaa: One is reminded here of Dunbar's "We Wear the Mask." But it's more than that. It's the fact that we often find ourselves masked against history. Or, more completely, hoodwinked.

Garabedian: "Let truth have its way with us" the speaker in "Safe Subjects" implores. Can poetry be employed as a method to arrive at truth?

Komunyakaa: Well, at least an approximation of truth—truth with a small *t*.

Garabedian: Then again, in "Venus's-Flytraps" the child wants to know— he's so very curious. At one point, he says, "I can hurt you with / questions / like silver bullets." Is poetry such a silver bullet?

Komunyakaa: Not really a "silver bullet" as much as . . . well, let me think about this. Because when we think of silver bullets, it is in a negative way. That is, to kill the werewolf—the predator at night. But if we think of the poem, we think of the poem as a place where we're trying to get to an approximated truth. And this involves our search into our own psyches that is an attempt to align the external with the internal. So, truth is always taking a step back—and it keeps us moving ahead—and there comes a point where what we really discover is, in essence, our own selves.

Barnstone: It's interesting, particularly if you think of the tunnel rat as digging for truth, since, if he finds the truth, he finds the enemy—it's kill or be killed. An uncomfortable truth!

Komunyakaa: Yes.

Barnstone: I'd like to shift subjects here and talk about your interest in music a bit. I'm thinking about the book *Copacetic*. *Copacetic* is a book with many dramatic monologues, often spoken in a very interesting idiom, by characters who have street names. And a lot of the poems are called "blues poems"—there's "Untitled Blues," or "Jumping Bad Blues," or "Woman, I Got the Blues." I'm wondering, do you come to this dramatic monologue tradition—as I said earlier, I came to write dramatic monologues myself after reading Browning, Masters, Robinson, Ai, and others. Ezra Pound. Do you come then from the blues or poetry, or both?

Komunyakaa: I grew up where the radio was always on, and consequently I internalized the blues to an extent. What I mean by "the blues"—I don't mean, you know, melancholy. The blues is really a combination of many different feelings. So, when I got to New Orleans, I would often have the radio turned to WWOZ—traditional blues, jazz—and in a way it connected me to those early experiences being four or five years old, listening to the radio. In some way I think it really helped me to write some of those poems. And I do see the blues as confrontation. I'm not talking in a strict political sense, but confrontation with one's mortality, confrontation with the essence of just being human. Pain, celebration—all those things mixed together—not creating a flotsam but creating a kind of relation, if possible.

Barnstone: The blues poems are also joined with a smaller number of poems about jazz, and about jazz greats—Monk and Mingus, for instance. Also, you've co-edited an anthology of jazz poetry. My question is whether the jazz poems versus the blues poems—whether you're trying to do something different in terms of mood, or rhythm.

Komunyakaa: Mood, yes. But essentially I think we cannot really have jazz without having the blues.

Garabedian: I'm thinking about the melancholy of your utterances—that "cruel happiness." A lot of times in *Magic City* this negativity in the text—or ostensible negativity—informs the present, and redeems it in that manner. Do you get that at all from the blues? It seems to me that there's a similar process happening in the blues.

Komunyakaa: In the blues, if you listen to the lyrics, they're singing about heartbreak, failures. But you realize that they're singing from the point of view of witness, of experience, but also an attempt to get beyond the pathos by singing about it, by laying it out, by "putting it on the line," as they say. It was, in a way, a departure into another day.

Barnstone: And structurally? In a poem that is structured as a jazz or blues poem, do you find yourself doing more repetition?

Komunyakaa: In a blues poem I think automatically you have to have—if you think about the classical blues—at least a refrain. Often what I'll do is I might write a poem with a refrain in it and then take it out, because a refrain pushes an intuitive imaging.

Barnstone: It becomes the underpainting.

Komunyakaa: Yes.

Audience Member: How do you try to get the oral quality of your poems across when you write them down? Just the way you spoke them carried its own meaning.

Komunyakaa: I'm quite conscious of spoken diction. But I also think the poem has to function on the page as well, and, for me, the white space is silence. Think about silence. We wouldn't have music if there wasn't silence, because we wouldn't have modulation. We wouldn't have tension or the space for tonal contrasts.

Barnstone: William Carlos Williams used to like to quote from Gertrude Stein: "a poem is made up of words, and the space between the words."

Komunyakaa: Yes.

Barnstone: I noticed when you were reading there were a lot of interesting pauses syncopating the sentences. I was wondering—because I wasn't following on the page—whether those correlate with line breaks?

Komunyakaa: Sometimes they correlate with line breaks. Other times what I do is I like to tell myself that I want to surprise myself in reading, if possible. And I do that because there is flexibility in language. It's elastic, you know. You can pull it this way and that, and it can endure that kind of tension, push-pull. In the same way I think musicians work. I'm not talking about Coltrane's idea about sheets of sound, but a kind of blues modulation.

Barnstone: One of the things the critics are tied up in knots about is what on earth Williams's "variable foot" actually means. But one of the most sensible explanations they've come up with is that it's essentially the same as musical notation. That any line or partial line in the triadic stanza of a Williams poem can be read incredibly slowly like a whole note, or many words will be eighth notes, and so that way you can expand or pace the poem. Do you see that happening in your poetry? Do you work with a variable foot, do you work with some kind of metrics? Or is it visual poetry, as some people say?

Komunyakaa: Early on—my very first poems—were over-controlled, traditional. A good example: The very first poem I wrote was in high school, and it was one hundred lines long, traditional rhyming quatrains—I remember being too shy to read it. So, somebody has it somewhere. As a matter of fact, I'm the one who has it. It's a well-kept secret.

Audience: [*Laughter.*]

Komunyakaa: But, I used to count out the metrics of the poem. Now, I read everything aloud to myself. The ear is a great editor. Even when poems are published I'm still revising. But one doesn't want to polish the heart out of the poem.

Barnstone: It's interesting. I usually think of metrics as a good training device to develop the ear; once you have the ear, you can dispose of the metrics.

Komunyakaa: That's right, but one has to be conscious of the poem's musical tensions or possibilities.

Audience Member: When you were writing that one hundred–line poem in high school, do you think of yourself then as a poet? When did you know?

Komunyakaa: I'll tell you exactly when it happened. I had been teaching at the University of New Orleans, and I said (I'd been teaching four sections of composition for a few years): "Okay. What I'm going to do is apprentice myself to a cabinet maker. And I'll become a cabinet maker in order to have time to do my writing." That's when I knew!

Audience: [*Laughter.*]

Ayame Fukuda: My experience tonight listening to you read was as if I was being amplified through your words. It was the most physical poetry reading experience I've had. I have heard other poets who have been influenced by jazz, but, for some reason, my head was the drum, and my body was full of insects, and it was the jungle, and I think the lack of finite resolution at the end allows the reader—or not the reader but the receiver, I guess—to reverberate back with you. Something like that. There's a reverberation happening.

Komunyakaa: Well, that's interesting because my idea is to—if possible—create a situation where the listener or the reader can be co-creators. And if possible, whenever that happens, we can say it's working. Often that's how I read poems. I'm very taken with poems that I can enter in as an active participant. Everything hasn't been told to me, it hasn't been resolved, it hasn't been neatly tied up.

Ayame Fukuda: A lot of your endings kept me on edge, awaiting, as if I were about to take that next physical step. I know I'm speaking sort of vaguely . . .

Komunyakaa: No, no! That's the same thing I feel with certain musicians. There's a certain kind of phrasing.

Ayame Fukuda: A phrasing that you had and that I would complete. I almost felt like humming with you or completing your phrases, or I would pick up on a rhythm that you dictated and I'd go "da-da-da-da" in my head. I really heard the stuff in my head.

Komunyakaa: That's interesting. I would like to know . . . can I have a dictation?

Audience: [*Laughter.*]

Ayame Fukuda: It was a very musical experience.

Garabedian: You preface parts 1 and 2 of *I Apologize for the Eyes in My Head* with quotes from Aimé Césaire's *Poetry and Knowledge* and Czeslaw Milosz's "Dedication," respectively. Césaire contends that the poet's "entire being [and] experience should become the poem," while Milosz suggests that "poetry which does not save / Nations or people" is deficient. The first poem seems to endorse a more esoteric or cathartic type of poetry; the second advocates a more exoteric, possibly didactic poetry. I'm wondering which of the two types—the reflective or the instructional—is more important for your poetry? Are the two necessarily distinct?

Komunyakaa: I think they're interwoven. I think I can't have one without the other. But I don't quite necessarily see Milosz as didactic. I see what's happening there as a presentation of a certain reality that embraces images that are often beautiful, frightening. I don't see at all how the attempt to get to the truth is didactic, the attempt to say "I witness this" is didactic. It's more presentational than anything else—this is what happened, so consequently you don't have to go through it. You only have to use your imagination to get there, necessarily.

Garabedian: Does this at all inform whom your audience is—those who haven't experienced these types of things?

Komunyakaa: No, I think all of us experience all kinds of negative things, and there's a whole commodity of distractions in which we try to escape them, and we realize that's impossible, finally. So I think maybe what I'm saying is that we have the capacity to have a certain empathy for those who come into contact with that which is horrific. We have the capacity to measure out the horrors against their existence. At least I hope so.

Barnstone: And the words in the poems, as I am understanding you—again, I'm thinking here of William Carlos Williams—there's a moment in an essay about Shakespeare in which he sees Shakespeare as one who didn't write *words* so much as write *actions*, and this is what he thinks a poem should do. Not print a copy off the face of the world, but make a world for people to walk into.

Komunyakaa: Yes. To not show them through it, to not guide them through it, but the world is placed there, you enter at your own risk and necessity.

Garabedian: You are located to some extent in academia. One friend of mine contends that academia is a means by which issues that society deems "radical" or controversial might be marginalized. Do you think this is true?

This would depend much upon what you see as the purpose of your poetry, but do you find your position in this setting hindering at all?

Komunyakaa: Well, I don't think so. For the most part, it keeps me close to what I like doing. Reading is one thing; I think it's important, and I think it has a lot to do with my own creativity. We have spoken about science. I tend to tell people to read texts in literature, science, history, philosophy, etc. The reason for science is that there's a line between beauty and terror, and it creates artistic tension. Poetry has to have tension. That's probably the only thing I embraced from John Crowe Ransom—the Fugitives.

Barnstone: For the last year I've been obsessed with chaos and imagination—where the two intersect. Often what I find myself doing for myself and my students is to—rather like having your students read history and science—is to show them that the brain is much better at making connections between two already-present objects than it is about taking one object and imagining what sort of connection might reach out to another, as yet undetermined, object. So, if you randomly fill your brain with a chaos of words from another discourse—science, physics, whatever it may be—while you're writing about making love, driving your car, whatever it may be, then you'll suddenly find a language for it that is utterly unexpected.

Komunyakaa: Surprise.

Barnstone: Yes.

Komunyakaa: The surprise is very important. That has a lot to do with the composition of a poem. One wants to surprise himself or herself, and consequently when that happens, often we say, "Where did that come from?" It came from some little place within the context of the psyche—some little door. That's the joy in the imagination, and it has a lot to do with possibility.

Yusef Komunyakaa

Toi Derricotte/1997

Originally recorded by the Lanaan Foundation on 11 November 1997. Reprinted by permission.

Derricotte: Yusef, I was told by someone that at one time you were a carpenter and I'm just wondering how did you get from carpentry to poetry?

Komunyakaa: Well, my father was a carpenter. Matter of fact he was a finishing carpenter, and he trained me by having me work with him measuring boards as a ten- or twelve-year-old; and he taught me something, I think, about patience; because he would measure a board five or six times, and once he cut it, it would always just slide into place, and only in retrospect do I realize that perhaps he also taught me something about poetry—about the attempt of being an artist.

Derricotte: The people that you write about in Bogalusa—the community there—there are so many hard things in their lives, but they seem to be such strong, resilient people . . . I'm wondering what you learned in that community. What are some of the things that people taught you?

Komunyakaa: Well, there was such an emphasis placed on work, and particularly I'm thinking about my father again. In a way he was a black Calvinist when I think about it. [Laughter] He thought that physical labor would lead to freedom and salvation. So I learned a whole lot about the rituals of work; but I also learned something about endurance, that there is a kind of confrontation and celebration within our everyday lives.

Derricotte: Turning now to the landscapes in your work: The people you write about seem very wedded to the landscape and it seems to be very nurturing. And then there is the way you write about animals—that wonderful poem tonight that you did is so compassionate. And I'm just wondering about the landscape in your work, the animals, the insects, and how you feel so much a part of them.

Komunyakaa: In retrospect, I suppose it was a semi-bucolic existence, but when I was there it was sheer hell in many ways. But I remember venturing out into the woods. Often I would. I liked being alone, and it was a kind of meditation on that landscape, but also almost a clinical look at the landscape because I wanted to know the rituals of animals. I wanted to know the rituals of insects. Consequently, in a way, for me those rituals came to parallel the rituals of people around me. It was a way of seeing for the most part.

Derricotte: Given the rituals that you talk about and the ones that appear in your poems, I would think you would be talking about Christianity in these environments. But what you appear to be thinking of now is not the Christian rituals; it's something else. You talk about sorcerers in your childhood and the name of your [recent] book is *Magic City*.

Komunyakaa: Well, *Magic City* is actually—every town has its nickname. My title refers to a place that is really controlled by the economics of pulpwood and the smells of chemicals and is nicknamed "Magic City." I thought it was rather ironic. In that sense, my title is satirical.

Derricotte: Yet there's a lot of magic going on there . . . the magic of rituals and—

Komunyakaa: The conjuring, yes, it's there. I grew up with people talking about hoodoo. I'm talking about salt sprinkled on the back porch and money powder and things of that sort. Later on, after living in New Orleans and teaching at the University of New Orleans, I began to look closely at some of the shops in that city and I found that, well, this wasn't a dream after all. These things do exist. I was quite surprised by that.

Derricotte: Frequently, I think that, as African American poets, we're asked to resolve the problems of race and to sort of give a hopeful look at things and to sort of provide uplift. I don't think your work is about that. How do you feel about this issue? Is uplift your responsibility?

Komunyakaa: I don't think it is my responsibility to do that. I'm thinking of the Harlem Renaissance writers. Some of them really short-changed themselves. I'm particularly thinking about a number of the poets who didn't embrace the work of Langston Hughes and we got into this whole debate about what's high and what's low culture. I think the writer has to take chances. I think the artist has to take chances just by the fact that we are born into such an interesting, problematic world for each of us is a challenge. It's not for me to really place any kind of design on experience or observations.

Derricotte: Your work seems to fall into projects and *Magic City* seems to cover a time period maybe of latency in a young boy's life. *Dien Cai Dau* also covers a certain period of time. I'm curious as to the period of gestation— fourteen years I've heard—before you wrote the book about the war.

Komunyakaa: *Dien Cai Dau* took fourteen years, but I actually sort of stumbled into that book. What I mean by that is, I was in the process of renovating a house in New Orleans. I'd been teaching at the University of New Orleans, and it was summertime. You know how those ceilings are in that city? I don't know how many of you have been to New Orleans. They have twelve- or fourteen-foot ceilings. I had this ladder and I was constantly going up and going down the ladder. I had a pad of paper at the bottom of the ladder and often when I would get down to the bottom I would write down an image and I found myself writing a poem entitled "Somewhere Near Phu Bai." That sort of uncapped this reservoir of images. The poems began to come forth, but, yes, it took me fourteen years. I usually work on three projects side by side, three collections of poems. One reason is that I want to be surprised. So I go back and forth between those collections—not that I'm straining to surprise myself or anything of that sort, but because this is natural for me.

Derricotte: You were a journalist in the war, is that right?

Komunyakaa: I had gone to infantry OCS and at that particular time they were searching for lieutenants who could perform as platoon leaders and somewhere along the line I heard that in a combat situation a second lieutenant only lasts for ten seconds. I said, "Well, why didn't I know that before?" [laughter] What happened is that I went off to jungle warfare training afterwards, and I applied for a branch transfer in the information field. And people were telling me, "Well, the army spent $10,000 on your training; you won't get a branch transfer into Information." And I thought, once the branch transfer came through, that I was lucky—until I got there. Because then I was in the field every day for six months, pursuing stories that happened in the area of operation. I was in the American Division, the largest in Vietnam, about twenty-four or twenty-five-thousand soldiers.

Derricotte: Wow, did you take any notes for yourself during the war? Did you write anything? Is there some way these images became embedded in you or did they just come forth?

Komunyakaa: I took with me to Vietnam two collections of poetry. I took Hayden Carruth's anthology *The Voice Great Within Us*, and I took Donald Allen's anthology *Contemporary American Poetry*. I wasn't writing poetry. I had written one poem. I had written a poem dedicated to my graduating class in high school. I don't know how that came about . . . I just found myself raising my hand one day saying I think I can write a poem. I'd been reading poetry, so I agonized over my decision for a long time; I said, "Damn, what did I volunteer for?" And finally I wrote a one-hundred-line poem, twenty-five quatrains. And then I didn't write for a long time until I came to the

University of Colorado in 1973. There I was in a creative writing workshop, and I've been writing ever since.

Derricotte: For our last couple questions I was going to ask you if you have any advice to give young writers, maybe especially African American poets.

Komunyakaa: I tell people that there's an intricate connection between writing and reading. I think that one has to know what the tradition is in order to break the rules, in order to become innovative. One has to know what is a sonnet, sestina, villanelle, or whatever, in order to break the rules. I also suggest that it's not just the reading of literature that is necessary; it's also the reading of science, psychology, anthropology, history, and so forth. It's all connected. And one has to have a need. Sometimes almost a severe need. So there's a dedication as such, and I talk about revision. Revision basically means to re-see. My method of composition is influenced by jazz. I write everything almost in an improvising manner. And then, very systematically, I revise the poem. Initially a poem could be a hundred lines long, and I very systematically cut it back to thirty or forty lines, focusing on the key images that are important. Often I think poems are resolved prematurely. I tell students to place a blank sheet of paper at the bottom of the poem and begin to work up to just to see how many possible endings the poem has. So poetry involves a process of re-seeing every day.

Derricotte: And finally, many poets keep relatively the same style throughout their writing careers once they have a voice that is unique, their own. With you we just never know. Every book seems to bring forth a different kind of consciousness. I mean, there's something there that's basically you, but there are these changes; your work seems to maybe I should say evolve, or maybe evolve is not the word, but it makes me wonder where your work is going in the future, what the forthcoming book is like, whether you see where the work is going, or whether you're waiting to be surprised yourself, or . . .

Komunyakaa: Well, the forthcoming book, *Thieves of Paradise*, is rather a longish book. I knew I wanted seven sections so in a certain sense there is an emotional or psychological symmetry within the collection. I tend to also be influenced by numerology. So that may even have something to do with the fact that I'm working on three books side-by-side always. I just like to know what the possibilities are of pushing that envelope. A good example is that I'm writing a book called *Pleasure Dome*.

The book has been developing for a long time. It grew out of the circumstance of my having students come to my office. . . . A great deal of my teaching happened within the context of conferences. . . . I would start talking to them about African American history, world history in the context of the black experience. I would throw out Pushkin. (You know Pushkin addressed his African background.) Or I would throw out Hannibal the Great or Charles Drew, responsible for the early research done on blood plasma. And finally I wanted to write a book that was a kind of excavation of black history, and I started writing poems with three-line stanzas. And what I discovered with this three-line, staggered stanza is that I could have a kind of lyricism that would at the same time include historical facts and so forth. So that was sort of a surprise for me. It's a book I will probably be working on for a long time. This is really a trilogy: *Taboo, Lust,* and *Bread.*

I should also mention the sixteen-line poems, in which I want to write about those things that we think of as insignificant. Here I want a kind of compression. Think about those artificial flowers that, dropped in water, expand—I want that kind of compression, if possible, so that you could spend hours explicating each sixteen-line poem, if you really desired.

Survival Masks: An Interview
with Yusef Komunyakaa

Sascha Feinstein/1997

From *Ask Me Now: Conversations on Jazz & Literature* (Indiana University Press, 2007, pp. 53–79). Reprinted by permission.

In 1995, Yusef Komunyakaa telephoned to ask for valuable biographical sources about Charlie Parker. He explained that he was writing a libretto, a long poem about Bird that would eventually be set to music by an Australian composer and producer. Over the next couple of years, he mentioned the poem in passing. (Yusef never easily parts with information about himself; when he won the Pulitzer, for example, he taught his class and told them *nothing*.) When he eventually said he'd completed his libretto, I fantasized about publishing the piece in *Brilliant Corners*, but I didn't want our friendship strained in any way so I simply asked if he would let me read it.

I received "Testimony" a few days later, and found it to be linguistically spectacular—a monumental tribute worthy of Charlie Parker's music. I called him right away and asked if he had sent it out for publication. He had. Worse: He'd sent it to a handsome, prestigious journal. I said, "I'm sure they snapped it up." Remarkably, though, this journal felt the poem was too long to run and wanted to print selections. The rest of our conversation went something like this:

I shouted, *"Excerpts? Are you kidding me? That poem's not meant to be excerpted."*

Yusef said, "Hmmmm."

I said, "That poem is symphonic."

He said, "Hmmm."

"Yusef, that poem's a very serious poem."

"Yes."

"That poem's meant to be read in its entirety."

"Yes, yes. I think you're right"—and shortly thereafter, he agreed to publish "Testimony" in *Brilliant Corners*.

At the last, however, this literary coup took place because of Yusef's generosity and kindness. The least I could do was feature the libretto as prominently as possible, which is why this taped conversation accompanied the poem.

Yusef Komunyakaa has published many books of poetry, including *Pleasure Dome: New and Collected Poems*, *Talking Dirty to the Gods*, and *Taboo*. He is also author of *Blue Notes: Essays, Interviews, and Commentaries*, and co-editor of *The Jazz Poetry Anthology* and its companion volume *The Second Set*. His many honors include the William Faulkner Award from the University of Rennes, the Hanes Poetry Prize, the Thomas Forcade Award, fellowships from the National Endowment for the Arts, and the Pulitzer Prize. He also received the Bronze Star for his service in Vietnam. In 1999, he was elected a Chancellor of The Academy of American Poets. He teaches at New York University.

This conversation focused on "Testimony." The interview took place at The Runcible Spoon (a coffeehouse in Bloomington, Indiana) on June 25, 1997.

Sascha Feinstein: What initially inspired you to write a libretto?
Yusef Komunyakaa: Well, Chris Williams at the Australian Broadcasting Corporation first approached me in early 1995 with the idea of a libretto, something that celebrated jazz's relationship with blues and gospel. I chimed to this wonderful idea because I feel that my work, my poetry, has evolved out of this musical tradition. In this first discussion, Chris described his admiration for Charlie Parker's musical ideas and then he mentioned that most likely Sandy Evans would compose the music.

Immediately I felt this was a healthy challenge. I had heard one of her three groups, Ten Part Invention, at a local pub a week earlier in Sydney and I remembered going away highly impressed. She has exciting musical ideas, and she blows that sax as if she was made for the instrument. However, the more I thought about the impending piece, the more I wanted to write something new and different. I began to play Charlie Parker, everything he did, and I clothed my psyche in his sounds again. Though I'd listened to him through the years, he was still new and traditional in the same breath, old and cosmopolitan.

I think Chris was thinking of a more traditional libretto but I wanted a flexible definition. With Parker, I felt that a traditional libretto would pull against his experimentation and his whole trajectory of working things out as he went along. I wanted the piece to emulate the musical ideas, how they would flow for him.

Feinstein: In essence, what did you keep and what did you pull away from?

Komunyakaa: I pulled away from the structure of the libretto. I wanted something to excite me and surprise me, so what I went for was a kind of composite. I started thinking about the actions of Parker, and also about the fact that many of the stories were erroneous, misleading. A good example is the story that Parker died in Baroness Pannonica's bathroom at the Stanhope Hotel with a needle in his arm. This is the story I had been told. So everything was rather melodramatic and less complex, and what I wanted to do was capture the complexity of this man.

Feinstein: Of course, the truth of his death—that he died watching a juggler on the TV—has often become melodramatic in the way that it's been presented and reported—

Komunyakaa: Yes, right. But at least there's something pleasing about the truth. Let's face it, he's *laughing*, and not sitting on the commode grimacing with a needle in his arm.

Feinstein: I know that often in your career a particular poem has triggered many others, even an entire book. Did a particular section or image generate the rest of this poem?

Komunyakaa: I tell you, the first idea that came to me was based on a photograph I'd seen of Parker where he's about one year, holding a brush in his hand. There's something about the severe innocence.

Feinstein: He looks like a girl.

Komunyakaa: Yes, very much so. I kept glancing from that photo to the photo of him at the Bird's Nest in Los Angeles in 1947. He's with Harold Doc West, Red Callender, and Erroll Garner, and he has a smile that suggests he has been initiated by hard times and joy. It is a visual moment of knowledge and acknowledgment. Cocky.

And, also, there's another photograph of Parker as a young boy, maybe a year and a half, astride a Palomino pony. I began to weigh this image against the image of him carefully listening to two Apache visitors, Swift Eagle and Bad Wolf, at the Royal Roost. He seems so attentive, it parallels something glimpsed of him in those early images. I wanted to at least attempt to unearth a moment of this somethingness, this mystery, through "Testimony." But I was also drawn to the later photographs of Parker. So I am interested in that contrast—the innocence and, later on, something close to a visual ferocity.

We tend to think of jazz and gospel as opposites. Blues is called "the Devil's music." One is secular, the other sacred. I tend to think of Parker as blowing both at the same time. I feel that the technology of sound through brass is his religion.

Feinstein: Obviously the music itself was the primary influence on your poem, but you also address biographical issues. Were there any literary sources that you found helpful?

Komunyakaa: I've read a number of works on Parker, such as Ross Russell's *Bird Lives!*

Feinstein: Which in fact takes many liberties with the truth—

Komunyakaa: That's the first one I read. Then I went to [Gary] Giddins's *Celebrating Bird* and Robert Reisner's *The Legend of Charlie Parker*—even to liner notes [especially Phil Schaap's writing for *Bird: The Complete Charlie Parker on Verve*], which are quite informative as well. So it was all of those things plus the imagination. I tried to create an emotional composite of the man.

Feinstein: I love how you make the effort to talk both about his life and the aesthetics of jazz, and my favorite section may very well be the third, with all the lush colors.

Komunyakaa: It's interesting, that idea of Parker being associated with visual arts. Colors and textures. Textured motion and emotion. I believe many visual artists have been influenced by jazz and the atmosphere it creates. I am thinking about Romare Bearden, Matisse's "Jazz" series, Otto Dix, Picasso, and so forth. Recently I saw an exhibit and I was quite taken with the fact there were so many visual images of Armstrong—literally hundreds—and there must be hundreds of Parker as well. I know at least one sculpture that captures him in stone, a piece by Julie MacDonald.

The idea of blowing colors is interesting to me, and I do think that there are certain tones that parallel certain colors. In a sense, that's the way I approach poetry. I think I've said somewhere that I wish I were a visual artist at times.

Feinstein: Many poets have said that.

Komunyakaa: Right. [Laughs.] The very first time someone asked me, "How do you define your poetry?" I remember saying, "I think they're word paintings?" In a certain sense, I think of Parker's tunes as pictorial.

Feinstein: "Testimony" seems to have changes in speaker. Do you hear vocal shifts?

Komunyakaa: I see this as many speakers, people telling different stories, or, at times, telling riffs on the same stories. Dealing with the space, I couldn't do *too* much of that. But this again emphasizes the complexity of Parker. I wanted a few of the pieces as multiple voices, with two or three people talking. I also wanted to give room to the director, where he could deal with these different voices. I think what Chris has planned so far is to use a thirteen-piece band and two actors, and a male chorus of four voices. So I kept thinking, "How would I do it?" and in certain cases I could see bringing in another voice in the middle of an idea or sentence.

This sort of parallels the way I construct poems often, in the sense that I love the idea of shifts happening where things are not completely resolved, where narratives do not necessarily have a lineal chart or continuity. In that way it parallels the idea of the psyche where there are many shifts.

Let's face it, Parker would have observed all kinds of things. He was a very troubled man, growing up in the Midwest, traveling around America and Europe, never really making much money, always living on the edge. But at the same time, I've seen so many photographs of him smiling—one where he's smelling a flower—which is interesting to me.

Feinstein: William Claxton selected the photograph that will be on the cover of this issue [Winter 1997] because he said he never caught Parker looking happier.

Komunyakaa: Parker seemed capable of being happy in the most troublesome moments, and I think that is the energy that people often relate to when they say "Bird" and give him this sacred dimension. I'm thinking of that Jack Kerouac poem ["239th Chorus" from *Mexico City Blues*] where he attempts to elevate Parker to Buddhahood. Parker had this capacity of embracing others, and at the same time he appears as a Trickster—trying to survive his habit, on the edge. But I don't think he ever tricked himself.

He wore many masks, multiple masks. I would classify them mainly as survival masks more than anything else. I don't know if he grew up lonely, but maybe he began creating survival masks early on, within the context of his family.

Feinstein: In the 1950s, poets dispersed Bird poems like napkins. [Komunyakaa laughs.] Some poets were much more successful than others, and I remember a few years ago when you said that Bob Kaufman had been an influential figure on your [early] poetry. Kaufman, of course, was almost obsessively attracted to Parker—

Komunyakaa: To the extent that he even named his son "Parker."

Feinstein: Do you still feel his presence guiding your sensibilities as a poet?

Komunyakaa: I'm not as quirky as Bob Kaufman. At times I wish I were! [Laughs.] He's full of surprises, and the other thing is his obsession: There's a body to that obsession which propels the music of the poems. You see that in Parker as well. I'm still quite taken with Kaufman, with his obsessive imagination.

Feinstein: You can tell that he really listened, and that he genuinely loved Charlie Parker as a human being and as an artist.

Komunyakaa: He respected Parker.

Feinstein: I think Kaufman's poems for Bird [compared to many others from the '50s] were most in tune with Parker's spirit.

Komunyakaa: Yes. He was able to penetrate the internal terrain, to get to the essence of Bird, the man. Maybe he saw part of himself in Parker. I don't know if I see part of myself in Kaufman, but it's interesting that Kaufman grew up in Louisiana [as I did], born into a complex family, with a black mother and Jewish father.

Feinstein: Many of Kaufman's contemporaries who tried to write Bird poems were, I think, emotionally removed from Parker. How did you solve that problem?

Komunyakaa: I really had to find myself meditating on the essence of Bird, and I'm glad I didn't attempt these poems early on—say, fifteen years ago. I don't know if I understood Bird early on, and I think it takes a certain amount of maturity to understand where Bird is coming from. I had to understand important things about myself in order to understand Bird. I was able to place myself, at times, in his situation. And at first it was terrifying, because people often talk about Bird and his habit—

Feinstein: Which, needless to say, did not literally parallel your life—

Komunyakaa: Of course. But I do empathize with him and understand how history helped to create him. I think he was more tender than he often wanted to appear—as hard edged as possible (maybe because he grew up in Kansas City). I was taken by the fact that Bird would wash dishes at Jimmy's Chicken Shack just to hear Art Tatum.

I think with Bird's alto there's a great lyricism, almost a tonal narrative. I'm also interested in the fact that he had such an intricate relationship with the blues—and a blues is not always a dirge. [Grins.] There's wonderment. There's laughter. There's a wholeness to his vision that I admire, and a bravery as well. There's also an ego he constantly wrestles with in his work.

Feinstein: The title of your poem changed several times.

Komunyakaa: Originally, Chris [Williams] suggested the title "Call and Response," and this idea of call and response as a dramatic device still interests

me of course. Then it changed to "Seance," but there's something about "seance" that didn't work because there's this idea of conjuring the dead. But
"Testimony" is a kind of coming forth, telling a story—a number of stories,
contradictions—braided into the fabric and design of the piece. At the same
time, it's a celebration.

Feinstein: Bringing emotional extremes together has been a central concern
of yours throughout your career as a poet, and this poem certainly does that,
sometimes quite directly: "Maybe that's when he first / played laughter &
crying / at the same time." And that's also at the center of the blues.

Komunyakaa: Yes. I think so.

Feinstein: Did you ever have an experience in your life that was similar to
Parker's artistic breakthrough when playing "Cherokee"?

Komunyakaa: That's an interesting question. When I went to Irvine in 1978
after living in Colorado for seven-and-a-half years, I wrote a poem called
"Safe Subjects," and after writing that poem I realized there was something
that taught me what I should try to accomplish in my work. It really became
a directive: "Let truth have its way with us / like a fishhook holds / to life,
holds dearly to nothing / worth saying—"

Feinstein: You've said before that you'll start a poem with a refrain and then
later extract it. I'm so glad you left the repetition in "Section V."

Komunyakaa: It's a riff on how stories come about, on possibilities.

Feinstein: What made you bring in [Anatole] Broyard [in section V]?

Komunyakaa: I wanted something to complicate the situation, and I visual-
ized Broyard walking through Washington Square Park, actually going past
Bird. I think Parker was very aware of race, even in relation to his half-broth-
er, Ikey.

Feinstein: Those issues certainly arise in section VI. And I love that image of
Bird being awakened by his mother's kisses.

Komunyakaa: When you think about it, the two brothers become a metaphor for the tensions of race in America, with Parker as a child hiding under
the bed.

Perhaps it was that tension of growing up in the 1920s that helped to create the lyrical tension beneath Parker's alto. In Amiri Baraka's *Dutchman*, the
character Clay says that Yardbird wouldn't have played with such urgency if
he had gone out into the streets and killed a white person. (Of course, this
existential act in *Dutchman* echoes Richard Wright's *Native Son*.) Indeed, I
feel muted screams underneath Parker's lyricism. There's a rage just below
the surface of a blues tonality that has been created out of need. He is sensitive to what is happening around him and to him.

Feinstein: Where did you first encounter the telegrams [in section X] that he sends to [Parker's wife] Chan after their daughter's death?

Komunyakaa: I don't even recall when I first encountered them. Maybe they are in Robert Reisner's *The Legend of Charlie Parker.* I do remember feeling that a cry sounded through the room as I read them. There's a quiet desperation in those telegrams—quiet because of the words chosen, but at the same time there's something frantic about them as well.

Feinstein: Phrase against phrase—

Komunyakaa: One after the other, almost as though he's forgotten the previous line, like words strung together by pain and regret.

Feinstein: And those strange signatures, "Sincerely, your husband."

Komunyakaa: Yes—almost as if he had to remind himself, out in L.A. I don't think he ever got along too well in L.A., that he was more at home in New York. He suffered in L.A. and found himself doing bizarre things.

Feinstein: At what point in making "Testimony" did you visualize the wondrous final images of the Chinese soldier and the engravings on Parker's horn?

Komunyakaa: That came to me as a breakthrough. One of the agonies of writing poetry is the question, "Where am I going to end this poem?" But midway through I started writing about the soldier, and the horn. For some reason I put that aside and then got back to it close to the end, and said, "Yes. This is the ending." It surprised me, and I do think it is the right stroke on the canvas.

Feinstein: "Testimony" is an individual section of your next book, *Thieves of Paradise,* which has seven sections. How does the poem function in this context?

Komunyakaa: It functions as a bridge. I think it's different from anything else in the book, and I'm glad that it's different because it sort of switches gears, but the emotional trajectory isn't broken.

Feinstein: Switching gears from what?

Komunyakaa: I think the subject matter's different, more urban. There are many shifts in "Testimony" that have to do with the possibility of many voices. Tonally it's different, though it's hard to say how exactly.

Feinstein: That's all right. Let other people chew the fat over those questions. [Komunyakaa laughs.] "Testimony" may very well be the longest poem you've ever written. Did you find the length liberating?

Komunyakaa: I had to surrender to its structure. I knew I wanted symmetry—not as a mold but as an organizing principle—and it liberated me in that sense. Two fourteen-lined stanzas. Fourteen sections. I seem to always get involved with numerology and destiny.

Feinstein: And you chose fourteen because—?

Komunyakaa: You can divide seven into fourteen twice. [Laughs.] Often this becomes an obsession of sorts, what I call an emotional symmetry.

Feinstein: There's a knockout line break in section VIII: "Wearing nothing but sky- / blue socks." That break on the hyphen is quite unusual for you. [Komunyakaa grins.] You often avoid breaks that might be seen as almost too clever—that bring attention to themselves. But I think it works marvelously well here.

Komunyakaa: For a long time, that was the very first image [in the poem] for me. And for some reason, when I initially wrote it, the break was there, and I kept it.

Feinstein: There's a truth to that image.

Komunyakaa: I hope so.

Feinstein: And I admire the way you address his stay at Camarillo [State Hospital] not merely as an emotional breakdown but also as a more positive revelation.

Komunyakaa: I was quite taken with the fact he experienced so much pleasure getting his hands into the dirt. It says something about Parker, and in a way it takes him back to his beginnings. For years I thought of the Midwest as restrictive and reactionary, but recently I've been having this idea about all the experimentation that came out of that part of the country.

So I could see Parker embracing a certain kind of space early on. It might even have something to do with his creative dexterity, you know? He was able to move from one musical idea to the next, and to embrace different people and musical situations. I think it has everything to do with the fact that physical space parallels emotional and psychological space. He was at home under that blue sky.

Discovering the Landscape
with Yusef Komunyakaa

Elizabeth Cho/1998

From *The Phoenix Online: Swarthmore College's Online Student Newspaper* (27 February 1998). Reprinted by permission.

This past Thursday, when I listened to Yusef Komunyakaa read in his deep voice that filled the Schuerer room, my first thought was that this man has a true sense of rhythm. As I absorbed the sounds of his words, I found my foot drumming along to the beat of his poems. Even afer he stopped speaking, my foot continued to tap the carpet. His style of reading is so powerful you internalize his poems when you listen. As Mr. Komunyakaa read, he leaned over the microphone and subtly moved his upper body to the rhythms of his language; it was as though he were trying to bury himself into the poems that were laid on the podium before him. He mostly read from his book, *Neon Vernacular: New and Selected Poems*, which was honored with both the 1994 Pulitzer Prize and Kingsley Tufts Poetry Award. His newest book, *Thieves of Paradise*, has been published but is not available for purchase in stores yet. Earlier that Thursday, I sat down for an interview with Mr. Komunyakaa. He was quiet and friendly. Often, his spoken sentences had the quality of poetry in the strength of their images and thoughts.

Liz: In "Fog Galleon," a poem about your hometown, Bogalusa, you wrote "The whole town smells / Like the world's oldest anger." What was it like growing up in Bogalusa?

Yusef: Well in retrospect, I realize that it is a place where I could discover the landscape. I remember my early rituals as being excursions out into the vegetation. It was a learning process for me because I was very inquisitive about everything but also I knew that there was a sort of violence overlaid with silence so. . . . There was always talk of Klu Klux Klan activities. . . . Usually, we talk about the violence in urban centers around the country, but

I think the most exact and scary violence for me is really rural violence because of that immense silence.

Liz: Do you feel comfortable with silence? I've noticed there's a lot of music in your poetry and that you edited a jazz poetry anthology so I'm guessing music is very important to you.

Yusef: Music is important, but I love silence. . . . We're talking about a different kind of silence, of course. It's not silence to cover up anything. It's silence to become part of because I don't think we can have music without silence.

Liz: How did you become interested in jazz?

Yusef: I remember my mother's . . . radio that was like a shrine, in a way, because it was huge, and I would ease behind the radio because I think it had what they call vacuum tubes in the radio and they glowed like bright invitations. I remember them being very hot, as well, because that was my first experience with fire, but I was sort of mesmerized by the voice coming out of the box. . . . Usually the radio station was tuned to New Orleans so that was blues, jazz, gospel music, coming into . . . that early environment. . . . I realize that as far as jazz [goes], especially modern jazz, I probably moved away from Louisiana to experience modern jazz, to experience Charlie Parker, Coltrane. My early experience with jazz is considered classical jazz, traditional jazz.

Liz: When you first heard the new jazz, what was your first thought?

Yusef: It was difficult the first few times, I think, to connect to that new sound, but because of the music itself . . . there was also a magnet. So I listened to it over and over, and I understood perfectly the link of modern contemporary jazz with traditional jazz that it came out of.

Liz: What gives you inspiration?

Yusef: I have this feeling that everything is about literature and this by the fact that we observe what's around us . . . we have to see what's around us in order to know what's happening to us because we're part of everything around us. . . . I think there's a kind of writing that's happening even when I'm not facing the fearful white space of the page. . . . It's informed by a certain kind of need and the need is informed by a certain kind of music so inspiration can be found. I wonder sometimes.

Liz: What was your relationship with your father like?

Yusef: It was quite an interesting relationship because . . . I was taught a lot about human possibility. He was a carpenter, and I learned . . . about precision, how he would measure a board five or six times at home, always going back and forth, always trying to get it right; and I think that in a way relates to my writing process, always revising.

Liz: What's your writing process like?

Yusef: I write everything down. Initially, a poem perhaps could be a hundred and twenty lines long [and I will] cut back to forty lines. So, I write in that way and I think that perhaps is related to jazz improvisation. But if we think about improvisation, it's not where everything flies apart; it's where everything connects, driven by a certain kind of need and a certain kind of energy and passion.

Liz: Is it like you're creating forms each time you write?

Yusef: Yes, but tone is the barrack structure of the poem. . . . It automatically takes us back to the most traditional forms of literature because early poetry I think would have been free verse and then those structures and literary conceits imposed on the language and such. But I do think that one has to know what those so-called traditional forms are, such as the sestina, sonnet, in order to break the rules.

Liz: How did you begin writing poems?

Yusef: In my graduating high school class, I raised my hand and volunteered to write a poem for my class. I'd never written a poem before but . . . I sat down and wrote a hundred lines, and then I didn't write again for a long time. I kept reading poetry. I wouldn't write poetry until I found myself at the University of Colorado in the arriving class in 1973, and I've been writing ever since.

Liz: When you look back on that high school poem, do you like it?

Yusef: I was too shy to read it [in high school]. The person who read it, [the Drama Club President] says she still has it and, consequently, she has promised to keep it a secret.

Liz: What was that poem like?

Yusef: I remember very pat rhymes, traditional poetry. The English language isn't really given to sophisticated natural rhymes, which is entirely different from a Romance language.

Liz: What made you raise your hand in high school to write a poem? Had you been reading poetry?

Yusef: Particularly, I'd been reading a lot of the British poets, memorizing passages of Shakespeare, reading closely Tennyson but even closer reading of Blake and Hughes. . . . Hughes led me towards the Harlem Renaissance poets and [they] sort of led me to read earlier African American poetry like Paul Laurence Dunbar.

Liz: What does writing poetry mean to you?

Yusef: For me, it's really a process of discovery. It's not so much to answer questions but just to discover what the various possibilities are. So it's a kind of a discourse with myself, often.

Still Negotiating with the Images:
An Interview with Yusef Komunyakaa

William Baer/1998

From *The Kenyon Review* 20.3/4 (Summer/Fall 1998). Reprinted by permission of William Baer.

In 1994 Yusef Komunyakaa was awarded both the Pulitzer Prize and the Kingsley Tufts Award for his collection *Neon Vernacular: New and Selected Poems*. Born and raised in Bogalusa, Louisiana, Komunyakaa served in Vietnam as an information specialist, saw combat, and received the Bronze Star. A graduate of the University of Colorado, he also received master's degrees from Colorado State University and the University of California, Irvine. After teaching at the University of New Orleans, Komunyakaa was a professor at Indiana University for over ten years, and, in the fall of 1997, he began teaching at Princeton University. Among his various books are *Dien Cai Dau* (1988), *Magic City* (1992), *Neon Vernacular* (1993), and *The Jazz Poetry Anthology* (1991), which was coedited with Sascha Feinstein.

Yusef Komunyakaa's poems have aptly been described as "razor-sharp pieces that tell us more about our culture than any news broadcast," and Toi Derricote, focusing on the poet's aesthetic, has written that "Komunyakaa's poetry is about art, about how it alters reality, how it changes the past, and how it is both a desperate and a redemptive act." Komunyakaa himself, keenly aware of both the social and artistic obligations of the writer, has claimed that "language is what can liberate or imprison the human psyche" and that "we are responsible for our lives and the words we use."

William Baer: In 1984, fourteen years after your tour of duty in Vietnam ended, you were renovating a house in New Orleans and began to reconsider your wartime experiences within a broader poetic context. What happened that day?

Yusef Komunyakaa: I was peeling back the old surfaces of my house at 818 Piety Street. Much had to be dismantled, and the dust from the horsehair plaster was flying everywhere. The old house, I remember, had high twelve-foot ceilings, and during the process of working and going up and down the ladder, I began to compose a poem inside my head entitled "Somewhere Near Phu Bai." When I'm doing such things, it's my method to have a pad of paper close by, so I'd periodically descend the ladder and write down a line or an image or an idea. So it wasn't a clearly thought-out process; it was just something that happened, and perhaps it had a lot to do with the fact that it was summertime, and there was a kind of familiar tropic heat that day. So it was the heat, and the dust, and the dismantling of things—and that's how it happened. If I hadn't written that particular poem on that particular day, perhaps I wouldn't have written about the Vietnam experience at all.

WB: Were you aware, at the time, that you still hadn't adequately dealt, both psychologically and emotionally, with your Vietnam experiences? And that you were, as you later said in an interview, "resisting those memories"?

YK: I don't think I was aware of it at the time, but in retrospect I think that was the case: resisting those memories, yet also moving on to other things that I thought were a more appropriate subject matter for poetry. Early on, my poetry was informed by classical surrealism, especially Breton and some of the other surrealist/dadaist poets.

WB: Weren't you able to use that, in a sense, to create much of the hallucinatory imagery that you used in the Vietnam poems?

YK: Yes, I think surrealism informed the psychological and emotional underpinnings of that experience.

WB: So when did you actually write "Facing It," your famous poem about the black vet visiting the Vietnam War Memorial in Washington, D.C.? I thought that it was one of the first completed poems?

YK: Actually, "Facing It" was the second poem that I wrote, and it was a real surprise to me. It was a poem that just ended itself, and I couldn't go any further.

WB: How recently had you been to the memorial?

YK: About a year or so.

WB: R. S. Gwynn has called that poem "the most poignant elegy that has been written about the Vietnam War," and you've admitted that the poem became the "standard" for the rest of your much praised collection, *Dien Cai Dau.* In what way did you see the poem as the "standard" for the others?

YK: Tonally, I believe, it informed the other poems. I wanted to deal with images instead of outright statements. That's pretty much how I remember the war—imagery that we sort of internalized, that was informed by the whole vibrations of the body.

WB: But in these poems, the images often comprise incidents, or are parts of incidents, and this allows readers who've had no personal awareness of such experiences, even more to hold on to—rather than just a series of striking images. Did you plan it that way or did it just happen?

YK: Well, early on, I'd always wanted to be a photographer, and I'd also wanted to be a painter, but I never really committed myself in those directions. Nevertheless, for me, poetry works best when it's aware of music and formed from a composite of meaningful images.

WB: During the Vietnam War, you saw combat and were awarded the Bronze Star. You were also an information specialist, a reporter, and an editor for the *Southern Cross*. What exactly did you do in those roles?

YK: "Information specialist" is a military term for reporter. For my first six months in Vietnam, I was pretty much out in the field every day. Whenever there was any kind of conflict or engagement, I'd be ferried out on a helicopter to the action—to the middle of it—and I had to report, I had to witness.

WB: Was there an expectation that your reports would tell things the way the military wanted them to be told? You've written poems like "Touch-up Man" and "Re-creating the Scene" which deal with how the truth gets known or not known during wartime. Did you feel pressure in any way?

YK: Not really. At least, I didn't feel that kind of pressure at the time, yet I think the pressure might have been there. But I pretty much reported things as I experienced them or saw them. I also had a column, "Viet Style," which was about the culture of the Vietnamese. So I was doing both side by side.

WB: Do you think that any of the wartime journalism had an effect on your poetry when you eventually got around to writing it?

YK: Yes, especially since I knew a good deal about the culture. I'd started reading about Vietnam and the Vietnamese culture even before I went over there. And when I arrived, I was especially struck by the land itself, the terrain. It was such a vibrant landscape, especially during the rainy season. There's vegetation everywhere, and I'd grown up with that in Louisiana. When you drop a seed on the ground, something automatically grows, so that kind of vibrancy in the landscape didn't frighten me.

WB: Your poems always have a powerful sense of place, especially the Vietnam poems. But you've wondered in the past whether your efforts to comprehend and appreciate the Vietnamese landscape were just a defense mechanism for dealing with the difficult situation that you found yourself in. How do you feel about that now?

YK: Well, the appreciation was mostly in retrospect. But I do remember that I had a certain feeling about it at the time, and I suppose that if I'd come from an urban environment I would have been frightened, definitely frightened, of that terrain.

WB: The various fears and horrors of these poems come not just from the startling almost hallucinatory images—a burning woman, underground tunnel searches, night ambushes—but also from the nerve-wracking psychological torment within the mind of each GI. The poem "Jungle Surrender" decides that "the real interrogator is a voice within," and this internal dialectic informs all of the Vietnam poems. These poems aren't just written from the perspective of a vet looking back at Vietnam, but, as Don Ringnalda puts it, a vet "watching" himself as he looks back at Vietnam. Was this concept with you from the beginning?

YK: I don't think I was fully aware of the tactic, the concept itself. It was sort of unintentional; it just expressed where I stood at that moment in history—where I stood inside my body. Let's face it, we internalize everything and that which is internalized informs the future and how we actually experience and see things later on.

WB: Some of the poems, especially "Starlight Scope Myopia," portray a real compassion for the enemy. Was this true at the time or was it an attitude that came only after years of trying to deal with the whole experience?

YK: I'm not sure if I felt that when I was there. I was quite aware of Vietnam's history, and I think that fact had a lot to do with my feelings. A crucial bond was the concept of the Vietnamese "peasant." I myself came from a peasant society of mostly field workers, and my father always believed if one worked hard enough, he or she could rise to a certain plateau—a black Calvinism. So I saw the Vietnamese as familiar peasants because that's what they are, and, consequently, I could have easily placed many of the individuals I'd grown up with in that same situation—especially the sharecroppers.

WB: No poem shows the interrelatedness of human beings in wartime more effectively than "Tu Do Street," in which the black soldier, after being rejected in a "white" bar, finds a "black" bar and temporary solace with a Vietnamese prostitute. [Reads from "Tu Do Street".] This is an amazing image of our connected humanity, but is the connection with "the underworld" just a harsh reminder of death, which should stir us to behave with more kindness, or is it a pessimistic reflection of the human propensity to divide and destroy ourselves?

YK: It was one of those endings which, once I'd written it down, just stopped where it was. There were many symbolic underworlds in Vietnam—the underground tunnel systems, some of the bars, and the whole psychic space of the GI—a kind of underworld populated by ghosts and indefinable images. It was a place of emotional and psychological flux where one was trying to make sense out of the world and one's place in that world. And there was, relentlessly, a going back and forth between that internal space and the external world. It was an effort to deal with oneself, and with the other GIs, the Vietnamese, and even the ghosts that we'd managed to create of ourselves. So, for me, this is a very complex picture of the situation of the GI—going back and forth, condemned in a way to trek back and forth between those emotional demarcations while trying to make sense out of things.

WB: In poems like "Hanoi Hanna" and "Report from the Skull's Diorama," you've described the racial psychological warfare targeted at the black GI. How prevalent was it? Was it constant or occasional?

YK: Occasional, but at the same time, the civil rights movement was going forward back home, along with the antiwar movement. So the problem was very much alive for black GIs, and there was always a discourse going on.

WB: Was it very alienating or was the overall situation so overwhelming that you didn't have time to think about it?

YK: The overall situation was extremely overwhelming. When you were out in the field in an ambush situation, you didn't have time to think about such things. You were keenly sensitive to surviving, and you knew that you had to connect to the other American soldiers. But when you saw friends getting killed or wounded, all kinds of anger would flare up, but let's face it, if you're placed in that kind of situation—and you've been trained—you're going to fire your weapons. You are going to try to stay alive. You're going to try to protect your fellow soldiers, black or white. But at the same time, there were those vicious arguments with one's self. One would feel divided.

WB: So it had its effect?

YK: Yes, it did. But it wasn't the first time that black Americans have encountered such dilemmas. Black American participation in combat goes back to the Revolutionary War. I think there were at least twenty-five hundred who served. During the Civil War, there was the participation of several black regiments, and, afterwards, there were those four black regiments in the West which escorted the wagon trains westward. I believe the Tenth Cavalry was responsible for the capture of Geronimo. And then there was the peculiar case of James Beckwourth, who was war chief of the Crows, had dealings with the Cheyenne, and was also implicated in the Sand Creek Massacre. Then there was World War I. As a matter of fact, my first connection with war happened through my great uncle, Uncle Jessie, who'd served in World War I at the age of seventeen with the ambulance corps. When he came back home, he used to have these horrific dreams, and the other grown-ups refused to talk about it. I must have been about six years old when I realized that his experiences in World War I informed his whole personality. He'd become a professional gambler, and I'm talking about in the rural South! He'd come back from the war, visited the turpentine camps, and gambled.

WB: What were the turpentine camps?

YK: They were camps where groups of blacks collected the rosin from the distilled turpentine. I can still remember my uncle wearing a suit coat, overalls, and carrying his .38 Smith & Wesson. But when he came to my grandmother's door, he would take out the gun, wrap it in a handkerchief, and then give it to her. It was a very strange ritual.

WB: You saw this as a boy?

YK: I did. I also remember that he always had a pocket full of dimes, bright silver dimes, which he gave away to the neighborhood children. But he would still have those terrible dreams, so one morning I cornered him and said, "Why do you have those nightmares?" and he told me a haunting war story. He said that so many soldiers were getting killed during the war that they had to bury the bodies in trenches. As they did so, they'd take the dead soldier's two dog tags, and one was placed in a collection bag, and the other was placed in the mouth of the corpse—so they could identify the soldiers when they came back to dig them up. It was a horrific story to tell a young boy, but I think, in a way, he was trying to tell me about war. It was a story that was supposed to teach me something about how to look at war.

WB: To be prepared?

YK: Yes, to be prepared.

WB: Eventually, in 1990, you returned to Vietnam. What was it like going back?

YK: I went with five other veterans, fellow Americans, and when we landed in Hanoi, I was quite shaken. I'd never before considered the possibility of actually *being* in Hanoi, and, for a while, I realized that I didn't feel safe. But, eventually, when I began to talk with the people and make friends, I felt more relaxed.

WB: So it was a matter of getting over the initial wariness of actually being in Hanoi?

YK: It was definitely that, and it was also the knowledge of what had been done to the Vietnamese people and trying to place myself inside their collective skin. It was quite difficult, and I felt that if it had happened to me, I'd be very angry. So I was very affected by how forgiving the typical Vietnamese happens to be towards Americans—especially towards the American veterans for some reason. It's still difficult for me to fully understand that special connection, but I think it has to do with the idea of the "shared experience," even if that experience was horrific and negative. It makes me think of that statement of Baldwin's where he says that, in the South, whites and blacks are closely connected—almost like kissing cousins.

WB: Are you planning to go back again?

YK: I'd very much like to go back, and I was supposed to return last year, but I didn't make it.

WB: A number of commentators have praised your Vietnam poems for not offering facile solutions—for being, as Bruce Weber puts it, "achingly suggestive without resolution." Yet many of the same reviewers have found a "redemptive," "salvic" quality in the same poems. Do you think that these are fair characterizations?

YK: It's difficult for me to say what's fair because I think I'm still negotiating with those images. I'm still dealing with them. I don't know if I'm going to write any more Vietnam-related poems. I feel that I won't be writing very many, if any at all, especially since I have a section in my forthcoming book, *Thieves of Paradise*, about Vietnam. The section is called "Debriefing Ghosts," and they're prose poems about returning to Vietnam—but there are a few other kinds of ghosts as well.

WB: In 1981 you returned to your hometown of Bogalusa, Louisiana, after an absence of over a decade, and you later told the *Times-Picayune* that your life had been "a healing process from the two places"—meaning both Bogalusa and Vietnam. Yet many of your poems about your childhood, especially in *Magic City* and the "New Poems" section of *Neon Vernacular* portray a generally pleasant childhood of sports, music, mischief, and rites of passage—a place where you could always "depend" upon certain relatives' "love to get us out of trouble." Have you gradually come to a greater appreciation of your youth in Bogalusa?

YK: I'm always rethinking my youthful rituals in Bogalusa. Recently, I was shocked by the realization that growing up in Louisiana there wasn't any place that I couldn't walk in the middle of the night—and I'm talking about two or three o'clock in the morning. But at the same time, there was an unspoken fear lurking underneath that youthful sense of freedom that greatly affected us all, especially the adults. I think that I personally connected with my environment because, early on, there was a youthful investigation going on. I would investigate pretty much everything, especially the terrain, and the social demarcations as well—even though I never crossed those boundaries. There was so much to look at, to query, within the context of my own environment that it kept my imaginative life very much alive. I was also, constantly, projecting myself somewhere else in the world. I would easily daydream about Mexico, Africa, or somewhere in Europe, and I later realized that those daydreams were actually connected to where I was growing up—that there was a unique space, an eminent silence, from where I could project myself to other possibilities.

WB: Was it because you wanted to get away, or was it the natural, imaginative, daydream life of a future writer?

YK: I think it had mostly to do with the quality of invention because I always could come back to that temporal space, that physical territory as such, and deal with it. I didn't have any problem about wandering for miles out into the woods, or things of that sort.

WB: In your memories of Bogalusa, the symbol of the paper mill is especially significant, and it appears in your poems—with its "acid fumes" and "chemicals / That turn workers into pulp." Yet even the factory is the source of financial security, camaraderie, and satisfaction about one's work.

YK: Yes, I've realized that growing up was intimately involved with the broad significance of "work." I started working very early on, physical labor. I had definite responsibilities, and, as a teenager, I realized that it had somehow become a competition between my father and me—probably because he respected physical labor so much.

WB: Yes, the most important aspect of these poems is the young narrator's complex relationship with his father. Maybe the most telling of these is "Songs for My Father," in which the dying carpenter father, who never approved of poetry as a vocation, asks his son to write a poem about him. Is this a true incident?

YK: It actually happened. He wanted a poem for his birthday, and it's strange to think about it now because within less than a year he was dead. So even if he hadn't received proper medical attention, he surely knew that something serious was happening. So I tried. It was probably the most difficult assignment I'd ever been given, and I couldn't write the poem. But I tried, and I can still remember reciting certain lines to him, although I'm not sure if any of those lines actually ended up in "Songs for My Father."

WB: But even though you were never able to produce the poem while your father was alive, it does seem that, at that point in his life, he'd accepted your vocation as a writer?

YK: Yes. But I think that what my father really hated wasn't the writing so much—it was the disconnection we felt when I left home. Early on, there'd been a very deep trust between the two of us. I remember, at about twelve years old, that he came to me around Christmastime, and he asked me to hold all of his money—and for me it was a lot of money, a couple thousand dollars. He could always trust me in that way; so there was a special kind of connection that I still don't fully understand.

WB: You were the oldest son?

YK: Yes, there are four brothers and one sister, and I'm the oldest.

WB: Another meaningful character in your narrator's search for identity is the grandfather he never knew—a man who'd once emigrated here from Trinidad and given up his "true name." Eventually, you took this last name, "Komunyakaa," as your own. Was this a problem with your father—or with other relatives?

YK: It upset my dad quite a bit, but it didn't bother my mother or my grandmother, interestingly enough.

WB: It was still a family name.

YK: That's right, but it still bothered my dad a whole lot, even though the rest of my family embraced me and dealt with it. In my youth, the very name itself was like a family secret, and I'm still trying to understand it. My great-grandparents had come to Louisiana as stowaways and slipped into the country. I can still remember visiting my great-grandmother, and there's a kind of pleasant mystery associated with it. I was probably about three or four years old, and I can still remember her and her house, which was raised on stilts above the water. But that's the only real-life image I have of her, and neither the name "Komunyakaa" nor my great-grandparents themselves were discussed very much in the family. So one day I cornered my grandmother about it, and she began to tell me a bit about my great-grandfather. But mostly, I remember my great-grandparents from a very large, framed photograph of them in my grandmother's bedroom. Often, as a child, I'd sort of meditate on that photograph because they were such grand-looking people.

WB: Do you know where that photograph is today?

YK: The large one got damp, and since it was so old, it deteriorated. As far as I know that was the only photograph of my great-grandparents, but I've been told that smaller versions of it were given to the older members of my family, so maybe there's still one in existence. I'm not sure. But I still have this mental picture of them together, just married, in that oval photograph.

WB: During your youth in Bogalusa, racist Klan activities were still present, and they're tellingly described in "The Whistle" and "Knights of the White Camellia" and "Deacons for Defense." How active were they? And did you see actual conflicts with the freedom marchers?

YK: Yes, I saw some of the conflict; the Klan activity was very much above ground. Yet, as I mentioned earlier, I'm still amazed by the fact that I could walk anywhere I wanted on my own. Maybe that had a lot to do with the direction that I would generally walk because I liked to head straight down the track, the railroad tracks, at any time of night. When I think about it, it probably has a lot to do with the ritual of one of my great aunts, my maternal grandmother's sister, who lived to be about ninety-five. Up until her death, she would rise daily and walk to the post office, which was about five miles away. She lived in a very wooded area, a very closed-off area, and when she went to the post office, she would always walk straight down the track.

WB: Was it a passage of safety?

YK: It could be. The railroad tracks were the demarcation in the South between different sides of town. But it represented another kind of "safety" as well because when we thought of trains, we thought of Pullman porters, and individuals who were able to move freely from North to South. So maybe that's all part of it too—and related to the fact that I would meditate on the passing trains. Often I'd count the boxcars and think about where they might be going.

WB: A less safe subject and theme throughout your work is the evil of sexual betrayal and the desperate need for meaningful love. For example, your poem "Boy Wearing a Dead Man's Clothes" ends with the uneasy child remembering the dead man from a few weeks ago. [Lines from poem follow.] And "The Heart's Graveyard Shift" describes a man "Between loves" who's so desperate for love he might actually "go off his rocker." Are these related problems especially significant in our contemporary times, or are they just inevitable facts of human behavior?

YK: Given the complexity of human social interactions, I see these realities as products of the whole social fabric of the society. I grew up seeing all kinds of things happening within the context of that society—unspoken things—things that were not talked about, just accepted, and that's how I began to understand the adult world—by examining the things that weren't talked about.

WB: Derek Walcott considers his poetic vocation both "votive" and "sacred," and you've described the spiritual in various ways in your poetry—the prayers of a Simeon-like grandmother; the "something" that saves the narrator's life in two of the Vietnam poems; and, more recently, the spiritual dimension of the Australian landscape. Could you discuss this aspect of your writing?

YK: I grew up with the Bible. As a matter of fact, it was probably the first complex book that I read from beginning to end. Several times, in fact. I was quite taken with the Old Testament, and I think I've said somewhere that perhaps the Old Testament, in a way, brought me to a clearer understanding of surrealism because, within surrealism, I could fire up my imagination again—as I'd done with some of the biblical images that are frightening, rather horrific—like visualizing mythic animals with nine heads. And the Bible and religion got me very close to the language itself. I especially remember the phrase, "In the beginning was the Word, and the Word was with God, and the Word was God." That was a phrase that really stuck with me and seemed relevant both to nature—the rituals that I observed in nature—and the rituals between individuals. I was also greatly affected by the fact that through language, especially poetic language, we can speak for others as well, others like the members of my family, or members of the larger community. Not that one should speak *for* them, but to share something that they have touched in a certain way and that has also touched your own life—informed it in some way.

WB: Do you see that use of language as having spiritual dimensions?

YK: Yes, I think it does have a spiritual dimension.

WB: And how about the Australian landscape which you've often described as having a spiritual significance?

YK: Spending so much time in Australia has taught me that my own rituals, my early rituals in Louisiana—like going out and looking at the landscape—weren't really chosen; they just happened to exist in the context of my own personality. I've talked to my brothers and sister about this, and even though we grew up in the same place, they always say that their memories are entirely different from mine—even though we were looking at the same things! So my experience in the Australian landscape, especially after talking to some of the aborigines, has helped me to understand how *they* looked at the landscape, and it's also taught me something about my own early experiences in Bogalusa. For example, it seems that, as contemporary people, we're very fearful of silence. But why? Why does every moment have to be filled with some kind of external vibration coming from the radio, or television, or some other technological device? I don't know, but I now realize that silence is not an endurance test for me, and it never was.

WB: Over the years, you've been involved, in various ways, with theatrical or dramatic writing. What have you been working on recently?

YK: Most recently, I was commissioned by ABC, the Australian Broadcasting Corporation, to do a piece on Bird, on Charlie Parker, and I thought that this was such a strange request that I agreed to do it. When Chris Williams of the ABC first suggested the project to me, we talked about the traditional libretto—the conceits of the traditional libretto—and I thought that I could negotiate those forms to the material. But once I started looking closely at Parker, I decided not to do a traditional libretto but rather fourteen symmetrical pieces under the title *Testimony*. So I sent Chris Williams part of the text, seven of the fourteen pieces, and he was initially concerned that it wasn't in the form of the traditional libretto. But when he talked it over with the composer Sandy Evans, she said, "I don't see how we can do it any other way!" So I finished *Testimony* a few months ago, and they're going to use a thirteen-piece band and four singers to actually perform it.

WB: For radio?

YK: Yes, for radio, but I believe that they're going to make a video as well, and I think it might even come out as a CD. Just a few years earlier when I was in Australia, they'd asked me to write something about Vietnam to be set to music. But I was so busy at the time that I couldn't do it. Then a few months later, someone sent me a news clipping announcing that a piece called *Fire Water Paper: A Vietnam Oratorio* had been done by the Pacific Symphony, commissioned by Carl St. Clair, and performed with Yo-Yo Ma and some others. This past April, the recording was released by Sony, and on April 13, I got to see it performed at Kennedy Center by the Boston Symphony. It contains only two of my poems, and it's really a collaborative text, set by the composer Elliot Goldenthal, who often does movie scores.

WB: Are you working on anything at the present time?

YK: I'm working on something that began a few years ago when I visited the La Brea tar pits. At the time, I thought it would be interesting to write a piece to be performed in the enclosed glass space at the tar pits. So I'm now writing it for "The Glass Ark" section in my next book, *Thieves of Paradise*.

WB: So it's a dramatic piece?

YK: Yes, it's spoken between two people, a woman and a man, back and forth. They're paleontologists, talking above all these ancient prehistoric bones, but actually talking about something entirely different.

WB: In a 1990 interview in *Callaloo*, you said that you were slowly working on a collection of poems in traditional forms called *Black Orpheus & Other Love Poems*. How's that project coming along?

YK: That project is coming along very, very slowly! It's one of those projects I want to savor—that I really don't want to finish. I remember when I was a kid slowly nibbling on a candy bar, for days it seemed, saving it, prolonging it, so it's like that.

WB: Does it include sonnets, and ballads, and couplets?

YK: Yes, all of those. That's how I first started. That was the kind of poetry that I first started reading, poetry informed by traditional forms and structures.

WB: You've often mentioned your early love of Poe and Tennyson.

YK: Yes, it's very interesting to me. Recently I wrote a series of songs for a jazz singer called *Thirteen Kinds of Desire*, and I relied on traditional rhymes in the twelve songs. In my youth, the other way that I came to poetry was listening to the radio. My mother always had the radio tuned to stations in New Orleans, and my impulse, as a child, was never to sing the actual lyrics, but to make up my own. I can remember, at eight or nine years of age, creating all these rhyming lyrics; so it's very interesting at this late stage to return to that impulse.

WB: What else are you working on?

YK: Well, the way I work is that I simultaneously compose several collections side by side, so presently, along with *Black Orpheus & Other Love Poems*, I'm working on *Thieves of Paradise*, which will probably come out next; *Talking Dirty to the Gods*, which is a longish book composed of sixteen-line poems, each with four four-line stanzas; and *Pleasure Dome*, which really started out as an excavation of African American history. Over the years, I'd read a great deal on African American history, but also on black history throughout the world. So the project began as an excavation of specific historical individuals such as Ira Aldridge, who played Othello—there's a bust of him at the Royal Shakespeare Theatre—and James Beckwourth, and other individuals whom I'd never, in the past, really thought about writing poems about. But once I started writing them, it made perfect sense to me.

WB: History seems untapped by contemporary poets who often seem afraid to use it in their work.

YK: Well, I'd never really thought about it before, but I do love reading about all these characters. Characters like Saint George, whom *The Three Musketeers* was actually based on and who became the bodyguard for the duke of Orleans' wife and was a classical composer as well! Or like Pushkin. It was very interesting being in Saint Petersburg and looking at the statue of Pushkin, thinking of his link to Africa. Another approach I'm currently exploring in my poetry comes from literature, not history. In the past, for example, when teaching Faulkner's "A Rose for Emily," I was always taken with the character Tobe, who never really gets a single line of dialogue. So as an assignment, I would instruct my students to write a poem in the voice of Tobe, asking them, "What do you think he witnessed?" But I never did the exercise myself, so, finally, I wrote a poem from Tobe's perspective.

WB: Do you usually compose in your head?

YK: I do. I see this as a kind of meditation, for the most part, so, in the beginning, I try not to impose a shape on the poem. For example, I know that I want to write a poem entitled "Quatrains for Ishi." Ishi, a Native American, was the last member of his tribe around Oroville, California, which is close to Paradise, California. Ishi ended up as a kind of museum piece in a way, and I've been meditating on what it would be like to be the last living member of one's tribe. I know I'll write it as a section of *Thieves of Paradise.*

WB: So, in general, you're meditating on several poems at a time, and you write them down when the time comes?

YK: Yes, they sort of choose their own direction.

WB: How often do you work at your poetry?

YK: Every day, if possible. I usually keep a pad of paper beside my bed, and I often wake up early and write for fifteen or twenty minutes before the busy day starts. That's when some of the images are most surprising to me for some reason. Over the years, I've realized that I can't rely on my memory to duplicate those images accurately—I would remember only a close approximation and it wouldn't feel right to me—so I write everything down now.

WB: Can you write when you're on the road?

YK: Not as much as I'd like to, but I can still read on the road.

WB: You're a firm believer in a poet "unearthing" his true voice. How does one go about that? What do you advise your students?

YK: Well, the first things I want to know about my students are the things they really care about—things that might not have a direct link to poetry, but which they're really passionate about. They have to have a *need.* Poetry, I believe, has to be informed by a need. Otherwise, it becomes a kind of artificial apparatus that the poet straps on, and it becomes more of a burden than a kind of telling moment—a poem is a moment of both confrontation and celebration.

WB: With that in mind, I'd like to finish things up by asking if you could read the end of "Facing It," a poem that, it seems to me, demonstrates that combination of sharp, telling images and dialectic complexity that uniquely marks your work.

YK: Of course. [Komunyakaa reads from "Facing It".]

Achieving Clarity through Contrasts:
An Interview with Yusef Komunyakaa

Shirley A. James Hanshaw/1998
Previously unpublished.

My name is Shirley Hanshaw, and today, Thursday, March 26, 1998, I am interviewing Pulitzer Prize–winning poet Yusef Komunyakaa. We are at the University of Mississippi where Mr. Komunyakaa has been invited to read from his poetry as a part of the John and Renee Grisham Visiting Writer Series.

Hanshaw: Concerning your book of poems titled *Dien Cai Dau*, I'm particularly intrigued by the recurring images of glowing, glaring light, as it relates to sunlight and fire. There is also the repetition of certain colors and the coalescence of colors, such as blue and violet and purple. In some instances, gleaming metal is depicted within a setting of haziness, mist, dusk, and shadows. Are these images deliberate, i.e., are they deliberately chosen or incidental to your purposes in the poetry?

Komunyakaa: I think they are incidental because of the way that I compose, which is a process of improvisation. Those are the colors that tumbled out of the psyche, and consequently, perhaps, they are associated with an internalized system of colors, system of "thought" colors. I think that they are part of an emotional composite. I grew up with shadows, with the mist of a paper mill.

Yes, in a certain sense, there is a kind of parallel when I went to Vietnam because of the rain, especially during the monsoon season during a downpour, when there would be shadows behind the grass. There is that system of shadows, then there is an attempt to introduce a certain kind of clarity. I think that is what I was talking about, in a certain sense, within all of these shadows between all the architecture and the fear, there is also a kind of reaching for clarity that has something to do with contrast, as well, so you have both things happening at once. You have the shadows, and then you have the brightness. All this is happening in concert with each other, and in a way, that's part of the confusion of the moment. I think a lot of the soldiers were completely confused. I know I felt confused. There wasn't any clarity. So in the poems, I think there is an attempt to at least impose some kind of imagined clarity on confusion. Does that make sense?

Hanshaw: Yes, it does. As a matter of fact, some of your poems are almost like a painter's palette to me. Maybe because I paint a little bit.

Komunyakaa: I think I said somewhere that I wish I were a painter at times.

Hanshaw: But you are, for me as a reader, you are a painter with words. For instance, I see the purple as a coalescence of the blood—the red blood—and the bluesy type of atmosphere that you're in. And I wondered if that had any validity.

Komunyakaa: I think so, I think so. I'm thinking about the fact that these poems . . . well, the whole book began in Louisiana back in that terrain. That terrain that is quasi-, or nearly Vietnam in the psyche. I was talking to somebody else about this as well. I was in the process of renovating a house on 818 Piety Street where they have those twelve-foot ceilings. I was going up and down the ladder, and there was dust in the place. I was doing it [the renovation] by myself. That is how I would deal with things. I had very systematically pulled back from things, and I wanted to just do this project on my own—to tear off the old wallpaper, sand everything back to its bare surface. And it's very strange, to get under the plaster of this house and then realize that the boards looked new although they were almost one hundred years old.

Hanshaw: That's interesting,

Komunyakaa: That's when I started writing the poem "Somewhere near Phu Bai."

Hanshaw: I have two brothers who went to Vietnam and a cousin who came back weighing sixty pounds because he was nearly blown to bits by howitzer fire, but he survived. I must say that I approach with trepidation the subject of the war with veterans because I know that some refuse to discuss it all.

Komunyakaa: What you might want to do also is . . . I'm associated with the William Joiner Center. That's in Boston. That's an institute, the Joiner Center for the Study of War and Social Consequences. We have a conference there in June.

Hanshaw: Of this year?

Komunyakaa: Of this year. We've been meeting there for quite some time. It might be interesting for you, if possible, to attend that.

Hanshaw: What are the days? Do you know?

Komunyakaa: I don't know the days off the top of my head, but I can give you the name of the director, Kevin Bowen, who is also a poet. He has a book out from Curbstone Press called *Playing Basketball with the Viet Cong.*

Hanshaw: Okay.

Komunyakaa: A lot of people go there. It would behoove you to spend a whole day there, because there is so much to do. You probably want to look at a special issue of the *Monroe Trotter Review*. I've forgotten when exactly it was published. It's a special issue. It has some stuff on him. Also, I did a short essay on Etheridge Knight.

Hanshaw: And that came out when?

Komunyakaa: That came out . . . I've forgotten exactly when, but that's associated with U. Mass Boston as well. If you're there, you can visit the Monroe Trotter Center. By the way, I just mentioned Etheridge Knight. Do you know that name?

Hanshaw: Yes, he is from Corinth, Mississippi. However, I've never met him.

Komunyakaa: You know he died a few years ago. When I said that, I just realized that no one has done anything on him.

Hanshaw: That's right.

Komunyakaa: There are some people working on that right now. I'm in the process of writing an introduction to a book about him that's being published by the University of Michigan. It has all of his letters.

Hanshaw: I'm focusing on the trickster character in black literature as it relates to the Vietnam War, particularly the fiction.

Komunyakaa: How much fiction has been done?

Hanshaw: I have found six novels: John Williams's *Captain Blackman*, Wesley Brown's *Tragic Magic*, George Davis's *Coming Home*, A. R. Flowers's *De Mojo Blues*, Clarence Major's *All Night Visitors*, and Larry French just came out in January of last year with *Patches of Fire*. Now I don't know if there are others. Do you know of others besides these?

Komunyakaa: No, I don't know of any others.

Hanshaw: Now what I noticed in reading them is that all of them mention trickster characters from the African American oral tradition, such as the Signifyin' Monkey, Shine and the Titanic, or High John de Conquer.

Komunyakaa: That's right.

Hanshaw: And, from my perspective, the protagonist of *Captain Blackman* is Ananse from West African oral tradition. In the African myth, Ananse has one long leg (signifying his connection with the gods in the heavenly realm) and one short leg (grounding him with humans on earth). Similarly, Captain Blackman, after losing part of his leg in a bombing attack on the battlefield, is left with one long leg and one short one. In your prose poem "The One-legged Stool" I also see an Anansean motif. Is that a stretch, to view the persona as a sort of trickster?

Komunyakaa: Well, it's a torture method that I understood was used, the one-legged stool—you fall off the stool, and you get killed. Whew! Isn't that interesting?

Hanshaw: Yes. So that's similar to the bamboo under the nails and the water thing. That's yet another form of torture?

Komunyakaa: Yes.

Hanshaw: Okay. And it seems to me that the speaker is having an internal dialogue with himself as well as an external dialogue. He is engaging the reader in an external dialogue.

Komunyakaa: He talks about a number of things, and he makes a lot of insinuations. It's the same way with blues insinuations. There are some prose poems in this new book. There are a few poems about Vietnam.

Hanshaw: What's the title of the book?

Komunykaa: *Thieves of Paradise.*

Hanshaw: Who is the publisher?

Komunyakaa: Wesleyan University Press. Also, I am working on a book-length poem about a Vietnam veteran. It's interesting because this veteran is white; but he's almost speaking as a Black man, which is interesting because of his experience and what he has seen. You see, maybe I can talk with you about some of these things because these things haven't been talked about. One reason is because in Vietnam there were at least fourteen or fifteen African Americans who threw themselves on grenades. That has never really been addressed. I'm moving toward addressing that because, you know, it's a well-kept secret. So the speaker in this book-length poem deals with it to an extent, not to an extent of the fact that there were fourteen or fifteen. That's a high number. Consequently, they were awarded the Congressional Medal of Honor. But I'm trying to basically understand what is within the psyche that would cause someone to do that. Of course, there's no time to think. . . . This is something that's within the individual, that type of sacrifice of throwing oneself on a grenade.

Hanshaw: Now this was to save a company of men?

Komunyakaa: Well, the grenade fell near them.

Hanshaw: In the interview with Vince Gotera you speak of poetry itself as "constantly changing, amorphous, and cumulative until it forms a vision." Elsewhere in that same interview you speak of the war as constantly changing, and in fact you speak of chimeras in the *Dien Cai Dau* poems. Do you see any relationship between war itself and poetry?

Komunyakaa: War itself and poetry? It's interesting you say that because when we think about Western history and poetry, you know, we go back to Homer and Virgil. That is the nature of the tales that we remember. They started with war.

Hanshaw: Well, you know in the *Epic of Sundiata* there is a praise poem that was always recited before the African warriors would go into battle.

Komunyakaa: For me, it was a way of trying to establish some kind of discourse, not necessarily with someone else but a discourse that involved questioning myself and trying to make some sense out of the war. I didn't really talk about the Vietnam conflict, even with my brother who had been there before. We still haven't established a dialogue about the war. So when I started writing about the Vietnam conflict, maybe it was just stuff in the context of my dreams that I wasn't even conscious of. Because when I was working inside of that house in New Orleans, going up and down the ladder, and I started writing this poem, "Somewhere Near Phu Bai," I don't know if I were fully conscious of what I was writing about at the moment. But the images started coming. I began to realize, "Yeah, I'm fully conscious of this, and it's something I haven't dealt with." So it was a way of . . . opening up a little door for me. And all these images started coming forth, not necessarily relived but just played back very visually. Working with veterans, I realized that is what happened. A lot of us, we came back and threw ourselves into various things. I threw myself into the classroom . . . into the university. Some other people threw themselves back into their communities, and what have you; some other people threw themselves into the streets, you know. So we dealt with it in so many different ways. For me, the university was like a Savior, I suppose.

Hanshaw: Of those novels that I mentioned to you, one came out in the late seventies, and the others came out much later. I read that it took you fourteen years to write about Vietnam. Do you think it took most African American Vietnam War veterans a span of twelve to fifteen years to be able to deal with the experience in order to write about it creatively?

Komunyakaa: Yes, yes. There is another novel, but I don't remember the title at this time. I don't even know if it's published by a large press. It might be published by a small press somewhere.

Hanshaw: Okay.

Komunyakaa: There is another novel and the writer is out of Indianapolis. Somebody sent me a novel. That was years ago, probably about ten years ago, but there is a novel. There is another black writer who writes poetry by the name of Horace Coleman. There is also Lamont Steptoe who has written about Vietnam.

Hanshaw: Now is Steptoe a poet?

Komunyakaa: He is a poet, but I think he has written some fiction as well. He is writing a novel. He just told me he was writing a novel that he has been working on for quite some time. He is in Philadelphia. I'm doing a special issue of *Callaloo*.

Hanshaw: When is that coming out? I remember your mentioning that in the classroom.

Komunyakaa: Charles Rowell is the editor of *Callaloo*, and he and I were just talking about it on Sunday, so it will be some time before it's coming out. But I would be interested in some of the stuff that you are writing research on.

Hanshaw: I have a copy of the article that I wrote for *The Literary Griot*, and I'll give that to you before I leave. I know that Clark Terry, who edited *Bloods*, was also a correspondent in Vietnam for *Time Magazine*.

Komunyakaa: Yeah, that's right. This is true.

Hanshaw: I wanted to know, did you go there as a journalist or were you drafted, or whatever, and then you did your journalism work after you got there as a solider?

Komunyakaa: No, I was drafted. I went to Vietnam as a combat correspondent in the Information Field. I was in the military.

Hanshaw: Already?

Komunyakaa: I was on-the-job trained as a correspondent.

Hanshaw: I see, okay.

Komunyakaa: In fact, I had gone to Infantry OCS and I got a branch transfer into OCS out of the infantry into the Information Field.

Hanshaw: Where did you go to OCS?

Komunyakaa: I went to Fort Benning, Georgia.

Hanshaw: Well, my classmates used to say if you were sent to Fort Polk, Louisiana, you knew the next stop was Vietnam. Everybody hated to get sent there. Were there many black journalists who were allowed to go out into the field?

Komunyakaa: In the Information Field, I think I came in contact with one other individual who was a master sergeant in WWII.

Hanshaw: I read that one of the reasons John A. Williams wrote *Captain Blackman* is that he was not permitted to go to Vietnam as a journalist. In fact, he was prevented from obtaining a visa to go. This was not the case for many white journalists, because many of the novels by white writers came about as a result of their being correspondents and going out into the field.

Komunyakaa: You're talking about most of those writers who actually experienced Vietnam as soldiers, particularly O'Brien.

Hanshaw: Yes, O'Brien wrote *The Things They Carried.*

Komunyakaa: I think there are many reasons for that. I don't think we have heard from that many black writers. There are many reasons for it. I probably could talk to you a long time about that.

Hanshaw: There is one anthology that I found as well, and I suppose it's the definitive anthology of Vietnam War literature by African American writers.

Komunyakaa: What is that anthology?

Hanshaw: Oh, here it is. *Vietnam in Black America: An Anthology of Protest and Resistance* by Clyde Taylor.

Komunyakaa: I don't know that anthology. That is interesting.

Hanshaw: It has excerpts from oral narratives, press releases, editorials, essays from black journalists such as Samuel Yette and Robert Brown. It even discusses Ron Dellums and Julian Bond concerning their stances on the Vietnam War and what happened to their political careers as a result. There is also an essay about Muhammad Ali's decision to become a conscientious objector.

Komunyakaa: What about Dr. Martin Luther King's anti-war speech?

Hanshaw: Yes, it is included. As a matter of fact his anti-Vietnam War speech was delivered at Riverside Church in New York on April 4, 1967, exactly a year before he was assassinated. I think that is quite significant. Thank you for this enlightening interview.

Yusef Komunyakaa and Paul Muldoon

Suzan Sherman/1998

From *BOMB Magazine* (Fall 1998). Reprinted by permission.

suzan sherman: Paul, Tim Kendall recently wrote a book, *Paul Muldoon*, defining the Irish vocabulary and bits of Irish lore in your poetry. Do you feel a reader needs this kind of preparation to fully grasp your poetry?

paul muldoon: Some uses of language are quite specific to a place, to the language I was brought up speaking and which to some extent still write in, Hiberno-English—usages I hope the context of the poem would clarify. I read Tim Kendall's book, I confess, very fleetingly. I tend not to pay too much attention to what people write about my poems. Not that I disdain it, not that I'm above it, but basically I don't want to be too conscious of what people say.

yusef komunyakaa: I'm wondering if immediate understanding is within an American readership's grasp, or if they are transported by the music of the narrative, if the listener isn't carried along by the sound of your Irish accent.

pm: I am interested in the musicality of language. Anyone who writes verse has some notion of the rhythm of the line. There's always an oral or aural aspect. I've lived here for ten years, and I don't speak the same language I did twenty years ago. Mind you, I was thirty-five when I left Ireland so a lot of it was ingrained, but things have changed. The poems now reflect the variety of language to which I've been exposed, and also to which many readers have been exposed. We're now operating, despite our insistence on the claims of the local and parochial, in a global context, where one *can* try to make sense of what's happening in contemporary Chinese poetry. That's not to say that there aren't complications. Yusef, do you find yourself thinking about a notional or ideal reader?

yk: I don't, but I realize that my work is immersed in Southern idiom, along with an acquired literary language. I'm trying to make both function tonally side by side to create music that doesn't have to achieve an absolute scale of meaning, but more or less to induce a certain feeling, because that's what literature is. How I like reading poems is to return, going to the bottom of a poem and finding myself again at the top reading down. It's a cumulative feeling.

pm: That makes me think of T.S. Eliot's remark about poetry being able to communicate before it's entirely understood. Each year a group of about fifty judges comes to Princeton for a weekend to talk to the faculty about their various subjects. Their questions are quite probing, as you might imagine. One of them asked me: "In what part of your body do you know that your poem is finished?" It's a pretty good question.

yk: Yes, the physicality of language. The tongue married to the heart, and emotions defined by flesh.

pm: Supposedly there's a chord called the Devil's Chord that evokes an extraordinary visceral effect, it makes the hair stand on the back of one's neck. That's the answer I gave; that there's some logic of the body, some disturbance that registers at a physical level in poetry.

yk: It's an emotional logic. The way the body operates makes me think of the blue note. That impossible note the jazz musician attempts to reach for, and it consequently becomes the engine that drives creative improvisation.

pm: When you sit down to write a poem, do you have a notion of a blue note?

yk: My process is to write everything down and not worry about the shape. Then I impose a structural frame. Since one is working with tools that one loves, he or she knows them well and can trust them. Rhythm extends the possibilities within the shape of language—it's reaching for that surprise, the blue note.

pm: The unexpected.

yk: The unexpected becomes the challenge, to achieve that and have the possibility of duplicating it, expanding it even further.

pm: The root of the word "poet" is "maker"—you've made wonderful analogies to your father's work as a carpenter, a man using tools—but that analogy breaks down for me. It's as if each time one has to make the tools for the task.

yk: Yes. Redefine the tool and test it against possibility, with slightly different adjustments and emotional calibration. We can achieve music and meaning simultaneously by trusting language.

pm: But that's the knowledge, surely, that you give yourself over to—whatever it will bring and whatever it will want to make through you.

yk: That's what I mean by improvisation. To the extent that there is not a complete frame around a poem, we're not forcing it into a preconceived mold. We are willing to be surprised and consequently, that mold is elastic.

pm: Do you do any work with your hands? Do you do carpentry yourself?

yk: I used to do quite a bit, too much as a matter of fact. Renovating houses—painting, scraping—there's exciting material underneath. I renovated a hundred-year-old house in New Orleans and was surprised to find that under the horsehair plaster the wood looked new, preserved. I often try to move back to the original because we tend to paint over things. Americans, for the most part, do not appreciate things that look old.

pm: Am I right in thinking that you were working on a house while writing some of the Vietnam poems?

yk: The poem "Somewhere Near Phu Bai." I had a pad of paper at the bottom of the ladder and I kept going up and down, writing phrases, words, images, and soon I had a poem. I hadn't thought about writing about Vietnam. My influences were Surrealism, especially Breton, and the Negritude poets: Aimé Césaire, Leopold Sédar Senghor, René Depestre, David Diop, Flavien Ranaivo, and Léon Damas. I was interested in the merging of different tones—where one can have the colloquial, the urgency of street language, along with a very technical and academic language. It has to do with switching codes—being able to talk with my father, who was not educated as such, and at the same time being able to talk to students and colleagues. One has to negotiate those different territories and realize that we're essentially cut from the same cloth. Because we're talking about communication, trying to be as concise as possible, and at the same time be provocative and surprising.

pm: Was your father able to read and write?

yk: No.

pm: The same with me. My experience is not unlike your own, in that I come from a culture where there were lots of horses knocking around, yet the tractor was taking over. I was born in 1951, and my extended family lived at the ends of lanes in houses that have not changed for a couple of hundred years, living in ways that have not changed for several hundred years. Forty-five years later and Ireland is one of the computer centers of the universe. It's quite an extraordinary leap.

ss: Yusef, you hadn't considered your experiences in Vietnam to be a proper subject for poetry before you began writing about it. I was wondering how your views in this regard have changed.

yk: Well, I came to poetry reading Shakespeare out loud, Tennyson, the protest sonnets of the Harlem Renaissance: Claude McKay, Countee Cullen,

James Weldon Johnson, Jessie Redmon Fauset, Jean Toomer, and Anne Spencer. Those are very formal voices, and I thought that was what poetry was about. And finally I got to Eliot, Langston Hughes, and Gwendolyn Brooks, modern and contemporary voices, and my whole perspective about poetry changed. When I first came to poetry, I definitely would not have said that you can put any- and everything within the context of poetic expression. But now I say, Yes, that's the challenge, to challenge the music in oneself.

pm: Consider some of the great seventeenth-century poets who dealt with a vast information explosion. John Donne had to find a way of dealing with the high and the low. We can still learn from him.

yk: Even Eliot, the shape of his imagination was informed not only by that which educated the psyche, but also by that which may be termed pedestrian.

pm: And he learned a huge amount from John Donne; he re-invented Donne to some extent. So, Eliot was big for you early on?

yk: Yes. "Journey of the Magi" and "The Love Song of J. Alfred Prufrock," along with *The Wasteland.*

pm: Same here. In many ways, he was *the* person when I was a teenager.

yk: It was informative to spend time in St. Louis, because I began to think of Eliot in a different way. He must have been taking in all kinds of things growing up there: music, Scott Joplin, the riverboats, all of that. When he talks about pianos in the alley in Cambridge, I think he's really talking about St. Louis. St. Louis pretty much created Eliot's tongue even as he attempted to betray it. I especially see signals of that in *Inventions of the March Hare,* where one also sees the misogynist, the racist.

pm: All the good things? (*laughter*)

yk: Yes, all those typical American tropes. Eliot's is really an American voice, which he seems to have wanted to deny. He was trying to erase part of his psyche, to reinvent himself as British. He was interested in the illusion of what art is: the demarcation between so-called low and high cultures.

ss: As readers, how do you negotiate a writer's anti-Semitism or racism when it's imbedded within the work? I'm thinking of the book *T.S. Eliot, Anti-Semitism, and Literary Form* by Anthony Julius.

yk: It wasn't until after I had read that line in *The Wasteland*, "The Jew squats in the windowsill . . ."—and put it together with "Gerontion"—that the poem read entirely differently. There are other racist remarks in T.S. Eliot; that's why I said he's very American. He was an instrument of his time, as artists are often shaped by their society. The Southern Agrarians, for example, the fugitives: John Crowe Ransom, Allen Tate, Robert Penn Warren, Lyle Lanier.

I'll Take My Stand is the title of their collection of essays; it's a line from "Dixie." Often intellectuals and artists have been the cornerstones of racist, regressive thinking.

pm: One would like to think that poets have an inherent moral sense, but clearly they don't. Bad men can write good poetry. Within the Irish context, you have people like Edmund Spenser and Walter Raleigh involved in violent—and I think inappropriate—action in Ireland. And yet I wouldn't want to say that one shouldn't read Spenser or Raleigh. This is a New Critical version of the world, but one has to try to read the work on its own terms. Eliot himself was a great proponent of the dissociation of the personality of the writer from what was on the page.

yk: The real problem is when it's also on the page. Hart Crane, in his letters from Cuba, made very racist remarks.

pm: I don't know if I agree with the use of the term, "We are the products of our times." I possibly reflect some view of the world that is absolutely flawed, but I hope that's not the case. I don't think being a product of our time absolves us entirely. The real question is, how do you respond to someone who is guilty of these offenses?

yk: I don't think we stop reading Eliot.

pm: Nor do I. But there are people who say that's what should happen. I couldn't go that far.

yk: I think Eliot's idea of dissociation was only an illusion. Perhaps it's something he wished to achieve but didn't. Those moments in his work are lived elements, not purely from his imagination.

pm: That's what's so complicated. One can never make that dissociation. Most writers' work reflects a small bunch of obsessions at the core of their personality. It may be presented in various ways, strategies may be developed for avoiding it, for making it seem different from the last time. That's just one of the things writers do to keep going—devise different strategies and vary the shots, to move around what's always there. The metaphor is perhaps inadequate—as all metaphors are finally—but there is a core, a core which is the self. I think that all writing is autobiographical at some level.

yk: What about language poetry?

pm: I'm not an expert on language poets. As I understand it, what they're doing is not so different from what Eliot did.

yk: That's right.

pm: The complete abnegation of the personality, as the language has its own logic and force. I believe in that to a great extent myself. I would argue with what I just said about autobiography, the personality shining through willy-nilly. I think it does, and yet ideally one tries to give oneself over when one writes, to have no sense of self. It's a paradox that there must be no sense of self and a complete openness and humility before the language. Language poets take it to an extreme. I have some sense of a regard for what they're up to, though I don't quite understand their insistence on nonsense.

yk: I suppose the influence is a Marxist principle. That essentially, the poet or the writer, the thinker, is seen as imperialistic, controlling meaning to the extreme. It is an attempt to untether language and meaning.

pm: Well, both sense and nonsense are tyrannical.

yk: But also, within that context, much of so-called language poetry has become grist for the theorists.

pm: I'm surprised that they agreed to be described as belonging to a group. I distrust all groups. I'm talking about being associated with any kind of movement. It's not about being special, it's about wanting to be free. So that one has no ties, so the next thing coming down the road, one might be able to go with it for a few steps, and then retreat. So that one is not in anybody's army.

ss: But I see you in the context of other people, because of how people have painted you.

pm: How do these people see me?

ss: As a contemporary of Seamus Heaney within a postcolonial structure.

pm: One really can't afford to think about those things too much. Not because one's an ostrich—circumspection is very important, having an intellectual grasp of things—but not on oneself.

yk: You don't want to be shaped by the terms of someone else's critique. You want the freedom to at least have the illusion of being outside of that. Although I think we are touched by reviews, all kinds of things.

pm: Have you done any writing for the theater?

yk: I've been asked by Northwestern University's School of Music to do a libretto on a historical individual named Arthur, no last name, born a slave in 1747, died 1768. Quite a provocative figure.

pm: Is there some aspect of his life that is particularly dramatic?

yk: His whole short life is dramatic. "I'm almost free," that's how he defines himself. That says a lot right there. But he was stealing horses, escaping with the American Indians. He lived short periods of time with the Mashpees, Nipmucks, and Wampanoags in Massachusetts. His whole personality seems to have been shaped by ritual and caper around Taunton, Massachusetts. But he always returned home to his mother. Finally he was charged with rape and hanged. And most of the people questioned. . . . It's really about the drama of public opinion.

ss: Paul, you've written a libretto too. Where does the title *Shining Brow* come from?

pm: "Shining brow" is the translation of "Taliesin," the Welsh bard, after whom Frank Lloyd Wright named a house he built for his lover, Mamah Cheney. There was a huge amount of drama in the writing of the libretto. I think there has to be some drama, some theatricality, in poetry as well. As a poet one sits around talking to oneself, and so it's a lot of fun to do a project with other people. I'm a great believer in fun.

yk: I think poets should be collaborating in theater, music, all types of projects. The Pacific Symphony Orchestra commissioned the composer Eliot Goldenthal to do *Fire Water Paper: A Vietnam Oratorio*, and he incorporated two of my poems, "You and I Are Disappearing" and "Boat People." Before I heard the poems sung and performed, I was prepared for failure. Hearing the performance started me thinking more about collaborations. Thus, I wasn't as apprehensive when Tony Getsug called me to suggest that 8th Harmonic Breakdown record me with John Tchicai's jazz compositions. Again, I was surprised by the outcome of the CD.

pm: The great thing about writing poetry is that you don't need much money. And if it fails, who cares? Nobody gives a hoot. Nothing has been lost if your new poem . . . (*laughter*) with a cast of thousands . . .

yk: We don't need a whole economic apparatus, do we? I still compose by pencil and paper, believe it or not. I do not, I can't even think of anyone composing on the computer.

pm: I compose on a computer.

yk: You do?

pm: When I started as a teenager, I always wrote straight onto a typewriter for the very simple reason that I wanted to know what it would look like published. The question of whether or not it would be published was completely irrelevant. I was interested, and still am, in the physical shape and the subliminal sense that shape conveys. We talked about the aural and oral traditions, which are extremely important, but then there's also the operation between the page, the eye, and the ear.

yk: It's the complete opposite for me. I love the idea of the pencil or pen pressed against the paper. The evolution of the brain has everything to do with the hand. I like the feel, the hand making, creating the letters.

ss: Paul, what place do you feel an Irish writer holds being in the United States? Does the distance give you a stronger understanding of who you are, and what you're writing of? Is being here like your poem "Wind and Tree," is it "telling new weather?"

pm: I am a citizen of both countries, insofar as one can be in two places at once, which I think one can. "Wind and Tree" is one of the first poems I wrote, a remake of Robert Frost's "Tree in My Window," although I was not conscious of it at the time. I've always been very influenced by American culture, not only literature, but films, music, and television. So it's not so strange that I came here, it's very familiar. And looking back home is not strange either, because it's not too far to look, even to go. I'm going to Ireland on Thursday and returning next Monday. It's like getting on a bus. To answer another part of your question—distance, I think, does not necessarily lead to perspective any more than proximity gives one a real sense of what's going on. When I lived in Belfast, which I did for many, many years, I don't know if I had a clearer sense of what was going on around the corner.

ss: Both of you are concerned with the plight Native Americans have suffered in this country and have dealt with this in your poetry. Paul, on the cover of your book, *Madoc*, there is a painting of Native Americans partaking in a Bull Dance ceremony. Yusef, on the cover of your new book, *Thieves of Paradise*, is a painting . . .

yk: By Benjamin West, of William Penn signing a peace treaty with the Indians. I suppose there is an ironic, satirical tone behind my title, *Thieves of Paradise*. Whether or not it makes us think of America as a stolen paradise, it responds to many kinds of thefts, small and big.

pm: I loved your poem "Quatrains for Ishi." Ishi, I must say, is one of my own great heroes. I dedicated a poem to him in my first book, "The Year of the Sloes—For Ishi." He was the last member of a tribe found in California in the early 1900s. It's a heartbreaking story of this man who spent his life in a museum where he made arrowheads as a kind of tourist attraction.

yk: One of the strange things for me to think about is how, as the last known member of his tribe, he goes about the rituals of keeping alive, the rituals of entertaining himself. That was part of my imaginative work, to try to place myself in his situation. His living in the Museum of Anthropology in San Francisco, gazed at and misunderstood—it's rather difficult to imagine.

pm: He was described as a Stone Age man. This little love poem I wrote was a spin-off of Dee Brown's *Bury My Heart at Wounded Knee*. The Native American names for the months of the year are the names of trees, and each section of it began, "In the month of . . ." using the Native American names. But it was really about Northern Ireland, and it ended up with this image of bodies lying in the road. It was written at the time of Bloody Sunday, when the British Army opened fire on a crowd of marchers and killed thirteen people.

ss: Did you see the connection between the Irish living under colonial domination and the Native Americans, before you came to the United States?

pm: There are a few poems that, in perhaps too crude a way, draw parallels between the condition of the Native American experience and the native Irish experience. One in particular called "Meeting the British," about Pontiac's Rebellion. I shy away from the parallel a bit. It's coming close to propaganda, which is something I've managed fairly successfully to avoid. On the other hand, it might be close to some aspect of the truth.

yk: "Ishi" means "man," and as I thought of Ishi, I kept thinking about growing up in Louisiana. My community has a kinship with many of the Southern Native Americans—especially Choctaw, Chickasaw—they are connected by culture and bloodlines to the African American. I have a poem, "Looking for Choctaw," about seeing an Indian in my grandmother's face. I must admit, as a child I was a bit confused by my community's link to Indians, because one begins to wrestle with demarcations, psychological ones, especially in the cultural and social apartheid of the Deep South. I remember the ritual of playing cowboys and Indians. Often, no one wanted to be an Indian. I always found myself volunteering, because I liked the idea of having the bow and arrow.

pm: Same here. I have photographs of myself as an Indian with the tepee in the backyard. I still have a bow and arrow in my house. But what does that represent? As I think about it right now, the experience of the Native Americans disturbs me. There are many, many people who have been mistreated, but frankly, that story in particular makes me want to cry. We were talking about poets and whether or not they had any morals—maybe it's not a matter of whether or not I'm a poet, but I always associate myself with the person having a bad time.

yk: Perhaps most poets do, in some ways.

ss: Yusef, why did you become a poet, as opposed to some other form of expression for the self?

yk: My sense of poetry has a lot to do with Louisiana where I grew up, my rituals. I was very tuned into the beauty and violence in the people and the landscape. It's a great, scary irony that the KKK call themselves the "Knights of the White Camellia"—as if language is used to pervert nature, to tinge the camellia with blood. I wanted a dialogue with the things around me, to understand them. Eels, mud puppies, cattails, Venus flytraps, fish-looking creatures with legs called Congo snakes, everything. I wanted to know the names of trees, plants, flowers. Naming became a type of inquiry. Poetry was also what I liked to read. The idea of coming back and forth to a poem became important. When a poem doesn't necessarily have a linear narrative, but invites one in to become a participant. Consequently, I found myself desiring to write poems. I volunteered to write a poem for my high-school graduating class, a hundred lines long, written with much agony. I still don't know why I raised my hand, because I had never written a poem before.

pm: Really?

yk: Well, songs had become important to me. Often I would hear songs, lyrics on the radio, and I remember making up my own words to the music. It was probably my first act of creation.

pm: When you were a child, did your father encourage you?

yk: My mother encouraged me; my father wanted me to work right beside him.

pm: Encouragement is extremely important. My daughter and I were in a restaurant the other night and in the middle of the dinner my daughter says, "Okay, I have a poem. Have you got a piece of paper?" One of the few times I ever put pen to paper, actually (*laughter*)—I wrote down this four-line poem. It's a natural impulse children have that needs little encouragement. Everyone else is trying to get back to something like that.

yk: It took some time, really, for my father to suggest that I had gone in the right direction. Actually, in March of '86, he said, "Could you write me a poem?"

pm: Did he?

yk: And it was a difficult task. It took a very long time to come up with anything. But at least it was a kind of recognition. Finally, I wrote "Songs for My Father" after he died in 1986, in September.

ss: Paul, you had mentioned that you have your students write their poems line by line.

pm: That's a small aspect of it. It's not the first thing I'd say about trying to write poems, because there are many ways of doing it. I find it effective because it makes my students think about the line as the unit of the poem. You get that line right and you move on to the next one. That establishes the cellular logic or progress of the poem.

yk: I don't have them go line by line, but I do express the idea about getting everything down. And then I have them isolate lines as part of the revision process. I think about revision as re-seeing, revisiting, if possible, a place in time. Placing a white sheet of paper at the bottom of the poem and very systematically working up, realizing that there are possibly two or three, sometimes five or six endings. Negotiating what has already been placed on the page. Reading is also such an intricate part of writing. I can't see how one can write and not read.

pm: As Yusef says, the two things are happening coincidentally, constantly. I think to be a decent writer, one has to be a decent reader. And to be an extremely good writer, one has to be an extremely good reader of oneself. Not that one ever, ever achieves the condition of not needing someone else to say, "You're missing something here. You can't get away with that."

yk: The workshop becomes an instant community. And that's what writers need. Usually I start the very first day of class by plotting out a community, and we have a certain protocol, and straightforwardness, and share opinions.

pm: Do you have particular friends that read your work and help you?

yk: I might get on the phone and read a couple of lines or a poem to someone. I realize that often I want to place a poem aside, and I'm almost a different person when I come back to it.

pm: I think one is. I just find that so difficult to do. I don't trust myself. I'm very interested in your process of working on several books at once. I think that's just wonderful.

yk: It's the idea of movement from one to another, about surprise. I don't know what I want to write on a given day.

pm: What are you working on at the moment, for example?

yk: A book-length poem titled *Autobiography of My Alter Ego*. I said I wouldn't write about Vietnam anymore, but this is a monologue spoken by a bartender, a white American. He comes back from the war and starts riding buses across the country. He cannot stay in one place. He might ride to San Francisco or Los Angeles, find himself the very next week in Alabama, crisscrossing the country. It's spoken many years after this obsession, and it starts off with this phrase: "If the President wants to know / What's happening / He should come in here / Order a Bloody Mary / Sit down / And I'll tell him. . . ." He's talking to someone there at the bar, and he just goes on and on. He's not conscious that he's trying to square a certain record with his observations and experiences. Also, I'm working on the sixteen-line poems—a book called *Talking Dirty to the Gods.*

pm: "Ode to the Maggot," is that one?

yk: Yes, that's one of them. I have about one hundred of the sixteen-liners.

ss: They're all animals?

yk: Animal insights, mythologies, histories, everyday rituals, and so forth.

ss: Paul, what are you working on now?

pm: Several things. I've been doing another opera, called *Bandanna*, set in Texas in 1969. It's about relations between a husband and wife, and between the Mexican and the white communities in a little border town. And then I'm doing a translation with a Greek scholar here at Princeton, Richard Martin, of Aristophanes' *The Birds*. And I'm giving some lectures in October and November, the Clarendon Lectures. They're on various aspects of Irish literature. And I hope to try and write a few poems.

An Interview with Yusef Komunyakaa

E. Ethelbert Miller and Zoe Anglesey/1999

From *The Writer's Chronicle* 33.2 (October/November 2000). Reprinted by permission of E. Ethelbert Miller.

E. Ethelbert Miller: For many of us, Komunyakaa's early poetry was like television bringing the Vietnam War into our living rooms. Maybe it is only poetry that can explain that war. Read Komunyakaa—he writes about Vietnam like Baldwin wrote about Harlem, the writer as witness and correspondent reporting back from the front lines. But before this war, he was a man shaped by the music of Louis Armstrong, Dinah Washington, Mahalia Jackson, John Coltrane, Duke Ellington. He heard this music on the radio, and one wonders about how the words began to take shape inside his head—like notes . . . Would you comment on the importance of Duke Ellington to our culture and to your own life?

Yusef Komunyakaa: I grew up with blues coming through the radio mainly from New Orleans—especially Robert Johnson, Mississippi John Hurt, Bessie Smith, "Big Mama" Thornton—and a number of other voices, including R&B and gospel. Ellington brought an urban feel to the blues, and that was instructive for me. It influenced me to look at the writing of the Harlem Renaissance, voices that came out of the Midwest or the landscape of the South that emerged in the North as part of the so-called Great Migration. I noticed a certain tenacity in Ellington's music; also a spiritual dimension as well. He says that music—I'm paraphrasing this—moves one closer to God. That's a rather audacious statement. He also insinuates that music is a seed for human discourse, so nature becomes a part of the musical design. I grew up in Louisiana and internalized that terrain. I know now how it influences everything I see and how my voice filters through it.

Miller: Is there such a thing as a jazz poem, and if so, what are its unique characteristics?

Komunyakaa: Understand that we internalize music, and consequently, the music one likes tends to influence the length of the line and pace of the poem. Richard Hugo talks about the use of long and short lines in *The Triggering Town*. I didn't know what that meant until I came across the statement that he was influenced by swing. It's then that I became aware of a kind of movement, an oscillation between lines of varied lengths and that between the lines is silence. We can't have music without silence.

When I was in New Orleans in 1981, I began to look very closely at certain poets who had been influenced by jazz—Langston Hughes, William Matthews, Etheridge Knight, Hayden Carruth, Michael Harper, and Shirley Anne Williams come to mind. There are certain poems by Gwendolyn Brooks and Philip Levine. In *The Second Set: The Jazz Poetry Anthology*, which I co-edited with Sascha Feinstein, there are 132 voices. I don't think the jazz poem means to mimic jazz music. Rather, it becomes subject matter or manifests itself in the care given to rhythm or making imagery clearly visible.

Miller: Do you consider yourself a jazz poet?

Komunyakaa: We can say that the music of many of my poems is influenced by jazz. My method of composition might be jazz-influenced because of improvisation. I don't worry about the construction of a poem. I write everything down as it comes to me, then I go back to the poem to systematically revise it. Revision means to re-see—to re-live in a certain sense.

Miller: Walk us through *Testimony*, which is about Charlie Parker.

Komunyakaa: I wrote that poem because Chris Williams, a producer at the Australian Broadcasting Corporation, asked if I would write a libretto on Charlie Parker. After agreeing, I agonized about it for a long time. Parker is rather experimental, so the traditional libretto wouldn't be appropriate. Finally, I came up with fourteen sections of two stanzas with fourteen lines each. At least it reflects a notion of symmetry. I wanted to capture the essence of Parker. I knew that people told hundreds of stories about him; I set out to retell them, but as poetry. Also, Parker himself liked poetry, and I was quite taken with that.

Miller: How important is clarity or the need to be understood? Joel Brower, who reviewed your last collection in the June 1998 issue of *Progressive* magazine, wanted footnotes to some of your poems. Is this a fair request?

Komunyakaa: I'll answer by mentioning my reading/writing process. I return to poems again and again. The poem is not an emotional ad where everything is understood from the first to the last line. Similarly, I prefer something more provocative than resolution in a poem, if possible. I strive for a last line or image that propels the reader back up to the poem's first thoughts. Poetry doesn't necessarily have to be easy, either. However, it should be emotionally engaging. Often I go along with the music of a poem and don't worry about linear narrative. This is the argument Plato had with poetry—that essentially, poets generate a non-reasoning form of expression. That's ridiculous. What he was really afraid of, I think, is that poets question. Basic to its nature, a poem seems to be more embracing when it avoids becoming an answer, and, instead, poses an active question.

Miller: Turning to your CD, *Love Notes from the Mad House*, I recall Ornette Coleman's album, *Free Jazz*. Once, with that music in mind, he walked into the studio and just started playing with musicians who were assembled there, whom he'd never played with previously. From what I understand, you had not met John Tchicai before the rehearsal and the recording in September 1997. I wonder how this happened.

Komunyakaa: Well, I had listened to John Tchicai's music before Tony Getsug of 8th Harmonic Breakdown called and asked to record my poems with jazz accompaniment. I thought about the failures during the 1950s. First of all, one has to rehearse. I don't think anyone can walk in and have a happening. There has to be mutual respect—the poet has to respect both the music and the musicians. In turn, musicians—by their listening and playing—must show respect to the poet's words. Then there has to be a working out of things: space has to be provided for both the music and the poem.

In reading the poem, "Twilight Seduction," dedicated to Ellington, I recalled that I had originally written the poem with the piano in mind for a performance at the Sydney Jazz Festival. Very seldom do I do that—write a poem to be accompanied by music. I want the poem to stand on its own.

It's interesting—Ellington makes me think of Whitman. There is an earthy aesthetic at the emotional axes of their visions. They both produce an elongated singing that reaches toward a tonal passion in their works—an insistence that goes straight for the heart. They seem to be searching for the muse wherever they can find it from the American landscape. This brings to mind Paul Gonsalves playing those twenty-seven choruses on "Diminuendo and Crescendo in Blue" at the 1956 Newport Jazz Festival and Whitman's robust refrain. In much the same way that Whitman writes the poems we return to most often, Ellington creates spatial colors that expand a composition to its visual manifestation.

I said that I don't necessarily write a poem with music in mind except when the time comes to record jazz-related poems, but writing librettos, the music is obviously left up to the composer. I have just finished writing *Slip Knot* in collaboration with the composer T. J. Anderson. Rhoda Levine has been so helpful in the formulation of this project. Now, I have numerous ideas for more librettos, and look forward to writing them, as long as I can stay close to poetry.

Miller: Would you comment on how you selected the painting *Penn's Treaty with the Indians* for the dust jacket of *Thieves of Paradise*? How does this image open the door to the poems?

Komunyakaa: John Crowe Ransom says that poetry has to have tension. That's probably the only thing I've taken from the Southern Agrarians. Reproducing this painting on the book jacket was one way of establishing a certain tension, and before someone opens the book.

Miller: How does the poet explore history, while at the same time entering into self-discovery?

Komunyakaa: I think that history cannot be on the surface of the poem. Rather, it has to be woven into the tonal structure. I'm in the process of writing *Wishbone Trilogy*. I want to excavate African American history, but by way of focusing on certain figures. There's Ira Aldridge. He was born on Greene Street in Manhattan; I've seen his bust at the Royal Shakespeare Theatre where he played Othello as well as other major roles from Shakespeare. Looking at Pushkin, Alexander Dumas, St. George, the personal bodyguard for the Duchess of Orleans, I discovered a way to intermingle poetry with historical figures and facts. I started to write jagged three-line stanzas, and consequently, a lyricism began to emerge that, in a way, parallels some jazz tonalities.

Miller: You have a tribute poem to Eric Dolphy. Was he an influence on your work?

Komunyakaa: Dolphy reminds me of the quality of listening. The way he explores space is interesting. This idea of him playing along with the birds, communing with nature, takes me back to Louisiana. I also grew up listening carefully to my surroundings. Baldwin says one has to know what's happening in one's environment in order to know oneself because we, too, are a part of everything around us. I believe that. I grew up with that conscious thought.

Miller: What are some of the things you like to focus on in your creative writing classes? What exercises do you like to use? What writers do you feel are essential for young writers to study?

Komunyakaa: Reading is important. I can't see how anyone can write and not read. I'm not just talking about only reading literature, but reading in the sciences, philosophy, mythology, history, about the arts, current events—everything that one can possibly read. This feeds the imagination. The other thing that I suggest is revising. Many young writers say, *aren't you afraid the inspiration will be tampered with or change the poem?* This is not the case at all. When I was in graduate school, Gwendolyn Brooks made a very memorable statement that I took to instantly. She said, "Art is that which endures."

I believe in and trust her statement. I come back to a poem again and again. In the process of compiling *Pleasure Dome*, I was still revising. Even after poems are published in journals and books, I find myself circling words and phrases, questioning them. In a certain sense, a collection of poems is an organism.

To answer your question more directly, the creative writing workshop fosters a small community of ideas seeking response. Working within a distilled moment when trust has been established by artists being firm and giving to each other, vital exchanges are made, and good poems come from this process.

As an important foundation, the writing workshop also relies on readings. I find myself referring to the so-called Western canon and culture-based literatures. We might discuss Shakespeare plays. My favorite, *King Lear*, often takes us to its poetry and beyond, to modern poetry, contemporary fiction and works for theater as with Naguib Mahfouz's *Echoes of an Autobiography*, *Krapp's Last Tape and Other Dramatic Pieces* by Samuel Beckett, Henrik Ibsen's *Peer Gynt*, and short stories by Yasunari Kawahata or Zora Neale Hurston. We talk about the history of literary conceits embedded in European and American poetry as we turn to Dickinson, Whitman, Wordsworth, Yeats, Coleridge, Hopkins, working up to Crane, Frost, Hughes, Pound, H.D., Eliot, Bishop, Brooks, and of course Hayden.

Usually, I don't give in-class exercises to workshop students; however, out of class, they are expected to write some theme-based poems. For instance, after having read Pablo Neruda's love poems or lyrics by Robert Johnson or Bessie Smith, I might have people in a workshop write amorous poems on the fifth week in order to understand the difficulties of writing a mature love poem.

Revision becomes the driving wheel of my workshops. Each word receives attention. We talk about the music of a poem in relationship to its meaning, how we come to trust what words are saying and how they make us feel. We create a space for what we have imagined and witnessed in writing poems, and we might examine Jerome Rothenberg's *Technicians of the Sacred*, Rainer Maria Rilke's *Letters to a Young Poet*, *The Odes of Pindar*, or Adrienne Rich's *On Lies, Secrets, and Silence: Selected Prose 1966–1978*. Reading such works inspires the impetus to revise.

[*E. Ethelbert Miller invites the audience to ask questions.*]

Audience: Could you explain what you mean by the "jagged line"?

Komunyakaa: Visually, the lines zigzag away from the left margin. That sets up a rhythm and syncopation in a poem's appearance on the page. Also, by adhering to unpredictable line breaks, the textual patterns suggest rhythmic structures. The poem achieves a symmetry, but not by falling straight down the page. I don't care if a line is exceptionally long or exceptionally short. Surprises might come with juxtaposition, by experimenting with a line's position. In this way, meanings change organically. This allows involvement in the emotional architecture of poems.

Audience: Has traveling influenced your writing?

Komunyakaa: I've written about Australia. *February in Sydney* was published in 1989 and is included in the forthcoming collected poems. I want to write poetry about New Guinea, but I haven't really internalized the images of that place yet. Traveling is important, but I avoid writing travel poems. First, I need to feel deeply about a place before I write about it.

Audience: How do you recognize that you've internalized aspects of a place?

Komunyakaa: I develop a certain love for a place. I've said that the poem itself is contemplation and celebration. The poem sets in motion a healthy query that delves into the relationships particular to place.

Miller: Thinking about your Vietnam poems—you've traveled back to Vietnam. How did you deal with that?

Komunyakaa: In retrospect, as I think about this, when I was first in Vietnam, I wasn't frightened by the landscape. It is semi-tropical and a Louisiana kind of place. In that sense, there is an apparent vibrancy that I identify with. I had systematically avoided writing about the Vietnam experience for fourteen years. Before then, my poems were informed by surrealism and also by the negritude movement. After finishing *Dien Cai Dau*, I said I wouldn't write about Vietnam again. Well, presently I'm writing a book-length poem entitled *The Autobiography of My Alter Ego*. The narrator is a white Vietnam veteran who doesn't spare us. You know that blues line, "start me a talkin,' I'll tell everything I know"? That's what he does.

Audience: Do you read out loud as you revise?

Komunyakaa: Yes, I do read the poem aloud because the ear is a faithful editor. That automatically takes us to the oral tradition, so it's important in that context.

Miller: Would you elaborate on what you wrote in the preface to *Listen Up! Spoken Word Poetry* (One World/Ballantine, 1999)?

Komunyakaa: Poetry has to survive on the page as well as in performance. Slam poetry is entertainment and as entertainment, it's quite fine. Anything associated with expression is fine as long as it doesn't become didactic or destructive. However, I think if slam poetry is in the realm of rap, it may be associated with commodity. When anger is commodified, I have real problems with that.

Miller: What are you working on now?

Komunyakaa: Besides writing poems, I'm finishing *Shangri-La*, another libretto, and editing with Sascha Feinstein and Zoe Anglesey *The Third Set*, an international anthology of jazz-related poetry that will be a little different from the previous jazz anthologies (*Jazz Poetry Anthology*, Indiana University Press, 1991; *The Second Set: The Jazz Poetry Anthology, Vol.* 2) because it will include translations.

Yusef Komunyakaa:
Blue Note in a Lyrical Landscape

Fran Gordon/2000

From *Poets and Writers Magazine* 28.6 (November/December 2000). Reprinted by permission of Fran Gordon.

Fran Gordon: Can you remember the first stories your mother read to you? Which myths you were exposed to?

Yusef Komunyakaa: Folklore more than myth. Southern folklore. Lots of ghosts.

FG: New Orleans folklore? Voodoo?

YK: As a matter of fact, yes. I would hear things whispered in the background—that gave people certain power over others. And I knew the people who were being named in these things, which was very interesting. In a way, it implanted a certain kind of apprehension about certain people—their power. Or their desperation—to have spells removed, or to cast spells. All those things were quite interesting to me and really prompted my imagination. Something else my mother gave me: I think you call them viewfinders, with this amazing false light. I remember being spellbound by some of the photographs of caves in America. Then there were travel photographs to other places: Mexico, Japan, Greece, Italy. And to have that false light enter the psyche, it does create a surreal moment in a certain sense—How one might look at something. I was drawn to mythology as a teenager, because it was another way of traveling in the imagination.

FG: Characters in the work of Southern writers like Faulkner always seemed to me to be closest to the shifty braggarts of Olympus. Is there something about the Southern landscape that brings out the fallible god in its inhabitants?

YK: Well, language itself. Language is an act of conjuring. I think the way language works in the South is its presentation—an argument with mystery, an argument with the past. Faulkner's idea of poetry is very Victorian, and yet

109

one can tilt that landscape a bit and realize that, yes, the poetry has informed the prose. The prose perhaps would have been dead on the page if the poetry had not been woven into it. The poetry releases his imagination to go many different directions, and let's face it, he also embraces the Gothic.

FG: You don't think of yourself as a Southern writer.

YK: I cannot deny that certain poems are influenced by the Southern land-scape. I've said in *Blue Notes* that when we internalize a landscape, every-thing filters through it—and I still believe that even though we try often to turn that landscape upside down, to see it in a distorted way, it is still there.

FG: What happens if there are too many landscapes—or if you're adrift?

YK: Well, it is just a more complex landscape, more to deal with. Maybe for the artist that is the gift—not this immense clarity from the onset. We're always trying to work things out, we're always trying to see, and not neces-sarily from the most enlightened place.

It was interesting, sitting in an African American barbershop today in Princeton. I felt a certain disembodiment, like I'm in the deep South, be-cause of the voices I heard from Virginia, from Georgia. Men were congre-gated there, telling their stories, recalling. It seems like a roll call from the dead sometimes. That's what it feels like. They know each other. Some of these men came in the forties, some came in the fifties, and even a few came in the thirties. And the young boys were sitting there, and I was thinking, "They're getting these very close haircuts." And I thought, "Didn't I experi-ence this once before? This is not new at all; this is the same place that I knew when I was a boy."

FG: There are good things about keeping a culture intact—little things like haircuts and food. On a larger scale it's great for African American literature to be available at the Schomburg Center, New York Public Library in Har-lem. . . .

KY: But this brings to mind a problem. If you go into some bookstores and they have a poetry section, and you're looking for Robert Hayden and you can't find him, something whispers in your brain, "Go and look for him in the African American section." And there he is—one or two copies of Hayden hiding out in the African American section, which, if you think of Hayden, is the last thing he wanted. Here is this great American voice—an American presence that should be even more than what it is—hidden in the African American section. My problem with education is that often we have individuals who really think of themselves as being very well educated; so I say, "Okay, now when I was in high school, junior high, I had to memorize long passages of Shakespeare. I knew Tennyson, Longfellow, Poe. But I also

had to learn some other voices as well, such as Langston Hughes, Gwendolyn Brooks."

FG: When was the first time you read Hughes?

YK: It was Negro History Week. God, I never read anything like that. And
yet I had heard it—but I hadn't read Hughes. That's how I came to Baldwin's
Nobody Knows My Name—but much had to do with Baldwin's picture on
the cover. I looked at Baldwin's picture and I said, "Oh, I know that face." Not
necessarily those long, passionate, driven clauses and sentences—although
he was saying some of the things I was thinking—but it was his photograph
that was so important to me. I was a teenager when picked Baldwin up. It
was in a small library that looked like a little house. I think it was the house
of the woman who ran it. She had been my kindergarten teacher, and my
mother's. She never had children. There was something matronly about
her—austere, big presence. She ran the library and I would go there and
choose books because we weren't allowed to go to the public library. That
says a hell of a lot when one thinks about education—that it was a no-no, it
was taboo, because education leads to questions.

FG: Power.

YK: It's the power of the questions more than anything else—and that's what
I still believe is so important about education.

FG: In *Magic City*'s first poem, "Venus's-flytraps," a child's questions are
weapons.

YK: Yes, because it is so important. And that's what art is about—it's one big
question. And not so much such a revised perspective, but it is that question
placed there for us to entertain, and come back to. I think that question is
what makes us human.

FG: It's not Write What You Know.

YK: Write what you're willing to discover. Why always give me something
that you know?! The poem isn't an ad for an emotion.

FG: As a senior in high school, you wrote a twenty-five-quatrain poem for
commencement, but were too shy to read it. What was it about this form
that even then interested you? Was there a particular poem you were trying to emulate? Or did you sense even then the fit of this form to reflection:
questions posed and answered aptly by contradictions. Did the distance inherent in the form suit your shyness?

YK: That's interesting. There is a kind of formalism in quatrain poems that
indicates the illusion of control. Then I was reading Locke and Tennyson. I
think I was caught up in the lyricism more than anything else. Then Robert
Frost's "The Death of the Hired Man" and "The Road Not Taken" became

important to me, as well as "The Witch of Coös," which is a poem Gothic enough to have been written by Edgar Allan Poe. It was so different from his other poems. But also he wrote about nature, so I was right there.

FG: Most Americans fear nature.

KY: I've been so distant from it, disconnected in a certain way, but when I lived in Louisiana, I trusted nature. I was thinking about this recently because I was in Santa Fe, looking out at this river, and along this river there was grass and what have you, and I said, "Gosh, I would like to walk through there"—and the words *scorpion* and *rattlesnake* kept entering my mind and kept me from doing it. But when I was growing up, there was no hesitation. I would have been out there right in the middle of it. I used to catch snakes. The rituals of animals are important to me. They just teach you a lot about life.

FG: You use science a lot. It comes into play in your work so much.

YK: Yes. But even with science there are certain questions that will remain questions. And that's fine. Because we're attempting to answer everything—and we create answers that pretty much erase themselves, I think. So why not be in awe of the mystery.

FG: That's part of Southern literature. The first poem you memorized was "Annabel Lee."

YK: I wrote an essay on this. "Annabel Lee" was a Southern name for me and I said, "Gosh, I know that name." It's interesting coming back to that poem because in a way it had a lot of playfulness for me—and even maybe sentimentality. I didn't think about class at all within the context of that poem. In retrospect, yes, there are statements about class. But Poe is problematic when it comes to his treatment of blacks. In his short stories, he has to cripple them, he has to maim them in some way; he cannot see them as whole people. He had to make them grotesque. But that has a lot to do with his imagination; his imagination has been perverted as well when it comes to the black person. I said somewhere that racism is a mental illness, and maybe that's what we're glimpsing—that mental distortion. Because as a whole person, as a whole black man, one that hasn't been crippled, I don't know if Poe can deal with me. And maybe it has to do with something very complex. Anything that distorts the personality in such a way we define as a mental illness. It's interesting, because Baldwin says it's not anger that sends the lynch mob out into the streets—it's fear. And fear taken to that extreme is, yes, mental distortion.

My first idea about education was actually to go into psychology, because I wanted to deal with just that element—those things I had witnessed in my lifetime, early life in Louisiana. Even then saw them as psychological constructions that were negative constructions that had everything to do with the downfall of the individual as a complete human. We're such an interesting one. Human life, human existence is always an ontological question, you know, just sitting there. It's such a huge question. All of these precise magical happenings that seem to be controlled by the brain—such an instrument. Such an instrument, and yet it's accidental. It has everything to do with chance and time, so even as a child I thought about this a great deal.

FG: You mean the system and the wisdom effected?

YK: Yes, "wisdom," and the capacity to do what we do—and that's why it terrifies me when I see people not fully engaged. I went back to Bogalusa, Louisiana, last month to revisit the old territory, and it seemed like everything was standing in place. By viewing the deterioration, I realized at that moment, for that system to work, blacks had to be psychologically, spiritually, and in every way at the bottom. Since this concept has been challenged, that little city deteriorated. Poor people once believed that if they worked hard, and excelled, they could move on.

FG: Your dad believed that.

YK: My father believed that, and others around me believed that. My whole neighborhood believed that in a way when I think about it. I knew men who had worked very hard and had been rather thrifty as well, and yet through the cost of living and what have you . . . I came back, years later, and they had their shoes tied with strings around their feet, and stuff of this sort. And this is not supposed to happen. Don't mention if one happens to work and get sick. There is a real . . . Come back and visit these empty shells. So that place where there was so much inspiration, disquieting inspiration, seems to have eaten itself barren in so many ways. And it doesn't have a spirit or heart any longer. It's just there, waiting to be. . . .

And at the same time these are the little communities artists come out of. They come out of the middle of nowhere. And for a long time, living and teaching in Indiana, I began to meditate on the Midwest, because there were similarities. I lived in New Orleans, and then I lived in Bloomington, Indiana, and I said, "Hmm, I am back home in the South. Deep South." When in fact New Orleans seemed like it could be anywhere in so many ways because it has twenty-four distinctive communities. In the Bywater area you might hear an accent and think you're in the Bronx. And when I came to the Midwest I began to entertain an idea of time and space. Now, time and space has a lot to do with the innovative spirit. I started thinking about some of the jazz musicians, some of the writers. William Burroughs comes from St.

Louis, and spent all that time in Lawrence, Kansas. Miles Davis is from East St. Louis. Or even Eliot—Eliot is from St. Louis and quite innovative, really, if you look at the Moderns, quite innovative in so many ways. And that voice of Eliot's was completely informed by the South. The River. And he's more British than the British. And you know he agonizes about his voice, how he sounds when he goes to Harvard. Yes, he must have had some black caretakers, wouldn't doubt it.

FG: Eliot wrote of himself as having been "a small boy with a nigger drawl." Now what was that about?

YK: That's Eliot trying to deal with himself. He's trying to wrestle himself down to the ground and dissect himself.

FG: He was talking about his speech.

YK: Yes! But see, that same rhythm informs Eliot's work, and you can definitely see this in *Inventions of the March Hare*. The early poems, some of those poems are racist, chauvinistic, misogynistic. All of it's right there in those early poems. And he's talking about, you know, playing piano in a back alley of North Cambridge, when in fact—C'mon, Eliot, that is St. Louis, man. Don't get confused!

FG: One of the interesting things about your new book is that although people might see you as becoming more formalistic, you're going back to your beginnings. *Thirteen Kinds of Desire* [a collaboration with jazz singer Pamela Knowles] seemed very formal, a little glimpse into *Gods*.

YK: Well, I thought about these things before—my obsession with insects, mythology. I didn't know I would write a hundred and thirty-two, but in retrospect there are more topics to explore. I wanted that form to move swiftly through imagistic territory, and moments between the stanzas where there could be meditations.

FG: I think of [Thelonious] Monk with your work.

YK: I think of Monk, of Monk and his silence.

FG: You liked silence as a child.

YK: We don't honor it as much. It's just not part of our culture. And what has happened to silence—if we're silent, we're still, and people say, "Are you daydreaming? Are you wasting time? Time is money."

FG: Gertrude Stein spoke of the importance of silence in a poem. Is it this silence that allows for the "surprise" you say a poem must have to work?

YK: Sometimes it's an image. Or sometimes it's a parcel of images.

FG: Can you use music to clarify an image?

YK: You mean the music in the words?

FG: I mean music literally. I'm talking about your jazz collaborations.

YK: That becomes an interesting question. I don't know if music helps clarify.

FG: It can warp an image?

YK: It possibly can. But I think the risk might be worth it.

FG: What about the influence of music on one's identity?

YK: It's interesting thinking of music as imposing or shaping one's identity. I remember reading an essay by Charles Black, who for years held the Sterling law chair at Yale. He's an interesting one, because he's a civil rights lawyer, white, from Texas. And he heard Armstrong as a teenager. And hearing that sound just pretty much reshaped his psyche.

FG: Blues brings a transcendence to your work. Hughes used blues to similar effect—a bounce from the pit with bebop. As in "Palimpsest": "I am going to teach Mr. Pain / to sway, to bop," or "Cenotaph": "I know shame would wear me like a mask . . . if I didn't slow drag to Rockin' Dopsie." There's almost a religiosity here—as despair is supposedly the worst sin of all.

YK: Despair is maybe the worst sin in a certain culture. Please . . . we're human beings. How can we not despair? In *Days of Obligation*, Richard Rodriguez talks about Mexico as being a country of tragedy and the United States as being a country of comedy. And he prefers, I think, Mexico in many ways because again I think tragedy can embody mystery easier than comedy can. Comedy is an attempt to laugh away mystery.

FG: Oh, but comedy is tragic.

YK: The good ones are. I know. I know. It's interesting to think about someone like Lenny Bruce.

FG: I kept thinking about Lenny Bruce in the lines of your poems "Hanoi Hannah" and "A Break from the Bush." I thought I was projecting. But he did make an impact.

YK: Yes. Especially when you think about the time he was coming out saying these things. He's confronting society. He's confronting what might be termed as the establishment. Just laying himself bare. Trusting the democratic impulse that is perhaps buried in the national psyche—not realizing that someone out there is going to dig his grave. But there's a great hope in Lenny Bruce as well. He's a person who I could see writing a poem about.

FG: "Hanoi Hannah" . . .

YK: "Soul brothers what you dying for?" Oh yeah, I know what you mean, when old Hannah comes out and says something like, "You know you're gonna die. You know you're dead men, don't you?"

FG: *Dien Cai Dau*, the book those poems appear in, did a lot to debunk the old heart-of-darkness take on the jungle, because, to paraphrase something you once said, it's the sun unfiltered that can kill, not darkness. In "Prisoners," ". . . prisoners look like / marionettes hooked to strings of light." And in *Talking Dirty to the Gods*, by aligning us all, and even bugs, with the gods, you disarm that old totalitarian strategy, whether used to run countries, schools, or libraries: the appropriation of mythology by oppressors—i.e., Nazis—for their own validation. Your work's done a lot to recover the lost as well as to bury the deadly. Have you started to write the poem on Matthew Henson, the Arctic explorer forgotten because he was black, and his cohort, Admiral Peary, was a lying egomaniac?

YK: Matthew Henson is interesting to me, because the first time he goes with Perry is not to the North Pole. They're headed to Panama. He goes on almost all the trips, and at the end he was the one who had the strength. He was younger. He had to live with the Inuits, and there was a word created for him in their language. And he most likely had children there.

FG: I believe someone criticized your Vietnam poems because they did not name things exactly, they used too many similes, they did not put a name to the kinds of horrors. . . . You're supposed to name that?

YK: You're not supposed to name that. Really. How can you name it? We're good for naming everything. Name something and you control it. Why have that feeling, the idea of controlling everything? We're back to the whole thing about mystery. There are so many interesting figures in history that I just happened to know about because I was reading about them in the seventies. There are so many interesting characters who are just buried, that have sort of scratched their way out. . . . Recently, they've been giving a lot of medals to World War II soldiers, black soldiers. First Lieutenant Vernon J. Baker called in fire on himself to save others.

World War I was even worse. A great-uncle of mine was in World War I—I think it was with the 371st—and he came back not the same person. My uncle always talked about France. "Someday I'm going to go back to France. I have a daughter over there, I think." That's what he kept saying. And he had been put on the detail to bury the dead—so many people were getting killed; it was so cold—to bury them, and then exhume them later on and send them back.

I'm talking about excavating historical figures with the purpose of honoring them in some way. That's why Matthew Henson is so interesting, but there are others who will also appear in my collection-in-progress entitled *Wishbone Trilogy*. Many people have seen the world change in such immense ways. It makes me think of the German painter Max Beckmann, who, speaking about World War I, says, "I am continually working at form in actual drawing, and in my head, and during my sleep. Everything else vanishes, time and space, and I think of nothing but how to paint the head of the resurrected Christ against the red constellations in the sky of Judgment Day." For me, as well, horrors are named through imagery. Aesthetics keep us from forgetting. But I don't think the writer or the artist can have the politics of the piece on the surface. Otherwise it becomes didactic, polemical—problematic as art. I do believe that. And yet we can't forget.

Kevin Bezner Interviews
Yusef Komunyakaa

Kevin Bezner/2001

From *Main Street Rag* 6.1 (Spring 2001). Reprinted by permission.

KB: Why did you title your new and collected poems *Pleasure Dome*?

YK: I have been influenced somewhat by Coleridge, and *Pleasure Dome,* is a phrase that has stuck in my psyche for many years. I felt that would be an appropriate title with a certain kind of irony as well.

KB: Is the irony connected to the sense that within pleasure there is pain, that split in a sense?

YK: Right. In that sense. It's a certain kind of built in tension.

KB: In choosing the poems for *Pleasure Dome* from over twenty-five years of work were you surprised by any particular poems?

YK: I'm surprised by the fact that there has been a constant evolution, but also the similarities in some of the earlier poems with the later poems. That continuity surprised me.

KB: The continuity that you're mentioning would that be your interest in musicians, both blues and jazz musicians?

YK: Yes, I think so, but also a tonal continuity. The image is important to me, and I see some of the images that are in the earlier poems relating to the images I have in the later poems.

KB: Can you give an example of a poem from your early work where you see a similarity with your later work?

YK: Not really. I'm just thinking about the tones for the most part. It's difficult for me to dissect the work. Yes? But it's a feeling that I have more than anything else.

KB: Concerning that feeling, what about themes? Did you see similar themes?

YK: There are social concerns in the poems, but also nature seems to come back again and again. I think that has to do with growing up in a rural community.

KB: Throughout your career you seem to be concerned with people. Sometimes they're famous, sometimes they're lesser known but with recognizable names, and some of them are unknowns as well. I want to ask you about the new poems that concern people. Can you tell us about the poem "Jasmine," where you mention the names of a number of well known Jazz greats, but then provide the names of two generally lesser known but still great figures. First, I want to be certain, are you speaking about Elvin Jones and Clifford Brown?

YK: Yes. I am.

KB: What significance do those two musicians have for you?

YK: Clifford Brown died so young, and yet his horn has a feeling that can be transferred to contemporary musical designs now. He seems to be now. That's why I thought of him at the Blue Note, at that moment. Of course, that's a ghostly figure.

KB: He's not really there.

YK: Right. Right.

KB: And Elvin Jones?

YK: Elvin Jones, yes, he was there. He was very much in the flesh and blood. Elvin Jones was in his seventies and he played with such unity and forthrightness that I was quite surprised.

KB: So this was an actual show you saw. Was that recently?

YK: It was a couple of years ago.

KB: Let me ask you about the poem "Never Land," which concerns one of our best known pop singers, Michael Jackson. You end the poem by directly speaking to Michael about his unnatural face. I'm wondering whether you hoped that he would see the poem, or whether there was a hope that you might reach younger African Americans to offset the actions of a popular figure who's altered his natural features, and, in a sense, has seemingly tried to remove what's African about him?

YK: I just felt that I needed to write about that particular topic at that moment. I found myself doing that. I didn't have Michael in mind as reader of the poem. It was just a moment I had to express. It wasn't really directed at anyone in particular, but I hope that different people read it and get different things from it, perhaps.

KB: It's a simple poem, in some ways, but so important, given our society and the emphasis we place on looking a particular way, or acting a particular way.

YK: And, just a summation of Frankenstein, the idea that one has to be responsible for one's creation is important, I think, but it's not just in looks, as such, but in everything that we do and think.

KB: How about the poem "Pepper," about the jazz great Art Pepper?

YK: I came to that realization by listening to Art Pepper and then finding out certain details about his life and his thoughts pertaining to African Americans. I thought there was a kind of built in conflict that maybe was driven by a certain internal terror. I wanted to try to wrestle with that idea.

KB: How do you see the conflict?

YK: The conflict is that he's playing jazz, something that's so African American, it's conception, and at the same time I don't really know how he feels about African Americans as flesh and blood, if he sees them as individuals or not. There's a conflict as an American, you might say.

KB: Do you think that that's a conflict that many Americans have?

YK: I think so. Well, jazz itself, I've said somewhere, or at least I've thought this, that many musicians had to go overseas to seek a livelihood, or even to have their work accepted. Before one's art can be accepted, the individual— or the individuals have to be accepted as real, whole people. That's the dilemma with African Americans creating art. Often the individual isn't accepted, so the art isn't either.

KB: Are we still stuck with this dilemma?

YK: We're still wrestling with a lot of things, but let's face it, within the last thirty or so years we've also progressed a whole lot.

KB: "South Carolina Morning." You give the woman in Hopper's painting a complete life as a woman, waiting for her jazz musician lover or husband. You see that woman as Hopper's wife, whom he has transformed into an African American. Do you see that as a problem or a conflict?

YK: I don't see that as a problem or a conflict, but I think Hopper is real interesting because his wife is a model for almost all of the women who appear in his work, and this black woman isn't any different. This is the way I see it. I kept going back and forth between those portraits that are clearly informed by his wife as the model and then going to this black woman.

KB: I looked at a few of the portraits and once you had pointed it out I was struck by that reality. Do you think this was an inability on his part to see an African American woman as separate or unique, or is it just that he's so enamored with his wife that he wishes to see her in every possible guise, let's say.

YK: He did that with other portraits as well. He doesn't paint that many African Americans. That was one. I had come across another one. So I've only seen two African American images. Perhaps there are more. I think there are painters, probably even contemporary painters, who haven't incorporated African American features into their work. It's hard to paint America and not.

KB: Tell me about "Ogoni," which concerns the death of Ken Saro-Wiwa. It transforms anger about the execution by a government of a writer into elegy. It seems as if that poem was extremely necessary for you to write. Was it?

YK: I think so. I had to write about him. I felt a certain kind of anger, a certain kind of frustration. And then I realized in writing the poem itself that in a way that anger on the surface doesn't do anything that's positive.

KB: But the poem can do something positive?

YK: I hope that it brings us to question certain things. Not to answer anything, but to pose questions.

KB: Another remarkable poem is "Tenebrae," which is written "in memory of Richard Johnson." I'm not familiar with Richard Johnson. Is he the drummer in the poem?

YK: He is. That poem also appears in a book of mine, *Blue Notes*, interviews and what have you, published by the University of Michigan. I have explained the whole circumstance of the poem, which is dedicated to the drummer Richard Johnson, who killed himself. He was a professor at Indiana University, a percussionist.

KB: Was he a friend?

YK: No, he wasn't a friend, but in a way he almost became a friend through my imagination, a certain kind of affinity.

KB: I was struck by how you depict him as a man who loves opera and baseball. Is that imagined?

YK: No, no, no it isn't. Apparently, yes, he did love opera and baseball.

KB: Why were you struck by that? Why did you include those particulars?

YK: It shows the complexity of an individual, that we are able to embrace so many things at the same time. That's what makes us whole in many ways, having that capacity.

KB: In your early uncollected poems included in *Pleasure Dome*, there are also poems about people, and as said earlier, this is an interest that has spanned your career. I want to ask you about one of those people, Langston Hughes. Besides blues and jazz, he seems to be one of your primary influences.

YK: Hughes is important to me because of when I discovered him. I discovered him as a teenager. I had been reading poetry and I didn't know much about African American poets. I knew about Paul Laurence Dunbar, but I didn't know about Hughes. When I discovered Hughes, Hughes seemed so natural for me, because born and raised in Louisiana, in a rural small town, his emphasis on the blues became natural for me.

KB: Was that a sound you were hearing in your life?

YK: Yes, I think so, I think so. It made me more conscious of that sound, more receptive of it.

KB: Your poem for Robert Creeley, "Recital of Water Over Stones." You note in the poem that a poet, and I assume it's Creeley, writes poetry filled with the sounds of jazz. Many people hear Creeley's poetry and think of him as a cerebral poet, and you hear jazz, which many people think of as a cerebral and yet emotional music. I think that's a great observation about Creeley. I was wondering whether you had come to this realization through a reading of his poems, or whether you had heard him read live.

YK: Actually, it was a combination. I heard him read live, but I had been reading his poems very closely and thinking, especially, the deliberate silence in some of his work is the same kind of silence that might parallel the silence in jazz.

KB: What do you mean by the silence in jazz?

YK: I've called Thelonius Monk, "technician of silence." And I believe that, in a sense, one doesn't have music without silence, but it is a kind of silence that has to do with the modulation of a given piece. That the notes are not really stacked on one another, there's space, almost like breathing space.

KB: I haven't checked this, but I can't imagine that Creeley was not affected by jazz somehow.

YK: I think he says somewhere that he was influenced by Miles Davis, which makes sense.

KB: You hear that influence?

YK: Yes, I hear it, somewhat. Again, we're talking about silence.

KB: *Talking Dirty to the Gods* has been nominated for the National Book Circle Critics Award. The book seems to me a departure in style for you and even in content to a degree, although it still has many of the same concerns that you see throughout your career. Do you see the book as a departure, or, earlier, as you said of your poetry, an evolution for you?

YK: Not necessarily a departure, but an embracing of some of the concerns that I had early on. I've always been drawn to mythology, folklore, ritual, and a love of satire. The forms are sort of satirical. Maybe it's just more condensed in these poems.

KB: Yes, very condensed. They're sixteen lines each, which doesn't give you a lot of room to operate.

YK: Correct. Correct.

KB: Did you find that hindering at all or was it freeing?

YK: I found a certain kind of freedom in it. Initially, I didn't know if I could write many of those, but finally it became a freeing exercise.

KB: Midway through the book you mention the Roman poet Catullus. I'm wondering whether Catullus was a starting point for you, or one of your muses.

YK: Probably one of my muses. I've read him quite closely in translation. Again, the levels of satire are interesting. In some poems, he's almost playing the fool that we see in Shakespeare.

KB: *Talking Dirty to the Gods* seems to move throughout, almost, the history of the world in poetry. You bump the present up against the past and retain either that satiric flavor that you mention, or the mythic sensibility. Was that something that interested you in writing this book?

YK: Yes, I think so. Where different moments of history rest beside each other, not in exact parallels, but as a kind of shared relationship, that's how history works for us as human beings. It places us in the present, but also links us to the future.

Komunyakaa's Riff

Lary Bloom/2001

From *Northeast Magazine: The Sunday Magazine of the Hartford Courant* (9 June 2002).
Reprinted by permission of Lary Bloom.

On Mother's Day, mother was away. For a seventeen-month-old boy, it is evidently an inconvenience to be the child of two poet-parents. On any given holiday, one of them can stray from Trenton's leafy capital neighborhood to give a reading in a place called New York City. And so Jehan—bushy-haired, bright-eyed, and blessed with a too-wide smile—made do with the parent who was available.

Yusef Komunyakaa returned from the kitchen of the five-thousand-square-foot, hundred-year-old house with a handful of Cheerios, which he deposited on Jehan's play station. The little boy clasped a few pieces, looked up expectantly at his father, and waited for a word. A melody. A little life lesson.

Komunyakaa is a musical man, though he plays no instrument. His voice, mellifluous and deep, has a soothing quality. He proceeded through Jehan's lexicon, in which "Cheerios" comes out as if it spells "enchantment." There is "apple" and "ball" and "pear" and, for diversity's sake, "agua," which the astute Jehan understands as the Spanish way to ask for water. Variations on "no" turned the word from stern rebuke to a pleasant alternative. These sounds transfixed Jehan, and he stared contentedly at his fifty-four-year-old dad.

In this musical admiration, the little boy was extending a family tradition. Music was the first poetry of his father. When Komunyakaa was a young man in Bogalusa, Louisiana, he made up his own lyrics to the songs he heard on the radio. Words that sounded good, and that came from the heart. It was, it turned out, a developing formula, influenced by the blues and the freedoms of jazz.

In fact, Alison Meyers, director of the Sunken Garden Poetry Festival, had emphasized the point when she explained why she chose Komunyakaa to lead off the eleventh season this Wednesday evening. "My first connection with his poetry was on the page—it engaged me immediately with its uniqueness, originality of language and complex sensitivity. When I heard him read it only deepened my engagement. He inhabits his work. He has the capacity to be moved by the emotion of poems. He isn't performing. He has an organic connection, and a kind of musicality."

Little Jehan is not quite so eloquent in his appreciation. But one word, "Papa," was enough for the moment. And the boy seemed content that a stranger from Connecticut, if not his mother (Reetika Vazirani—author of *White Elephants*) inhabited the living room and played with a toy. It was something called a Dell, and it opened up, like a clam. Jehan couldn't take his eyes off it, and wondered what those words were.

They were words about a man whom Garrett Hongo, author of several acclaimed volumes, calls "the most original poet of his generation." Komunyakaa, a Princeton professor who has won the Pulitzer Prize and an array of other top poetry awards, is the author of twelve books, including the recent collection *Pleasure Dome* (Wesleyan University Press). It is a CV that clearly puts him among the most popular poets in America—an eye-opening circumstance for a man who has no intention of pandering to the reading public.

On the one hand, he is well aware of the standing of poets in American popular culture. When people ask him what he does, he replies in one word: writer. And then he hears, commonly, something like this: "Oh, you write novels. Have you written anything that's becoming a movie?" When he reveals he is a poet, he is likely to be asked, "Well, have you ever thought about writing a novel?"

On the other hand, Komunyakaa believes in the resources and innate abilities of readers who open themselves to poetry. It is his view that readers (or listeners) contribute to the poem, as co-readers, by bringing their own experiences to it. And so he is unusually harsh on his own words—slashing away at them, paring to syllables that matter. In this, he is influenced by Thelonious Monk, the late jazz composer and pianist, whom he referred to as a "technician of silence." Komunyakaa refers to silence as "part of the text," and argues that generally we all "say too much to little effect. Writers often do not trust the reader. We want them to understand every word and gesture—this extends to novel writing, and especially memoir writing. I've been asked to write memoirs many times. I've resisted. Memoir tells too much. It would take away from my creative effort."

His poetry relies on a certain level of "verbal innuendo," and does not resolve neatly. This isn't an impediment, even to an audience that doesn't qualify as poetry scholars. When I mentioned that the Sunken Garden attracts some who have little experience at poetry readings, and who worry they won't "get it," he argued on behalf of an inherent human capacity to get the point, in one way or the other—"people will go along with the musical language." He also related an experience in a manufacturing plant near Cincinnati. "I spent a whole day talking to people who'd been there thirty years, and I saw how individuals working at a factory could be drawn to poetry. They pulled out poems from their pockets to show me. They talked about Carl Sandburg, Robert Frost, Langston Hughes. I had assumed that workers were not reading poetry. But when I thought about it, it made perfect sense. In the 1930s, in the labor movement, workers were listening to folk songs and poets."

At the heart of Komunyakaa's own work are portraits from a period just as rich and difficult. As a young man, he went off to Vietnam with two anthologies of poetry in his duffel. As an information specialist, he reported on the "progress" of the war, but more than that, he recorded in his memory and his notebook scenes that, once translated to verse (beginning in the volume *Dien Cai Dau*), became as eloquent as any fiction and memoir that came out of Vietnam.

"I resisted the topic for so long. It was only fourteen years later that I found a way to write about it. If I had written a year after, the work would have been different. I had to discover the importance of aesthetics, the importance of the images." Images are the key to the Komunyakaa body of work. Consider "You and I Are Disappearing." [Text of "You and I Are Disappearing" follows.]

In *Blue Notes*, a book of his essays and interviews, Komunyakaa says, "I realized a kind of beauty in the overall landscape (in Vietnam). And many times that is what we have, beauty and violence side by side. We have been taught to see that as a contradiction, but, to me, contradiction is a sort of discourse. You have this push and pull in everything. It's underneath everything. That's what nature is about. And that is what creative energy is about. That's what the chemistry of the mind is about as well."

Vietnam, then, was an ideal subject—a place of stunning physical beauty, and where "we were creating more enemies than we could kill." It was the custom of the time—actually a custom that remains today—to portray the enemy as something less than human. "I never called anybody a 'gook' or a 'dink.' I had grown up with derogatory, negative terms. I felt insulted when I heard those words. I understood that one has to dehumanize the enemy before they're killed."

In his wartime job, he wrote about the intricacies and significance of Vietnam culture—a way to point out the importance of his own, and all cultures that are not "mainstream." As a black man, he was involved in a war that exploited his community. As a result, he felt an extra burden to address the war in his work. We were dehumanizing the Vietnamese, even as black soldiers were dehumanized.

"The literature that came out of the Vietnam experience erased the black presence, and it grew out of the inability to embrace black soldiers as citizens. It isn't the first time it happened in situations of war." Komunyakaa can recite contributions of black soldiers in all American wars, though popular histories largely ignore them.

His background and upbringing put him in a position to provide a rare historical service by documenting the black experience. He was able to maneuver and accommodate Vietnam in a way others couldn't. "Had I grown up in New York or San Francisco or LA, I wouldn't have adjusted to Vietnam. In Bogolusa (its name means dark waters), I explored everything I could explore in my rural environment."

And he had been—at least in spirit—something of an adventurer. Even at a young age, he decided that his given name, James Willie Brown, didn't adequately reflect his heritage. And so, over family objections, he changed Brown to Komunyakaa to honor his grandfather, who had that name until he left the West Indies. In the poem "Mismatched Shoes" he addresses this decision. [Text of "Mismatched Shoes" follows.]

His childhood in Bogalusa did not offer a world of artistic encouragement. "I remember the first time I heard a live musician—a blind teenage boy. He had a goat tied to his wagon, and he was playing a guitar and singing the blues and spirituals. I thought, in a sense, he is an artist. I remember being quite taken with him. It influenced me to listen to the music coming out of the radio. The radio was shrine."

His own gravitation toward poetry was gradual. "My father was pragmatic, but my mother encouraged me to read. When she bought a set of encyclopedias I read volumes A to P thoroughly." Extensive reading, he argues, is essential for every writer. In *Blue Notes*, he says, "I do impress on my students the importance of reading everything—not just literature but also history, economics, psychology, philosophy—everything."

As a youngster, he read Shakespeare, Edgar Allan Poe, Emily Dickinson, and Alfred, Lord Tennyson. He said, "I was introduced to American literature (written by blacks) in what was termed 'Negro History Week,' which were brief moments in our education before we went back to the regular curriculum—history and literature dominated by Europeans. In the works of Langston Hughes I remember being struck by the surprises in his poetry, that it was close to a spoken diction, with blues—a metric shape."

In recent years, students everywhere have come to learn—and more than on special commemorative weeks—the contributions of black writers. On the other hand, some things have not changed. When he came to Hartford to read to high school students a year ago, he saw something he hadn't even seen back in Bogalusa, "where blacks and whites were kissing cousins." Komunyakaa was shocked to see de facto segregation—nothing but black faces. "A throwback." There was another kind of segregation, too. After he looked around the room at Charter Oak Cultural Center and saw that the attendees were limited to one gender, he asked where the boys were. "They told me they were all at football practice."

Komunyakaa does not dismiss sports. When he considers little Jehan's future, he says he hopes the boy will inherit his sports interest and, perhaps, his own love of playing centerfield. ("It is a place of meditation, while waiting for a fly ball. Poets are in the outfield. A poet is definitely not a pitcher.") Of Jehan, he says, "Sports is something he can participate in, have fun doing, but he doesn't owe his life to the instruments of sports. There's a danger in that."

Surely, Jehan is not deprived in terms of being introduced to poetry and narrative. His father makes up little tales for him, and writes a few lines of verse regularly. Komunyakaa is an old hand at the obligations of nurturing a child. Jehan is his second. He also has a thirty-two-year-old daughter, the product of his first marriage, who lives in Indiana. And he struggles for the time required to be a father, a teacher, a poet, a husband.

In fact, on the day we met, he moved back and forth between two images. One was life as a Princeton professor, living a dozen miles from campus in a beautiful old house on Trenton's loveliest street, with spacious plaster walls to display colorful work by Jacob Lawrence, Ed Clark, and Romare Bearden, and bookcases of poetry, featuring Philip Levine, James Merrill, William Meredith, Galway Kinnell, Robert Hayden, James Dickey, and Hayden Carruth, as well as other genres of works (he is currently reading biographies of Ho Chi Minh and Paul Robeson).

Here's the other image: life as an LSU professor in Baton Rouge, where a "great offer" awaits and where Komunyakaa would have to teach only half the number of courses he now teaches, allowing him much more time for writing. When I asked him if he was staying or going, he just shook his head—there are obvious attractions in both places—but he must make a decision soon.

As he talked of it—of the work ahead and of the practical considerations of balancing everything—he looked at Jehan, who was, he thought, approaching nap time. "Maybe he's getting a little cranky." But before the interview ended, and father became lullaby-man, he revealed something of the poetry in the works—much of it exploring the minds of others.

Komunyakaa was in Australia, on sabbatical, when the Oklahoma City bombing occurred in April 1995. When he came back, "Everyone seemed so dazed. And then Timothy McVeigh's face surfaced out of all of this. Well, he must have told somebody. I kept thinking, what a burden it must be to have that information. What would it have been like to be his psychiatrist?" The poet was obsessed with the idea of responsibility—what if you know someone's terrible secret? What do you do with it? This is the subject of "Chameleon Couch," the title poem of a new volume in the works.

"The Autobiography of My Alter Ego" has so far taken eighteen months. He is writing it from the point of view of a white Vietnam veteran speaking about his experiences and observations—"a composite of some people I've known. The intention is to address the complexities of the American culture through an individual who has witnessed certain things from many different points of view—and through my imagination. I realized this was the way to go—using the imagination, outside of the observed facts. One has to take the risk. I wanted an individual who returned from the war and never really felt at home. He began riding buses, crisscrossing the country. I wanted him to be literate, and informed by everyday experiences, and trying to come to terms with what he really knows. I needed to find the voice of the alter ego—to get slightly outside of myself, and yet create a voice that addresses some of my own concerns. I need a character to do that, the way a novelist might do it."

In recent years, Komunyakaa has also returned, in effect, to where he started—the lyrics he heard from the radio. He has written the words to accompany the music of several composers. Currently, he is collaborating with William Banfield on a piece based on the life of Edmonia Lewis, a nineteenth-century African American sculptor. He was drawn to her because of the drama and power of her work and because, "I suppose that she had the audacity to be an artist with black skin. It is an attempt to encapsulate certain moments of her creative experience, and also try to trace where her fears were."

Ten days after the Trenton interview, it was the turn of "Papa" to leave Trenton for New York City. The venue was the Makor/Steinhardt Center in Manhattan, a branch of the 92nd Street Y.

My own experience hearing Komunyakaa read until then was limited to a videotape I had borrowed from Alison Meyers. The tape, which recorded a California appearance several years ago, had worried me. I had a little trouble making out some of the poet's words. I had not mastered the Bogalusa-born dialect.

But at Makor, I learned how to listen to that baritone voice. At first, I watched the poet's face intently. He seldom looked down, searching for text—it was as if each piece was presented not from the podium but the soul. I closed my eyes, put myself in the place of little Jehan, and concentrated on the music of the mind.

Komunyakaa was one of two readers on the program that night, so his presentation was short. And yet in a brief period he had affected those assembled. He had told me, "Poetry is not an ad for the emotions." Well, why could you hear gasps when he read "You and I Are Disappearing," as he described the burning girl? And then, during "Anodyne," I thought of him not so much as Yusef Komunyakaa but as Joe Brown, riffing in the manners of Charlie Parker, Art Tatum, or John Coltrane. [Text of "Anodyne" follows.]

American Voices and the Cakewalk of Language: Yusef Komunyakaa in Conversation with Terrance Hayes

Terrance Hayes/2002

From *Black Renaissance* 5.1 (Spring 2003). Reprinted by permission of Terrance Hayes.

On April 4, 2002, Cave Canem sponsored a conversation featuring poets Terrance Hayes and Yusef Komunyakaa at the New School University in New York City. Founded by poets Cornelius Eady and Toi Derricotte in 1996, Cave Canem hosts a summer writer's retreat, workshops, a yearly first book prize, and readings and other literary events featuring African American poets around the country. In this lively and compelling session, Hayes and Komunyakaa discuss the work of Gwendolyn Brooks, Robert Hayden, Alexandre Dumas, and Etheridge Knight, as well as the experience of living, researching, teaching, and writing poetry in the "varied territory" of the contemporary United States.

Robert Polito, Creative Writing Program Director, New School University: I'm pleased to say that we have two poets of such grace with us tonight: Terrance Hayes, the author of *Muscular Music*, which received the Kate Tufts Discovery Award, is also the recipient of the Whiting Emerging Writer's Award, and his work has appeared in such anthologies as *American Poetry: The Next Generation* and *Giant Steps*. He teaches in the Creative Writing Department at Carnegie-Mellon University, and his second collection, *Hip Logic*, is forthcoming from Viking/Penguin later this year and is a selection of the National Poetry Series Open Competition.

Yusef Komunyakaa was born in Bogalusa, Louisiana, in 1947. His numerous books of poems include *Pleasure Dome: New & Collected Poems, 1925–1999* (Wesleyan, 2001), and *Talking Dirty to the Gods* (FSG, 2000). His book *Thieves of Paradise* (Wesleyan, 1998) was a finalist for the National Book

Critics Circle Award, and he received the Pulitzer Prize and the Kingsley Tufts Poetry Award for *Neon Vernacular: New & Selected Poems 1977–1989* (1994).

His prose is collected in *Blue Notes: Essays, Interviews, and Commentaries* (University of Michigan Press, 2000), and his honors include the William Faulkner Prize from the Université de Rennes, the Thomas Forcade Award, the Hanes Poetry Prize, fellowships from the Fine Arts Work Center in Provincetown, the Louisiana Arts Council, and the National Endowment for the Arts, and the Bronze Star for his service in Vietnam, where he served as a correspondent and managing editor of the *Southern Cross*. In 1999 he was elected a Chancellor of The Academy of American Poets. Yusef Komunyakaa is a professor in the Council of Humanities and Creative Writing Program at Princeton University. He lives in New York City.

Please join me now in welcoming Terrance Hayes and Yusef Komunyakaa.

Terrance Hayes: Well, I guess the program said, "conversation," but to me it's really more of an interview, because I just have all these questions that I want to ask Yusef. Questions I think you might not answer except for under these circumstances.

Yusef Komunyakaa: Oh, is that right?

TH: And you still might not answer! The beginning questions come out of *Blue Notes*, which came out from the University of Michigan Press pretty recently—2000, I think. I suppose if you follow Yusef's work, you've read a lot of the interviews, and this is what I think: I think, traveling and doing this kind of stuff, Yusef—you've done this many, many times—so that after I read maybe two or three of your interviews, I started seeing the same answers.

YK: That's right.

TH: So that's my point. So I was thinking, "Well, I have to figure out a way to get him to answer some of these other questions." [laughter] What I really want to start out with is a series of questions about your mentors. I think you've influenced a lot of people—myself, Sharon Strange, Kevin Young, Major Jackson. Could you just start by talking about who were some of your influences before you were a Pulitzer Prize–winning poet?

YK: I suppose my influences come from all over the place. I was introduced to poetry early on, particularly poets coming out of what we might classify as the Harlem Renaissance. I suppose I was particularly taken with some of the protest sonnets, but then I started thinking about the fact that many of those Harlem Renaissance poets were pretty much writing "service literature" and responding to a certain kind of traditional form. I began to think about some of the poets standing outside that tradition, particularly someone such as Helene Johnson, who was, I think, a modernist who comes out of that movement, because she was so young at the time. But, someone such as—there was another Johnson as well—Fenton Johnson was an amazing voice, and the things that he dealt with were inspiring. Langston Hughes really connected with me because I grew up with the radio as sort of the shrine, the centerpiece of things, and I heard a lot of blues and jazz coming out of New Orleans but also out of places like Jackson, Mississippi, and Memphis, Tennessee. And I heard people around my town singing the blues as well. I've been thinking about this recently because the very first individual I connected with was this teenager, Pete Burrell, who sang the blues, and was blind.

TH: You knew him? He was in your home-town?

YK: Yes, yes. I mentioned Professor Longhair in that poem, "You Made Me"; Professor Longhair grew up in Bogalusa as well, born in 1918. But Pete Burrell played guitar, so I was—probably at six or seven—drawn to his voice, technique on the guitar, and surprises in language. But we think about someone like Robert Hayden: Robert Hayden has been a constant influence, because of—he studied with W. H. Auden, interestingly enough—his care for poems. I really see him as an American voice. In the 1970s, during the Black Arts Movement, I think Hayden probably caught sheer hell, even from someone such as Gwendolyn Brooks, interestingly enough. Hayden would have written a lot more, but he polished everything, he was a very meticulous individual; but really an American voice.

TH: This is like a magic show, because you have the card before the person says what they planned to, but here's my next question: You've mentioned in interviews the essentially American voice of Robert Hayden's poetry [laughter]; can you talk a bit about what it means to write in an "American" voice and how that term might be applied to your own work? What does it mean to have an "American" voice?

YK: A good example of that is probably one of Hayden's last poems, "American Journal." There's vernacular within the context of that poem, and the poem is actually spoken by someone from out of this world—from Mars or somewhere like that, from the universe beyond—and he sort of comes into this world speaking the vernacular of black expression. But also there's something else within the context of that voice; there's a marriage of the vernacular with a very educated diction as well. So, in a certain sense, I've seen this alien from another world as a code-switcher, and that's what Hayden is. That's what I mean by American voice, he has that capacity to be in two worlds at once—at least two worlds at once, or even more than two worlds at once—that ability to incorporate, especially, Anglo-Saxon diction into those poems.

TH: You talk a lot about the two worlds in your own work, for instance in the essay that was in *The Best American Essays of 2001*, "The Blue Machinery of Summer." Towards the end of that essay you talk about being in at least two worlds; is that how you think about your own poetry, as kind of functioning in multiple dimensions?

YK: Growing up in the South, in a place called Bogalusa, Louisiana, I think early on—probably when I was four or five—I knew the dynamics of switching worlds because I saw those worlds being dealt with within the context of my own family. I'm talking about growing up in the segregated South. I suppose that has everything to do with survival in a certain sense, but there's a kind of education of the psyche going on as well. One develops a certain kind of dexterity in both of those worlds.

TH: I wonder about how that has changed. How do you think emerging poets have that dilemma of separate worlds? Of course it's not there in the same way; there are no "whites only" signs anymore.

YK: There's a kind of cultural apartheid within the context of the national psyche, so in a certain sense it is still there. It's how we negotiate it, I suppose, that might be different. Baldwin said—I think he left the States for fourteen years—and he said he had to come back in order to be shocked. That was rather instructive for him, because it had everything to do with his subject matter as a writer. Also, he says somewhere else that when he was writing *Another Country*, he took with him some Bessie Smith records and a typewriter, and went to Switzerland. He said he had to re-create what he had come out of, basically to renew the cadence of expression. So, I think we're all negotiating varied territory.

TH: OK, well let me read you something here.

YK: Something I said? [laughter]

TH: [laughs] Yeah, something you said. It's still in the vein of influences, "outsiderness," and some of the things we're talking about: "I feel that Gwendolyn Brooks has been undermined by lesser talents who happen to have been popular during the 1960s and '70s. She was an outsider to them and had to compromise for acceptance (not honor or love). They coerced her into becoming a turncoat against who she really was, thus her art and creative spirit seem to have suffered greatly. They're the ones who should have been learning from her, but she gave in to their arrogance and bravado."

I remember reading this and I was like, "Whoa, is Yusef saying that?" I mean, there's anger there. I want you to talk a little bit about that: What kind of changes occurred in her work? I know she wrote, I guess it was *In the Mecca* around that period, which is an interesting book. What kinds of things did you see happening in her work, coming out of what I think you're talking about here—the Black Arts Movement poets?

YK: I think what happened was that the anger is on the surface of the poems. However, I do remember her saying to me—because I posed the question, I said, "What is art?" She said, "Art is that which endures," and that was such an important statement to me at the time. I think her last real great poem is "In the Mecca," for the simple reason that there is so much care for language within the context of her earlier works, aesthetics, and what have you. She's clearly influenced by the Harlem Renaissance, especially the voices of those protest sonnets, and I think maybe she's trying to break away from that as well, but that's a certain kind of strength in her earlier work. It's almost as if she's in the observation tower, sort of looking down from the kitchenette, viewing everything out in front of her, and there's a certain kind of strength and witness that seem to have been compromised in later poems.

TH: But compromised for what? Do you think it was compromised in a general sense and she just stopped doing it, or was there something that replaced it?

YK: I think she had this great need to belong. I didn't intend to get into this here, but I think I should get into it because I have a feeling that a lot had to do with how she looked as a person—within the context of her own community—so she had to compromise herself in a certain sense in order to belong to that larger community that was really at her fingertips.

TH: Well, the Black Arts poets are pretty good-looking people for the most part, and that wasn't an accident. At any rate she definitely didn't look like some of them.

YK: Yeah, yeah.

TH: So you definitely think that the politics of color within black culture were significant in her work.

YK: Yeah. Which she really addresses in some of her work, especially the character Lincoln, the boy. She's not really comfortable within the context of her own community.

TH: This is one of the questions that you would probably say, "Don't ask me those kinds of questions," but again, in all responses I wonder—the first thing I wonder is about that notion of compromise and community. Do you ever feel those pressures, as if there are these kind of communities-at-large of poets that made you think, "Maybe I need to be in that?" And the other question—this is the question I really want to ask, and you actually told me not to ask this kind of question [laughter]—about complexion, dark skin, and recognizing those kinds of dilemmas in Brooks because you can identify with your own experiences.

YK: I realize, I was very observant. I think I want to write some essays dealing with that; it's a thing that doesn't really get talked about that much, and I suppose as Southerners we can talk about it here in the Big Apple.

TH: It's true. I remember when I was in college I had a roommate who was dark-skinned—James. He was from Georgia and it never occurred to me—we hung out, we had a real good time—and I remember going back home and taking him with me to meet some of my friends—and I'm still friends with some of these guys, from third grade—and we were hanging out, and when he left they were saying, things like "God, he's dark, why are you hanging out with him?" And I was shocked. But, yeah, maybe it is a Southern dilemma, the politics of race.

YK: Yes, but it is more than a Southern thing—

TH: Well I'm only talking from my own experience, as a Southerner.

YK: It's a national issue. Brooks was born in Topeka, Kansas—

TH: That's not the South?

YK: Well, yeah, that's the South, but she's—are you saying everywhere is the South?

TH: Yeah, at this point.

YK: Yes, in a certain sense. I live in Trenton, New Jersey, and I've been saying to myself for the last year, "I feel like I'm living in the South." And it becomes an interesting dilemma, because when I go back South, I feel like the greatest changes that have happened in this country have happened within the Deep South, and consequently in the Northeast or West, or what-have-you. But in those other areas, those changes are not as—they're not there, really. Maybe my expectations were different from the realities.

TH: So Indiana, I guess, would be the South; you felt like you didn't change environments so much, going from New Orleans to Indiana in the '80s?

YK: When I got to Indiana, I had come there in a visiting position, having said, "I can stay anywhere for a year." But I ended up staying there for ten years.

Since we're talking about the Midwest, I do believe that the most innovative voices have come out of the Midwest. It has everything to do with time and space. I'm particularly thinking about certain voices that have come out of the Midwest; Hughes is a good example, coming out of Joplin, Missouri. But it isn't just literary voices, I'm thinking of musicians as well. T.S. Eliot comes out of St. Louis, Miles Davis comes out of East St. Louis. William Burroughs—

TH: It sounds like you're talking about St. Louis in particular. [laughter]

YK: No, no, no, but that has something to do with the river as well. William Burroughs coming out of . . . St. Louis, I think. [laughter] Also living in Joplin and Lawrence, Kansas, believe it or not. Kenneth Rexroth came from South Bend, Indiana.

TH: Do you have any ideas about why it has that significance?

YK: I think there was a sense of individuality, and there was space, so one could hone one's individual ways of expression. A good example would be, if you think about music, Kansas City, and someone such as Charlie Parker.

TH: Do you think that the relationships between blacks and whites were different in the Midwest?

YK: Oh sure, there was certain attention paid to education. There are a number of voices coming out of the Midwest in the 1920s; Joseph Seamon Cotter is a good example, coming out of Louisville. His son, Joseph Seamon Cotter, Jr., died very young, but he had gone to Fisk, and he probably would have been on the forefront of the Harlem Renaissance if he had lived.

TH: I want to ask you one question about Etheridge Knight, who was born in Mississippi but died in the Midwest, in Indiana. Can you talk a little bit about his influences, your impressions of his work, and the importance of his work?

YK: I suppose I first came in contact with Etheridge Knight through an anthology that he had edited in prison, and I continued to follow him through Broadside Press, when Dudley Randall was the publisher there. I think [Knight] was such an unusual voice because there was a kind of earthy, Mississippi-informed diction there, but also something else. Etheridge wanted to appear as if he had not been really educated; that was part of his persona. But he read a little bit of everything, I think—he had time to do it, I suppose, in prison. That's where he started writing, and of course, he was a close friend of Gwendolyn Brooks.

TH: Is it that persona that appealed to you?

YK: Yes, I think so. Again, there is the ability to exist within at least two worlds. Etheridge was really a code-switcher. I mentioned to someone—maybe I shouldn't say this because it's an idea that I have that someone could really do a biography . . .

TH: You mentioned that to me; we were talking about this in Pittsburgh.

YK: Okay, then I probably shouldn't talk more about it.

TH: No, no, go ahead, because I'm not going to do it. I'm too lazy. [laughter] I hope somebody does it.

YK: This idea was that someone could go through the country—because Etheridge did this continuing workshop, it seems, wherever he happened to arrive, and there are all these stories about Etheridge Knight—and I said, if someone went through and recorded all of those stories they would have a great biography of Etheridge.

TH: Well, this actually comes out of something I was going to ask—and it's kind of connected to *Pleasure Dome*. In '97, you said that you were working on these poems that were excavating black American history, and at the time you were saying that they were *Pleasure Dome*.

YK: That's right, yes, yes. But it isn't *Pleasure Dome*, though.

TH: Yes, but I guess you could do *Pleasure Dome* Part Two. [laughter] But that impulse to say, "Someone should write about Etheridge"—is not Etheridge part of that scheme of African American history that hasn't been tapped into? Does he not appeal to you that way? You have that poem, "Troubling the Water" about Frank O'Hara, and I'd like to know, why don't you write the Etheridge Knight biography?

YK: I think it's more that I don't have the time, because I think someone would have to go through and just record all of the people that he knew, and there are a lot. We have the negatives and the positives side-by-side, which really shows the complexity of Etheridge.

TH: You talk about his ability to tap into his feminine side in his work, and I wonder, what does that mean, the process of "tapping into one's feminine side," particularly as a male poet, and as an African American poet?

YK: To Etheridge I think it was a certain kind of sensibility. A lot of people argue with that premise, but I do think that having been in prison there is that masquerade of maleness at work, and talking with him one sees the other side of that. I realize how close he was to his sister and to his mother— a certain respect that I was able to detect—and his relationship to people around him made me start thinking about his poems as such, how he seems sensitive to that side of his experience.

TH: When you read Knight, or Hayden, or Brooks, and you see a project at work there, do you take those ideas and try to render them in your own fashion, or do you look at the craft and you say, "Oh look, he's doing something in the persona of a woman. I'm going to try and write a poem in the persona of a woman?"

YK: No, not really. I admire what the accomplishments are, but my head is somewhere else as well. When I said I was "excavating" African American history through poetry, that project has changed. The title of it has changed to *Wishbone Trilogy*. It's three books: the first one is *Taboo*, the second one, *Lust*, and the third is entitled *Bread*. I think I've written forty or fifty of those poems, so I'll probably go back to that.

I realized how large of a project that was. At first it was on African America, and then it broadened to cover blacks in the world—someone such as Pushkin comes to mind, because we know Pushkin as the so-called "Father of Russian Literature," but he acknowledges his African background in his work. Or also someone such as Alexandre Dumas, who was actually taking from his own lived history and observation—I'm thinking of *The Three Musketeers*, with the character based on St. George from Haiti, who was a personal bodyguard for the Duchess of Orleans. Dumas was also a composer, interestingly enough, and I think about what it would be like to find some of those compositions, and to try and live with those for a moment.

TH: You said something about Hayden being an anthropologist; would you consider yourself an anthropologist? You're saying these things and I'm feeling like I need to go read up on Dumas. I know that it is, whether you want it to be or not, what you do: you bring us these people in your work. But are you conscious of that? How do you decide that you're going to explore Dumas or Charles Drew, who you've mentioned elsewhere as being a part of that series?

YK: When those individuals stay with me for a period of time—some of these individuals stayed with me for twenty or twenty-five years. A good example would be Ira Aldridge, who was born on Greene Street here in New York City, and became a Shakespearean actor; there's a bust of him at the Royal Shakespeare Theatre. When we think of black acting in Shakespeare's plays, we ordinarily think of Othello, but Aldridge actually appeared in all of Shakespeare's major plays.

I'm doing a different project now that involves a sort of excavation of the work of Edmonia Lewis, who is a neoclassical sculptor. She was born in Greenbush, New York, and went to Oberlin in the late 1850s. Her style never really changes from neoclassical to a more modern style—and maybe that could be a shortcoming in her work—but as an African American sculptor at that particular time, going to Oberlin, then to Boston, from Boston to Florence, and from Florence to Rome where she would spend the majority of her life, she is a significant figure in history. Those are the kinds of concerns I'm looking at.

TH: Those poems seem to be of a different nature—a more public, historical nature—than those in *Magic City*. Every now and again you'll throw some personal stuff up in there and it's usually masked or disguised, or at least layered. In discussing your creative process and your aims, you often talk about psychological overlays, using terms like "excavation." In *Blue Notes* you said, "It is difficult for me to write about things in my life that are very private, but I feel I am constantly moving closer to my personal terrain, to the idea of trying to get underneath who I am." What are you doing to get closer to this more private terrain, and how do you draw the line between the Private and the Public, as a poet?

YK: It's difficult. Those two terrains, at least, begin to merge sooner or later. I suppose I'm dealing with that personal information in the context of essays, and not necessarily in the poetry—at the moment.

TH: Why is that? What is it that you can do with a nonfiction essay that you can't do with poetry?

YK: I think it has a lot to do with how I came to writing in the first place. I admired James Baldwin's essays. I read very closely his novels and short stories, but I still admire him as an essayist, and that would have been my direction early on, how I thought of myself as writing as a teenager. I'm interested in a kind of revelation that happens in his essays, and I think one of the things that is interesting with Baldwin's essays is that one has the Public and the Private side-by-side.

TH: I'd like to talk some about satire in your work: there is *Lost in the Bonewheel Factory, I Apologize for the Eyes in my Head, Thieves of Paradise, Talking Dirty to the Gods,* and even *Magic City,* which is not a collection I thought of as satirical until I heard you talking about how it came out of the environment where you grew up, which felt far from a "magical" kind of place. Is the notion of satire something you consider as a weapon?

YK: That's interesting that you would say "weapon." One of my favorite titles is Gordon Parks's autobiography, *A Choice of Weapons,* where Parks deals with the fact that he picks up a camera and uses it as a weapon . . . .

TH: He's from the Midwest too.

YK: Yeah, he's from the Midwest too, that's right. [laughter] He's from Kansas.

But satire—I'm interested in satire and the blues, because I've always thought of the blues as political. A lot of other people will probably say, "No, it is anything but political," but it is very satirical on a personal level, and also on a political level. When one goes back and looks at the Delta blues, one realizes that these are not passive voices. They were voices of protest, they were often disguised—there was a kind of "cakewalk" in language that was going on.

I grew up with people who were rather satirical, in Bogalusa, Louisiana. That's also the area where the Deacons for Defense and Justice came out of. Jonesboro, Louisiana, is where the Deacons for Defense was actually formed, but the most significant history of the Deacons comes out of Bogalusa— individuals I knew who were friends of mine were part of that. The reason I bring them up is that they were anything but satirical; they were pretty straightforward. [laughter]

TH: Before I ask my last question, I'd like to go through some definitions.

YK: Some definitions? [laughs]

TH: Yeah, maybe I'll just throw some words out and you can say the first thing that comes to mind. [audience laughs]

YK: Oh no. [laughs] I'm not going to do that.

TH: Alex Blackburn! Do you remember Alex Blackburn, who was your first creative writing teacher? We have him waiting backstage! [audience laughs]

Really, though, when you think of him, what comes to mind? This would have been your first creative writing class; what did he teach you? What were your impressions?

YK: Yes, this would have been my first creative writing class, in 1973, at the University of Colorado. It was more or less reading at that point; I began to look at voices I hadn't looked at—the whole of American literature—so it was a widening of my perspective for the most part.

But [Blackburn] helped me toward reading in a different way, I think, bringing certain kinds of thought processes to the reading of literature. And since writing has to happen side-by-side, that was rather instructive.

TH: No one will ever know where your stuff comes from.

YK: That's good to know. [laughs] But really it comes from everywhere. I tend to tell students that there is no topic that's taboo; it's the aesthetics that are important.

TH: That seems to be separate from the notion of Private and Public, though. "No topics are taboo . . . but I'm not going to tell you about this and that." [laughter]

YK: Right, right. [laughs] Somewhere else I've said that the poem isn't an ad for an emotion, and I definitely believe that.

TH: Do you make distinctions between truth and emotion?

YK: "Truth" might be an elaborate abstraction—a layered abstraction, but an abstraction.

TH: Alright, I'll ask my last question and then we can open this up to others. What was your obsession at age fifteen? When you think about being fifteen years old, what do you remember being obsessed with?

YK: Strangely enough, I was obsessed with building a greenhouse. I had drawn up all these elaborate plans and I thought that's what I would really do. Growing up in Louisiana I thought I knew everything about plants—I knew a lot about plants—and I had made all of these plans, and I began to learn about drafting and to learn the scientific names for plants as well as their vernacular names. It's just one of those things.

TH: Wow, I didn't realize that. You write about flowers a lot, but not about plants in general; that's interesting. How about when you were between thirty-five and forty? What was your obsession then?

YK: I probably was most obsessed with jazz through that whole period.

TH: Interesting. I had expected that for the first answer. And now, what are you obsessed with?

YK: My obsession now? Gosh, I wish I knew. [laughter] One realizes that one wants, pretty much, to engage everything. I was thinking about this coming in on the train: I had written a few notes down about Australian Aboriginals, and had written the title "Corrobery" down, and I believe that the corrobery was probably the first poetry—art performance—where songs, the instruments—not just the didgeridoo, because that becomes the cliché for aboriginal instruments—the method of painting the instruments is part of the performance because of the painting on the body and what have you.

I was thinking about how, if you think about the Aboriginals being here for in excess of forty- or fifty-thousand years and having everything invested in the landscape—where one is conceived and where one is born has to do with one's name—that relationship to landscape interests me, and I'm very much interested in the fact that they were performers of their work.

Also there is "dreamtime." I have a feeling that this idea of "Dreamtime Mythology" isn't a mythology as much as the fact that it is a recording of things witnessed.

TH: It sounds like, from connecting the dots of what you've said, especially in that last answer, that in terms of your current projects your obsession is the nuances of cultural histories.

How about we take a couple of quick questions from the audience as a wrap-up?

Audience Member #1: This question is for Terrance . . .

YK: Good! [laughter & applause]

AM#1: Do you feel conflicted teaching at a program like Carnegie Mellon, where it's a mainly white creative writing department?

TH: Oh yeah. I told them that when I came in; that's why they gave me a lot of money. [laughter] I did; at the interview I said, "There's just a lot of white folks there."

AM#1: But how do you deal with that?

TH: Well, I'm a black person, so there's one more black person there than there was before.

This question—about teaching at Princeton or Carnegie Mellon, the notion of the poet in academia—I just feel like teaching is raceless, the problem is what the students will allow and what they'll resist. I can teach the blues to black students, and they may be more susceptible than white students, but I guess we could debate that too.

And it still is only to a point. I lived in New Orleans for two years and I taught at Xavier, a historically black university, and that was the hardest part of leaving. I taught lots and lots of classes—I taught four classes per semester, whereas now I teach two per semester—and it was for much less pay, but the reason I didn't want to leave was because of the students. It was a very difficult decision to make. I mean, every time I come up the stairs and I see Andrew Carnegie's face right there and I've got to go to my office and I start thinking about *Invisible Man* and the "Great Benefactor." [laughter] I've thought about painting his face brown or something—so now when I do this, my students will know it was me.

YK: Okay, go for it! [laughter]

Audience Member #2: In some of your comments about Gwendolyn Brooks it's clear that you had some reservations about the quality of the work of some of the poets of the Black Arts Movement. As you move from the Renaissance forward, I'd be interested in your comments on those poets of the Black Arts Movement of the '60s and '70s whose work you find of merit and value.

TH: I had a question like that too. [laughter] Do you want me to read it?

YK: I thought that was a question for you! [laughs] Who was that question for?

AM#2: It was for you.

YK: I'm going back to that statement that Gwendolyn Brooks made; she said, "Art is that which endures." If I went back to the Black Arts Movement, yes, there are individual poems that definitely endure from that period. When I started trying to formulate *Pleasure Dome*, I realized that many of those earlier poems had been directly influenced by the Black Arts Movement, so yes, I was certainly reading some of those poets.

Amiri Baraka, I think, is a very important voice from the Black Arts

Movement—if I had to really just go to a voice from that movement. The plays are important, the short stories, *Tales* are very important stories. For me, the book that is the most successful of his books is *The Dead Lecturer*, but of course many of those poems are, if not directly influenced by Black Mountain, they are at least partially influenced by the Black Mountain Movement.

TH: With this notion of art that endures, the question is how does it endure? Does canonization make it endure? I think about that in terms of someone who no one knows, like James Booker—someone who was clearly talented and whose work was of merit—the question is, "has he endured," or "will he endure?"

YK: That's a good example of endurance, the fact that while most people don't know James Booker, there are individuals—at least a few thousand individuals—in this country who will definitely keep Booker alive because of the passion in Booker's work. And that's the same thing about the passion of some of those voices from the Black Arts Movement, or individual poems from the Black Arts Movement. Larry Neal is a good example of a real thinker and poet of merit, but one has to go to certain individual poems to see that. An individual such as Bob Kaufman, who isn't really part of the Black Arts Movement, is systematically left out of discussions of the Beat Movement, and yet he endures.

AM#2: Speaking of James Booker, as a Midwestern artist, I was wondering if you could talk about a Black Arts poet from the Midwest, Henry Dumas.

YK: Henry Dumas was actually born in Arkansas—he's a southerner. He lived in East St. Louis for a while, but he has the South in him. Look at those poems, and it's there. [laughs] But I think Dumas is outside of the Black Arts Movement.

TH: I think the notion of the Black Arts Movement should be opened up. It's like what you were saying about Gwendolyn Brooks: too many people try to narrow the definition of it as a movement, but if you really were to expand the definition and what it achieved, you would have Lucille Clifton—she published her first book in 1969—definitely Kaufman; there would be different corners, but that spectrum gets complicated quickly. [laughter]

With that we must end, I'm afraid. Thanks to everyone for coming out.

Robert Polito: The great thing about these Cave Canem evenings is that they never really stop, they just pause. I want to thank Yusef and Terrance for this amazing evening full of surprise and wonder. Thank you all for coming.

A Finer Form: T. J. Anderson and Yusef Komunyakaa in Conversation

T. J. Anderson, Trudier Harris, and Jerry W. Ward/2004

From *Callaloo* 28.3 (2005), 585–91. © Charles H. Rowell. Reprinted with permission of The Johns Hopkins University Press.

In 1996, the George Moses Horton Society for the Study of African American Poetry was founded at the University of North Carolina at Chapel Hill, with the purpose of promoting the creation and scholarly evaluation of African American poetry. After conferences in Chapel Hill in 1998, 2000, and 2002, the Society met jointly with the second Furious Flower Poetry Conference held at James Madison University in Harrisonburg, Virginia, in September of 2004. The featured activity for the Horton Society was a luncheon at which Pulitzer Prize–winning poet Yusef Komunyakaa and internationally famed composer T. J. Anderson discussed their collaboration on an opera entitled *Slip Knot.*

Their comments on their unusual adventures into creativity make clear the myriad possibilities for collaboration across traditional creative boundaries. Komunyakaa appreciates the rhythms of Anderson's compositions, and Anderson embraces the musicality of Komunyakaa's poetry. The two artists discuss the importance of valuing each other's work, of trusting the collaborative process, and of the need to allow the result of their creativity to rest in the hands and minds of the other. Where to nudge and where to "bid the vassal soar," as George Moses Horton would say, is a line that they adhere to almost without discussion, for both Komunyakaa and Anderson have tried and true histories of sustained creation.

In an engaging exchange in which they informed and entertained the audience of luncheon guests, Komunyakaa and Anderson provided a glimpse into the expansive possibilities of language and music—and the sound that is integral to both of them. By sharing insights into how creativity works, whether it is scanning lines of poetry or limning words that "sing," these art-

145

ists illustrate that the boundaries between disciplines are always permeable, that the desire to collaborate can always leap over obstacles, and that art can be limited only by imaginations too fragile to push boundaries. By pushing their imaginations, by embracing the differences that have led them to an intertwining oneness, Yusef Komunyakaa and T. J. Anderson have stepped into a sea of diversity and yielded a product of a finer form than either could have produced individually. The path they offer is one that many creative persons might find worthy of emulation.
—Trudier Harris

From Jerry W. Ward's opening remarks at the George Moses Horton Society Luncheon, September, 2004, at James Madison University, Harrisburg, Virginia:

Jerry W. Ward: *Slip Knot*, the opera, composed by T. J. Anderson with a libretto by Yusef Komunyakaa, tells the story of Arthur, whose last name remains uncertain, a man born into slavery in Massachusetts in 1747, and executed for rape in 1768. During his brief life, he exercised a degree of freedom uncommon for a person with no property in New England. He lived a devil-may-care existence of considerable freedom, moving back and forth between Massachusetts, Connecticut, and Rhode Island. He worked a number of jobs, loved a number of women—often casually, sometimes seriously—tried the sea-faring life, and, when in need, pilfered. Because he was often in conflict with the law, he was often imprisoned, but he escaped numerous times with the aid of both white colonists and Native Americans. He ultimately was accused of rape. Though he insisted he was innocent of the crime, he was tried, convicted, and hanged. As it became known, Arthur's story played a role in turning public opinion in the North against slavery.

The dramatic action follows Arthur as his life becomes increasingly threatened, and his influence increases in the growing New England abolitionist movement. The three main characters, Arthur, his accuser, and his betrayer, are placed among such important social groups as the Christian Massachusetts townspeople, the African American community, and the legal religious establishment. Based largely on court records, *Slip Knot* is both an intense musical drama and an intriguing exercise in the retrieval of the history of ordinary people. The composer and librettist for this opera are not strangers to collaboration. Perhaps we could begin this conversation by asking: What motivated the two of you to collaborate on this project?

T. J. Anderson: I certainly want to thank you for that marvelous, kind introduction. . . . And I also want to thank Trudier Harris for the invitation for us to be here. I'll start off by answering the question that Jerry raised. The writer Leon Forrest told me I should find Yusef Komunyakaa, which I did. The opera, which has had a workshop performance at Northwestern University, started when I heard a lecture by Timothy Breen at the National Humanities Center in 1996. Timothy talked about a slave named Arthur. Arthur was fascinating. We only know a little bit about him, but what we know is a fine basis for an opera. It was marvelous—it had both sex and violence [Laughter]—and that's usually a good thing.

However, there were other things that we found attractive, and that is because Arthur had a great desire to be free; his whole life was spent trying to be free. His return to the plantation in Barre, Massachusetts, in about 1750—his return to Barre Manor, which is where his mother was a slave, is interesting because in the literature Arthur is listed as a Mulatto, so one can assume that the plantation owner was Arthur's father. Arthur went to sea at one point. He lived among the Indians when the French and Indian Wars wiped out a number of Indian men. He also spent a lot of time in jail; he was a drunkard. He was also a ladies' man; and all of these virtues make him human—there are a lot of people like this. The thing that Arthur—that made Arthur distinctly unique, was his brilliance. He actually wrote a testimony regarding what happened to him when he was in jail before he was to be hanged. So therefore he had—he was certainly a literate person in a society that was highly illiterate. When I found Yusef, I explained to him my interest in Timothy Breen's discoveries and the story he wrote about them in Northwestern's newspaper. I told him that I had been the resident composer at Northwestern, and I thought they would be interested in commissioning the work, which they did. And we had a workshop, what? Two years ago? And we had an excellent review in the *Chicago Tribune*. I guess we can start talking about collaboration, since we've done that. . . . The background is, we've been collaborating on another project, but we don't want to talk about that one because that one's in the process; but we'll talk about *Slip Knot* and our collaborative effort.

Yusef Komunyakaa: That's interesting because I'd come prepared to talk about the other. [Laugher] I suppose the thing that really drew me to the hero of *Slip Knot* as a character had to do with what he said. He defined himself as "almost free" early on, so consequently he had established a certain point of view about his life. He stood himself up against everything around him—everything that was happening to him. And I wanted to stay very close to poetry. I knew that that had to be the element to tell the story, so the piece really became a poem narrative; and I knew that with T. J.'s musical background, his genius as a composer, that the music would become part of the narrative. So these things worked together in harmony to recreate the essence of Arthur. The most difficult thing was really not beginning the piece, but the question of how to end the piece. It's my intention to always stay away from melodrama, although—although I know that is a component of opera—melodrama. But I wanted to end on a visual image, and the visual image is almost a crucifixion that takes place. And it's through light and design, as opposed to outright statement.

Anderson: Last night you had the opportunity to see a marvelous play [Eric Quander and Daniel Bryant's *The Bard Meets Black and Unknown Bards*, commissioned especially for the conference by Joanne Gabbin], and I want to talk about that for a minute because that exemplifies collaboration. I was very much impressed by that.

What most people don't seem to realize is that the artist is really a "recreator," and that what we do is we document the culture, the time and those things have that particular significance for our lives. Take Shakespeare, and the possible view of Shakespeare's language as the basis for [Bryant's] play, in which the repetition of Shakespeare's lines weave in and out in a sort of rich melody. And to offset this view, as Bryant does, by introducing the African American poets was certainly a beautiful idea and well executed; and of course what happens is that it turns out to be a sort of call and response—the African form. It also turned out to be a vehicle in which we witnessed dance; we witnessed singing which is beautiful, we witnessed the links between gospel music, spirituals, and other forms of musical expression. And to have all of those things coming together, to me represents what the new art forms are going to be. In other words, what I'm saying is that collaborative efforts are key . . . because within the last fifty years we all became products of a television generation. Television has changed the manner in which art is going to exist in the future. When one has a hundred channels and can immediately click a button when bored, one begins to realize that, to make a statement, one must address oneself to this medium, which is a collaborative medium. And therefore that is very important.

Komunyakaa: The artists in collaboration cannot focus on entertainment because entertainment can be a kind of distraction. However, there has to be an element of truth that vibrates underneath everything. So in capturing the truth, or, rather, in approximating the truth—the listener or the viewer comes back to my definition of poetry. Under this definition, one has to emphasize that the listener and the viewer are co-creators of meaning. . . . That's why I rely so heavily on the image to express emotion.

I've worked on a number of other collaborative projects, and I do think that poets are going to go in that direction more and more. Working with T. J. I think has been a foundation for me, helping me realize in how many directions collaborations can actually go. The other important thing about collaborative spirit [is that] one has to trust one's collaborator. That becomes very important. You have to really know what that artist has created, in order to know what the possibilities of the piece are. Otherwise, it's merely a technical experiment that could undermine one's vision.

Anderson: It's obvious that since Yusef and I are both college professors, we could talk forever. [Laughter] But we don't want to do that. What I would like to do now is open it up for questions. I would feel more comfortable, answering your questions rather than going on talking. . . . Are there any questions from the audience?

Audience Member: Why was the opera produced in a workshop?

Anderson: The opera was produced in the workshop mainly because the Dean was going out of office at Northwestern. And the new Dean happens to be an African American woman, and I didn't want her being saddled with having to do the total opera. In other words, they did excerpts—and it was very well done, I might add.

So the complete opera has never been done, and we would certainly hope that some opera company will be interested. But again, that's easy to say, and very difficult to do. I think the cost of opera makes it almost impossible for people to undertake, unless there are heavy donations and so on. Because when you consider you have to have a music director, you have to have a stage director, you have to have costumes, you have to have a conductor, you have to have a librettist, a composer—I mean, the list just adds up and up and up. So, you're talking about a lot of money. It's a medium that's almost out of reach. And it's unfortunate because opera's future cannot depend on doing things in the past. In other words, sooner or later the medium will die if it continues to do what it is doing now. We notice a great deficit in the major symphony orchestras now. Sooner or later, if any medium is to survive, it must become relevant, and when it becomes relevant then these other things such as adequate levels of funding, we feel, should come into play.

Audience Member: Could you talk a little bit about the relationship between collaboration and improvisation?

Komunyakaa: The relationship between . . . it's not really a good question for me. [Laughter] However—well, I've done a number of these projects . . . I should talk about the one called *Testimony*. It was originally written for [Australian] radio. Again, we're talking about cost. In *Testimony*, I really wanted to capture the spirit of Charlie Parker. Initially, it had been set up in a very formal, formalized way; but I came back to the United States, and I said to myself, "the essence of Parker has to be somewhat experimental." So I sat down and constructed what I call a flexible design for the piece. I wanted the illusion of symmetry. I composed fourteen pieces all relating to the history of Parker, two stanzas in each of the pieces, fourteen lines each, that was the symmetry I wanted. But I also desired improvisation within the context of those forms. And to see it on page, it looks very formalized, but when it is performed, the element of improvisation bleeds through. Initially it took thirty-two musicians, ten singers, and an actor, for the radio broadcast. Recently, it was performed at the Sydney Opera House, where it was a more expanded project. . . . So that is an example of improvisation—the whole piece was done as an improvisation. All the people concerned actually helped to compose the piece. It is a slightly different piece than the ones T. J. and I are working on.

Anderson: My latest experience with improvisation was a commission by Harvard University to celebrate my seventy-fifth birthday. I wrote a piano concerto all based on "boogie-woogie." [Laughter] And it's unusual in that I had a former student—his name is Donal Fox—who is a phenomenal pianist, as my soloist. And what makes it unusual as a piece is that it is a concerto for the piano in which not one note is written for the piano. The piano part is totally improvised, so I was at the mercy of Donal Fox, which made me look good, because he can play. [Laughter] I'm currently working on a piece for the hundredth anniversary of the University of Iowa School of Music, and that piece is also a piece in which I will use Donal Fox, but it's totally different from the piano concerto—it's really a fantasy. . . . And the major influences are J. S. Bach and Thelonious Monk. And Fox already has an album out combining the music of Monk and Bach. So he sent me the album, and I told him I won't even listen to it. I'll do my thing and then let him do his thing when it comes to the piano. So I do have sections in which he improvises, and that's a new work. . . .

Audience Member: Yusef said how important it is to trust your collaborator. Can the two of you comment on what makes it easy for you to be collaborators? What's this love going on between you? [Laughter]

Komunyakaa: Well, I'm quite aware of T. J.'s music and I listen to it and I love it—I love the spirit of it. So, in that sense, I trust his dexterity in music, but also his musical ideas. He has ideas, and that's what I trust the most I think—this kind of extended possibility that happens when I listen to his work. So it gives me the freedom to be more expansive as well. In that sense it's a kind of trading notes in a way, because I'm writing a narrative that's flexible in a sense, and I think T. J. is writing a parallel narrative that dovetails with mine.

Anderson: When I spoke with Yusef about the project the first thing he told me is that he was one of the few people who heard my opera *Soldier Boy, Soldier*, based on the libretto by Leon Forrest, that was commissioned by Indiana University. It's the story of a black veteran returning to the United States after the Vietnam War, facing greater violence than he faced in Vietnam. And he is killed on his wedding day. So Yusef had this awareness of what my music was and certainly I knew of his poetry and I had read some of his poetry. And what I noticed about his poetry—it's very important in collaboration—is that the music fits the written word. In other words, if his poetry didn't sing to me, I could never use him. And there have been a lot of poets whose words sing to me. I'm talking about M. B. Tolson, Robert Hayden, and I could go down a long list of people—Michael Harper, Harryette Mullen. I mean, there are certain poets who just sing to my ear; when I read them, I hear the music. That's what the connection *is*. And if you have this sense of respect . . . (addressing Komunyakaa) I don't think I've ever asked you to change a line; I may ask you to change a word, but not the line. [Laughter] And of course, Yusef is very receptive . . . I mean he was able to say, well, can we use *this* word you know, so I mean it is a collaborative effort in that sense. And this sense of trust and respect has to be the basis of a collaboration; if it's not there, it won't work, it won't work. Because you have to have confidence in the ability of your collaborator.

Audience Member: I just want to sort of emphasize what you're saying because I had a piece of poetry that was done—put into music by a composer. And he came to a word, and he said, "Do you need this word?" I said, "Yes." He said, "It won't sing." And I had never heard that expression before in my whole life. I said, "What do you mean it won't sing?"

But I want to get back to this collaborative work, because I've done some. There's a metro station that's opening up in Washington, and I've done poetry for the sculpture in that station—my poetry is going to be written in steel all over this station. The conclusion that I came to working with the sculptor is that I had to complement her work. I had to respect this sculptor's work, and she had to respect mine. It wasn't a matter of my doing my thing and her doing her thing, but the two of us had to get together and complement each other. I wonder if that makes sense to you.

Komunyakaa: Well, essentially, that's what I mean by two parallel narratives dovetailing. It's almost where two things form a third, and that third thing that emerges is filled with surprises.

Anderson: For us both, for us both. . . . Another question, any other questions?

Audience Member: Yes, could you address the issue of working with the historical texts—that is, selecting a historical text and taking it and making a creative piece. How did you work with poetic license versus the issue of historical accuracy?

Komunyakaa: We allowed ourselves the freedom of artists. You know, I'm not producing a documentary. The foundation of it is a document, but for the artist, he or she has to go beyond that. Otherwise that would misshape one's passion; one has to come to the piece with a certain passion.

Audience Member: Okay, but my question gets to the issue of Arthur. Do you feel the passion for Arthur or do you feel the passion for the creation of the opera?

Komunyakaa: Well, it's going back to that idea of what Arthur actually says: he defined himself as "almost free." Yeah, I felt the passion for that expression, so consequently I related to the individual behind the expression.

Anderson: And another dimension of your question is Timothy Breen, the historian who developed all this through his research. We were fortunate, and I told Timothy, I said, "Now you have to realize, once Yusef reads this, he's going to do what he's going to do." [Laughter] And I said, "I'm not going to put any restrictions on him," and I said, "You may not recognize Arthur. Or you *may* recognize him." I said, "But he has to be free to do whatever he wants to do with your historical document. . . ." Timothy did not wholly understand it, but he had trust. He had trust that the two of us would maintain the integrity of Arthur. And most of the story *is* Arthur's story. It's not a story that Yusef made up; it's Arthur's story. And we had faith in Timothy Breen's research; we had faith that we could change anything we wanted to change because we both needed that for our creativity, and that's how Arthur was developed.

Further questions? This will have to be the last question.

Audience Member: Did you agree on the colors that represent Arthur's mind?

Komunyakaa: It came about when Arthur began to speak; when Arthur began to speak for himself, basically, within my text. Which means being able as a writer to actually align oneself with the historical individual and to realize that an element of him is still alive. So that was the energy behind the piece, I think—and trust, to trust the language. This is all part of a process of discovery. So I discovered certain things about Arthur, and I don't think that it really misshaped the essence of Arthur. It enlarged him. And the music also enlarges him.

Furious Flower II:
Cross-Pollination in the Diaspora

Tony Bolden/2004

From the videocassette *Furious Flower II: Cross-Pollination in the Diaspora* (California News-reel, 2005), produced by the Furious Flower Poetry Center at James Madison University (executive producer: Joanne V. Gabbin). Reprinted by permission of Furious Flower Poetry Center.

Bolden: How do you think African American poetry has influenced poets, writers, and ordinary folks in the African Diaspora?

Komunyakaa: I am surmising that a lot of poems are memorized. In particular, I'm thinking of Langston Hughes. Some of his poems are memorized. It keeps us conscious of history, of culture. So there's that influence; it's an influence of necessity. I was very conscious of how the poet fits into a society because I was in Chile recently in celebration of Pablo Neruda, and children who memorize lots of Neruda are just everyday citizens. I don't know if poetry could ever function that way in this society because there are so many distractions. Again, going back to entertainment—it's to be processed and put aside. Poetry cannot be processed and put aside that way. Poetry calls for meditation and reflection, something that we revisit.

Bolden: You suggested that art functions as social critique and that beauty doesn't have to be escapist, that it can confront the evils of our time with a sort of dressed up kind of representation of life. How is that reflected in your work?

Komunyakaa: Well, when we think of beauty, we think of something defined for us.

Bolden: Okay.

Komunyakaa: I would like to think of beauty in a different way, as something that we are defining as we are experiencing it. Monk has a title; I think he calls it "Ugly Beauty." I like to think about that in a way. I have a friend whose interest is visual arts. Some of the things that she paints, the individual who views it initially might say, "My gosh, that's almost grotesque isn't it?" It's interesting. I've gone back to those pieces, and I've seen the severe beauty in those pieces. It's a kind of beauty that isn't on the surface. It's a beauty that comes through experience and intensity of observation. Sometimes the beauty that is on the surface becomes rather problematic because it's a beauty that knows it is supposed to be beautiful. Consequently, it is ugly inside.

Bolden: This is sort of a blues concept in the sense that it contains these contradictions. I'm struck by the visual appeal of your own work. So how were you able to accomplish that?

Komunyakaa: I think it is informed by my early experiences. I grew up in a small town, Bogalusa, Louisiana, and the woods were so close to me. Within a matter of minutes I could be there in the midst of all of that, and early on I was quite taken with what I saw around me and realized that there's a kind of activity underneath, moments of silence even. And so, saw things visually, and I began to think about the rituals of animals and how those parallel human beings and what have you. I took my very first writing class, I think, in 1973, and some people asked me, "How do you define your poems?" I say, "They are word paintings. That's the only way I could define them because I had entertained the idea of painting, but I don't think I have the endurance to do it.

Bolden: I wanted to ask you about your poem, "Ode to a Drum." I think that's one of the great classics of African American literature. How did the poem come about?

Komunyakaa: The poem came out of the idea of how in Congo Square, the drum had been banned by time of slavery. What interested me about this idea of the drum being an object is that it could come alive and be instrumental in its necessary passion as such. It's also a tribute to the idea of the daughter in the poem as well.

[Komunyakaa reads "Ode to a Drum."]

Bolden: There's that ending—Kadoom, Kadoom—which is a kind of paralinguistic imagery there. It seems that sound is actually part of the meaning of the poem at that point. Do you want to comment on that?

Komunyakaa: Well, it also takes us back to an idea that I have as far as language goes. It is our first music and has a lot to do with how something is expressed. The body knows deeply what the language is about. The body is an amplifier of emotion, images and everything; an image somewhere that says the body remembers in the same way that the drum remembers life.

Bolden: In traditional Western thought, there is a split between the mind and the body, that the two are mutually exclusive, and your comment there seems to counter that.

Komunyakaa: Well, one is married to the other. It's all part of the same thing. Matter of fact, the whole development of the brain, I think, has everything to do with the dexterity of the hands, and that is still happening. That's why it's difficult for me to think of people composing poems on computers and typewriters because of the fact of that tactile relationship of the pen or pencil pressed against paper is still sending signals to the brain.

Bolden: How do you know when a poem is finished?

Komunyakaa: Some poems tell me that they're finished.

Bolden: They talk to you?

Komunyakaa: They talk to me, but my process is quite improvisational, so I write everything, and then I begin to edit the poem down. Initially, the poem perhaps is 150 lines long, and I edit it down to 30 or 40 lines. And at the very end I begin to go back up through the poem from the bottom realizing often that I've written past the most important, the most provocative ending. The poem shouldn't resolve; it shouldn't be a resolution. This is what I feel.

[Komunyakaa reads "The Same Beat."]

A Poet of Suffering, Endurance, and Healing

Chris Hedges/2004

From *The New York Times* (8 July 2004). Reprinted with permission of PARS International, authorized licensor on behalf of *The New York Times*.

It is morning on West State Street, a wide expanse of asphalt hugged by brick and clapboard houses, some refurbished and others in need of help. The city has yet to hum to life. Sitting in a living room filled with books, Yusef Komunyakaa explains why he fled from Princeton, where he still teaches poetry at Princeton University, to New York, and finally settled four years ago in this city whose segregated neighborhoods and urban poverty remind him of the Deep South, where he grew up.

A decade after he won the Pulitzer Prize for poetry, Mr. Komunyakaa (pronounced koh-min-YAH-kah) is teaching classes to African Americans of all ages and walks of life, in the belief that poetry is not simply about verbal dexterity, but about meaning, about experience, about the intimate and sacred struggles of human existence. His classes here are sponsored by Cave Canem (Latin for "beware of the dog"), a group committed to discovering and promoting black poets.

His voice dips low, dripping with the honey inflections of Louisiana. He keeps his eyes downcast. He mumbles at times, or draws his words out in odd syncopations that give them a disarming intimacy. He knows enough of pain and discrimination and suffering not to be too impressed with his status, not to forget where he came from and why he writes.

Mr. Komunyakaa was born James Willie Brown Jr. fifty-seven years ago in Bogalusa, Louisiana, the eldest of five children. His great-grandparents, stowaways on a ship from Trinidad, had given up their surname, Komunyakaa, which he legally reclaimed. Mr. Komunyakaa's father, a carpenter, was illiterate and not quite sure what to make of his son's love of books, but he pressed the child to write his mother apologetic letters on his behalf after violent arguments that drove her from the house. Words, young James saw when she walked back in through the door, had power. They were his tools.

"My great-grandfather Melvin had been a carpenter—so was my father— and they taught me the value of tools: saws, hammers, chisels, files, and rulers," he said. "It all dealt with conciseness and precision. It eliminated guesswork. One has to know his tools, so he doesn't work against himself."

The boy went to church and listened to the preacher, reading the poetry of the King James Bible. He wanted to be a preacher, too. But by the time he came of age there was a war in Vietnam, and he found himself clutching the black metal of an M-16 assault rifle, not a book. "I never used the word gook or dink in Vietnam," he said. "There is a certain kind of dehumanization that takes place to create an enemy, to call up the passion to kill this person. I knew something about that growing up in Louisiana."

It took him fourteen years to write about the war in two books of poetry. In many of his poems, like "Starlight Scope Myopia," he writes with compassion about those he fought. The Vietnamese peasants reminded him of sharecroppers.

He came back and went to college and then to graduate school at Colorado State University and the University of California at Irvine. And he began to write. His dozen or so books of poems, including *Neon Vernacular: New and Selected Poems*, which won him the Pulitzer in 1994, use the experience of being black and often poor in America to speak of suffering and endurance, and most importantly healing.

His life, he said, has been a "healing process from the two places": Bogalusa and Vietnam. But darkness has stalked him beyond the bayou and Southeast Asia. His two-year-old son, Jehan Vazirani Komunyakaa, named for Shah Jehan, the emperor who built the Taj Mahal, was stabbed to death last July by Jehan's mother, the Indian-born poet Reetika Vazirani, who then took her own life. At the funeral, Mr. Komunyakaa sat as a poem he wrote to his son, which began "I am five," an age his child never would reach, was read to the mourners by a friend. He has an adult daughter from another marriage.

He has just finished a performance piece called *The Trial of Chief Standing Bear*. The chief was arrested in 1879 while taking the body of his son home for burial from the reservation where his Ponca tribe had been relocated in Oklahoma. In the resulting trial, a federal judge declared that American Indians had legal rights.

Mr. Komunyakaa wonders at how quickly we forget the injustices perpetrated in the name of God and country, on the Great Plains, in the segregated

South, in the soporific heat of Vietnam, in the slums of Newark and Trenton, and in Iraq. He fights against this forgetting, for only in remembering is there healing. "I excavate history," he said, "I look at lives buried under too much silence. Periods of time, like slavery, have to be revisited, reimagined, so we can move through them."

In his poem "Tu Do Street," after being expelled from a Vietnamese bar for white soldiers, he walks into a bar for black soldiers and sees the Vietnamese bar girls, "wounded by their beauty & war," noting that "back in the bush at Dak To & Khe Sanh, we fought the brothers of these women we now run to hold in our arms."

Komunyakaa and the Kolkata Book Fair: Entries from a Diary of a Journey to India

Goutam Datta/2004

From *Callaloo* 28.3 (2005), 734–747. © Charles H. Rowell. Reprinted with permission of The Johns Hopkins University Press.

Entry 1: *The Idea of an Anthology*

Between September 25 and September 27, 2003, the largest gathering of Indian intellectuals ever held outside India took place at the Manhattan Center in New York City. The occasion was a conference on Indian literature sponsored by Bharatiya Vidya Bhavan USA, a New York–based organization dedicated to the promotion of Indian culture, philosophy, and arts; and the Bharatiya Sahitya Academy, the central organization for letters in India. In attendance were poets, novelists, and academicians representing fourteen languages. Also present was the then prime minister of India, Shri Atal Bihari Vajpayee, who himself is a poet. I was one of three conveners for the Bengali language, the fifth largest spoken language in the world.[1] The renowned poet-novelist Sunil Gangopadhaya and the academician Nirmal Kanti Bhatyachariya from West Bengal, India, joined me as fellow "Bangla" representatives.[2]

During the conference, I met many poets who were making their first visit to the United States. Mrs. Priti Sengupta, a fellow Gujarati writer from New York, and I were constantly attending to these colleagues, who shied away from asking simple questions of the hotel concierge because of their lack of confidence in English. However, all of them wanted to go sightseeing in and around Manhattan. I acted as a guide, helping them make sense of local maps. In the course of doing this, I had an unfortunate experience with a poet from southern India. This gentleman asked me where to go for sightseeing in Manhattan, stressing that he wanted to avoid the "Negro" part of the city. He had come to the conference with a preconceived, stereotypical image of African American community. I had a long and heated conversation with this so-called intellectual.

Then I reflected and realized that the world we live in is a "propaganda" world, where the individual's perception of reality is influenced by the news media's tendency to rely on some stereotypical image or other for every community. Of course, in the wider world, there are stereotypical images of mainstream America, too. At the time of the conference, the U.S. war with Iraq, and related government policies, had already caused most of the world's population to feel strong anti-American sentiments. These thoughts led me to a further realization—that apart from "Hamburger-Budweiser-MTV" culture, there are many American cultures that are not represented in India. In particular, I had in mind African American "blues-jazz" culture and African American literature.

Thinking further about the man who wanted to avoid black neighborhoods, I remembered that the modern education system in India originated under British rule. Therefore, it is not surprising that there is a strong influence from white Anglo-Saxon culture throughout the Indian education system. In school, we read Eliot, Pound, Frost, Cummings, Ginsberg, Kerouac, and Burroughs. But we had very little exposure to the history of the Harlem Renaissance, the Black Arts Movement; we learned nothing about the Beat poet Bob Kaufman, nothing about modern African American poets such as Yusef Komunyakaa and Rita Dove, or the younger generation of poets such as Natasha Trethewey, Elizabeth Alexander, Major Jackson, Terrance Hayes, and Kevin Young.

We had little reason to look beyond opinions like those expressed in the 1930s by the Bengali poet Bishnu Dey when he said, "T. S. Eliot is the only poet who can enlighten us in our search for true poetry after reading Marx and Engels." But seventy-five years after Dey's statement, I feel that focusing only on Eliot and his peers deprives us of another possible, even obvious, source of enrichment for Indian literature: African American literature. There is no reason why the major African American writers should not be better known in India. This is all the more true because, in my opinion, there are so many similarities between jazz and Indian classical music, and between blues and Indian vocal semiclassical Gazals, that it seems likely that these ancient cultures, African and Indian, probably somehow connected in the past.

Like jazz, Indian classical music thrives on improvisation; the same "raga" played by two masters will feel different because of their individual improvisations. Both forms inherently call for improvisation, as opposed to Western classical music, which is more frequently tied to strict notations. I think this is a basic difference between Western and Eastern cultures, Old and New World culture. Examples of the improvisatory impulse in India abound. The paintings inside Elephanta Caves, for instance, were done by Buddhist monks to express their freedom-filled state of the mind. And like their African equivalents, old Indian mythologies were an oral tradition for generations before being written down (that's why old Hindu text is called "Shruti," or "remember by listening"). In modern culture everything seems formula-based—even filmmaking and poetry sometimes seem to be taught by the numbers. But improvisation is more fundamental: I think in Africa when the first humans fought their way through unforgiving nature, they had to improvise every moment of life just to survive.

During my years as a student in Kolkata (which is anglicized "Calcutta" in most Western texts), students sang an immensely popular protest song (directed in many instances against autocratic government troops present): "They do not let us sing our song, O Paul Robeson—Negro brother of mine." Paul Robeson's name and the song associated with it was introduced by left-ist intellectuals in the 1950s because of Robeson's association with the Communist Party of America. The name Paul Robeson is very familiar in West Bengal, where communist and leftist movements have long been a part of public life. West Bengal has been ruled by a democratically elected leftist government for twenty-seven years. Memories of Bengali identification with Robeson, together with the parallels between African, African American, and Indian culture, helped convince me that Bengalis would embrace an African American poetry anthology. Therefore, I undertook the task of re-butting the man I argued with at the conference by editing the first African American poetry anthology in the Bengali language.

My first step was to write an article in the poetry magazine *Krittibas* that I accompanied with a translation of sixteen African American poems by authors from Dubois to Dove. The article created great excitement among both Bengali poets and poetry readers. I therefore approached the *Krittibas* editor, Sunil Gangopadhaya, and suggested that we collaborate on an anthology of African American poetry. Sunil, who visits the United States frequently and is a world traveler, is always open to new ideas, always trying to infuse new concepts into Bengali literature to keep it modern and alive. He responded as I had hoped, promising to handle both the distribution of poems for translation among Bengali poets in Kolkata and the publication of the results. All that was left for me to do was select poems for our anthology from the last hundred years of African American poetry.

In undertaking this daunting task, I was fortunate in that I already knew two prominent African American poets, Rita Dove and Yusef Komunyakaa, to whom I could turn for advice. In October 2004, only two months before the publication deadline, I spoke with Yusef about my determination to publish an African American poetry anthology in Bengali. The deadline for publication was December 2004, but Yusef extended his helping hand,[3] introducing me to the work of many young poets. In addition, Yusef agreed to travel with me to the Kolkata Book Fair to participate in the opening ceremony for the anthology, entitled *Ami Amar Mrittur Por Sadhinota Chai Na* ("I do not need my freedom when I'm dead"[4]), which he helped shape.

Entry 2: *An Interview with the Bengali* Vogue

To publicize both the anthology and Komunyakaa's journey, my comrades and fellow poets Subodh Sarkar and Mallika Sengupta formed a plan. Mallika is the poetry editor of the most popular fashion and family magazine in West Bengal, *Sananda* (similar to *Vogue*), and she went to the magazine's editor and arranged a special article on both Yusef and Rita Dove. My job was to interview both poets. Here (translated into English) is my interview with Komunyakaa, which appeared in *Sananda* on January 15, 2005:

Goutam Datta: The trip to the book fair will be your first visit to Kolkata. Do you have any expectations?

Yusef Komunyakaa: My poems are driven by images. I am anticipating that Kolkata will surprise me with numerous images. I will ask Kolkata—"please surprise me." I also hope to connect with new people, to make new friends.

Datta: Do you remember your feelings at the moment you heard that you had received the Pulitzer Prize?

Komunyakaa: When I heard the news, I was preparing to teach a poetry workshop at Indiana University. I was pleased. But I was also a little worried that the excitement and publicity might interfere with my concentration. I needed to complete the book I was then attempting to finish.

Datta: You are the first African American male poet in the past hundred years to receive a Pulitzer Prize. Do you think that racism is at work in even the arts and literary world?

Komunyakaa: Remember, artists and writers come out of the same society as everyone else. How can we expect that they would be outside the society's psyche? However, I believe that artists should not obsess about awards. They should concentrate on creating.

Datta: You took part in the Vietnam War. Please comment on your experience.

Komunyakaa: Vietnam divided the heart and soul of America. There was a narrow bridge between good and evil, black and white, rich and poor. . . . But I try to say whatever I want to say through poetry.

Datta: Most of the poets and writers in the United States voiced opposition to George Bush in the last election. However, Bush still won the election. Do you think that as a result poets became alienated from the mainstream American population?

Komunyakaa: A large percentage of the population (48 percent) voted against Bush. A large portion of the population also voiced their objection to the war in Iraq. But fear of the unknown helped Bush win reelection. Poets are always against war, because war is against life—and poets always celebrate life. Even when poets are writing about the guts and blood of war, still they write against war. And I believe most Americans are against war.

Nevertheless, we cannot forget that America was born out of "Manifest Destiny." That is why Native Americans suffered in such an extreme way.

Datta: What is your opinion on the war in Iraq?

Komunyakaa: We poets are against this war. Goutam, do you know how many Iraqis are dead? Thousands of Iraqis are dead because of this war. We have only tabulated the 1,200 American dead. Just as we created more Vietcong by mistreating ordinary Vietnamese, so in Iraq we are pushing some Iraqis toward insurgency. As if history never taught us anything.

Datta: Please let me know your last word to the people of Kolkata before your visit.

Komunyakaa: Please, surprise me. . . . Kolkata, please challenge me.

Entry 3: *A Komunyakaa Poem, Brand New*

As this interview went to press in India, Subodh, Mallika, Shrijato, Rahul, and many other young poets (with the help of Sunil Gangopadhaya) were hard at work organizing Yusef's trip to Kolkata. They arranged a weeklong series of events celebrating poetry and designed to initiate a conversation between cultures. To get the process started, and to make the brochure being prepared for our gala opening program memorable, Subodh asked me to get a new poem from Yusef that could appear in the brochure. The result was that within twenty-four hours of my calling Yusef with Subodh's request, he faxed me an hour-old piece, with the following message: "Hi Gary: Well, here is my most recent poem written this morning about 7 a.m." Then came the remarkable poem (actually a portion of a longer work), which I reproduce here.

[Reproduced excerpt from "Love in the Time of War" omitted.]

Entry 4: *Kolkata, Sunday, January 23*

Finally, the day of our journey arrived. Yusef and my friend Nupur Lahiri (who translated Nikki Finney's poems for the anthology) took the long flight (almost nineteen hours) from New York to Kolkata. After changing planes in London, we flew on to Mumbai, which is like the "LA" of India, on the west coast, before again changing planes and flying on to Kolkata, which is like New York, on the east coast. We landed at 3:30 a.m. local time on Sunday, January 23.

Even at this early hour, Kolkata welcomed Yusef with an open heart. Subodh and Avik (a young poet and assistant professor of comparative literature at Jadavput University, Kolkata) were waiting to receive us, and we got a special Kolkata police escort as VIP guests of the city. It was a little foggy and chilly—a perfect temperature for us. The roads were empty. Kolkata was still sleeping; street people lay under their blankets on the city sidewalks. Yusef, with his unapologetic eyes in his head, started to absorb the metropolis.

That afternoon in his guesthouse room, in the presence of several reporters, Yusef rehearsed an operatic, antiwar poetry piece with the author, Subodh, as well as two other poets and a musician. Subodh's plan was that each poet would perform antiwar verses to the accompaniment of narration and music. Yusef read the section he had faxed me of "Love in the Time of War," mesmerizing everyone in the room with his words and immense voice.

Entry 5: *A Rose in Burdwan*

On January 25 we went to Howrah Station (the Grand Central Station of Kolkata) to catch a train to Burdwan, a large rural town about seventy kilometers from Kolkata where we had two programs scheduled. Burdwan is almost at the midpoint between Kolkata and Shantiniketan, and the train reached the town by noon. We were greeted by Rotary club members and little girls who gave us garlands and red roses.

The whole group was split up into several cars for the trip to the venue for our first scheduled program. Yusef, Subodh, and I squeezed into a tiny Hyundai. But before the car could move, it was surrounded by child beggars who, having recognized Yusef as a "foreigner," started asking him for money. I gave him what local coins I had, and he gave them away as fast as he received them. But there was one seven or eight-year-old boy who just would not go away. With no more coins to give, Yusef gave him his red rose. The boy took the flower and was elated. He examined the rose and started to dance as he crossed the road. Before we understood what was happening, the boy sold the rose to a very young man waiting at the bus station.

We three poets speculated on this incident together. I said there must be a woman involved. Yusef laughed and said he would write a poem about this experience. Subodh said the same. Following is my own poem about the incident, which I call "The Stranger Comes to Town." (The stranger here is Yusef.)

[Text of poem follows.]

Entry 6: *Town Hall*

After the incident with the rose, we went on to the government guesthouse where we were staying, to get ready for the first of the two public events we had scheduled for that day. (This section of the trip was arranged by our poet friend Angshuman Kar, a professor in the department of English literature at Burdwan University.) At the government guesthouse, we went to the dining hall for a Bengali lunch. We dined on potato with ground poppy seeds (a delicacy in West Bengal), fresh fish curry, and a mango chutney desert. It is impossible for me to describe how those serving the food and the other local people welcomed us and how proud they were to have us there.

After lunch we hurried to Burdwan University for the first of our two events. Because Yusef's books are unavailable in India, Angshuman had collected Yusef's poems and articles from the Internet and copied and distributed them among his students. The students were therefore ready to engage with Yusef after he read his poems: indeed, questions from this dusty rural town hit him like little pebbles whirling around in a storm. Yusef answered them all attentively, pleased that his poems had reached and touched these students, and began the conversation between two cultures for which we had all hoped. At the students' request, Subodh and I read our own poems, and I read my translation of Yusef's famous poem "Tu Do Street."

The evening session was held in the town hall. All of Burdwan came down to the venue to welcome the first African American poet ever to visit there. The town hall walls were covered with "Welcome Yusef Komunyakaa" banners, and as the evening unfolded, the hall echoed with the poems of Subodh Sarkar, Mallika Sengupta, Rahul Dasgupta, Shampa Sen, Bithi Chattayapadhaya, Krishna Basu, Shibashish Mukherjee, and above all Yusef Komunyakaa. Angshuman's three-year-old daughter listened to poems for more than two hours, until she couldn't take any more. She came up to the stage and started to recite a famous Bengali children's poem written by Tagore. I thought that was the height of our poetry session!

After the program ended, we went back to the guesthouse, traveling through a night draped in winter smog, the temperature around 50 degrees Fahrenheit. The organizers had four bottles of Indian whiskey waiting for us at the guesthouse to keep us warm. Although Yusef generally does not drink, this night he joined us. Yusef and the young poet Rahul (with whom I coauthored the 2005 book *Face to Face: Two Poets*) traveled well into the depths of poetic theory. Shampa, Subodh, and I started to laugh for no reason. But two other companions, Shibasish and Krishna—who is in her sixties and is one of the leading female poetic voices of Bengal—became agitated discussing one of the major new formalist poets of Kolkata, who is trying to bind Bengali poems with his iron fists of meter and rhyme. As the poetry editor of the only major Bengali literary magazine, he is excluding everyone who opposes him, banning the publication of their poems in this journal. I could feel the heat even on this winter night, in this unknown town.

The next morning I was awakened by a knock on the door. A guesthouse worker informed me that my poet-comrades were already in the dining hall having breakfast. That day, Yusef and I would travel to Shantiniketan—Tagore's place—while most of the rest of the group would return to Kolkata. Shantiniketan, the palace of peace, is about two hours from Burdwan by train. As we said goodbye back in the dusty Burdwan station, it was clear that everyone had been touched by Yusef, not only because he is a poet among poets but also because of his simple lifestyle, his humble and undemanding character.

Entry 7: *Looking for Bauls*

Shantiniketan is approximately ninety miles (150 km) from Kolkata. If you are a poet and come to West Bengal, you must go to Shantiniketan, where the first Asian Nobel laureate, the poet Rabindra Nath Tagore, established his now-famous university "Viswabharati." Shantiniketan has since become renowned as a university town in West Bengal.

According to a promotional Web site, "Rabindranath Tagore's father, Maharshi Debendranath Tagore, established Shantiniketan (abode of peace) in 1863. In 1901 Rabindranath Tagore set up a Bramhacharya school here, which later came to be known as the Patha Bhavan. With the financial backing of the Maharajah of Tripura, the Visva-bharati Society was established in 1921. Tagore envisioned a center of learning that would have the best of both the East and the West: "Open air education, as opposed to being cloistered in the four walls of a classroom, became a reality here. At the Kala Bhavan and the Sangeet Bhavan the arts were given their rightful place in the Indian education system. Eminent people from all over the world came to Visva-Bharati during its peak period. Visva-Bharati became a Central University of Bengal in 1951."[5]

The university has become a cultural hub in Kolkata. Almost all the famous painters, writers, and singers have a place of their own in Shantiniketan.

On the day we visited Shantiniketan, we later traveled thirty kilometers farther to visit Kenduli, which is famous for its mid-January folk-song festival and the sect of wandering minstrels, known as Bauls, who gather for the annual event. Yusef, who had already heard Baul songs on the train, was eager to see the singers perform in Kenduli, so we hired a car and traveled two hours—but found no Bauls! As it happened, we had just missed the festival, and the Bauls had gone elsewhere.

That night we stayed at Nupur Lahiri's house and enjoyed local booze as poetry filled the night air. Getting the 6 a.m. train back to Kolkata the next morning proved to be a memorable experience. Nupur's housekeeper had already reserved two rickshaws for our early morning trip to the train station. However, they didn't show up and we began to worry about making the program we had scheduled at the American Center in Kolkata that very afternoon. We couldn't afford to miss this train. Yusef and I gathered our luggage and five newly purchased paintings and started to walk. We finally found two rickshaws on the road and hailed them. But before we reached the station, our previously reserved rickshaws caught up with us in the middle of the road and demanded payment. To avoid confrontation and catch the train, we gave them a portion of the fare and moved on.

Entry 8: *The Book Fair*

After a successful reading and question-and-answer session at the American Consulate, the final major event on Yusef's itinerary was the Kolkata Book Fair. Our book-launch ceremony was scheduled for Saturday, January

28. The Kolkata Book Fair is the second-largest festival in the state of West Bengal. Thousands of temporary structures are erected in the open area of Kolkata Maidan (similar to Central Park in New York) in order to accommodate all the publishing houses that participate. It seemed like a city within the city had been built overnight. Every day half a million people visit the fair, which lasts twelve days. Each publishing house does more than a year's business during the fair.

Each year the organizers select a theme country, and 2005 was France's year. Many poets and writers came to Kolkata for the 2005 fair. Even the German Nobel laureate Günter Grass was in town on this occasion. Salman Rushdie and V. S. Naipaul had come a few weeks earlier. Kolkata is a city that reveres arts and literature. Everything was working out as planned. However, at the last moment, Mother Nature opposed us: it started raining on Friday evening (January 28). We had planned to go to the book fair after completing a poetry reading seminar at Jadavpur University. But it had rained lightly throughout the day, then at around 4 p.m., it started to rain heavily. Because of an electrical problem the year before, the book fair closed down. It stayed closed on Saturday. I couldn't sleep all night. I was waiting for dawn. I knocked at Sunil's door at around 7 a.m. Saturday. Then Subodh and other poets came, and we decided that we would ask Yusef to stay one more day in Kolkata so that we could hold our book-launch ceremony on Sunday afternoon at the fair. Sunil, with his extensive connections, was able to reserve a small auditorium at the fair. Then we spent hours contacting all the invited poets and reporters to advise them of the change of venue. Susan Sultz, the director of public affairs at the U.S. consulate, was nice enough to send a well-connected person with us to change Yusef's flight. By around 4 p.m. on Saturday, everything seemed to have been settled. This was, for me, an example of what people could do if they stuck together and worked hard in spite of the odds: It is almost impossible to get a time slot at the Kolkata book fair. No one wanted to cancel their program. However, to accommodate us every group sacrificed a few minutes from their scheduled program, and we were able to get an hour slot. Saturday evening Yusef, Sunil, and I went to a party at the Lake Club that Nupur Lahiri had organized to honor Yusef. At last, we could relax a bit after a long day of fighting against nature.

Most of the poets who contributed to the anthology came for the ceremony. George Sibly, the U.S. Consul General also came in unexpectedly and recited Langston Hughes's "Dream Deferred." The small auditorium was wall to wall with people. Another highlight was the appearance of Taslima Nasreen, an exiled poet–novelist from Bangladesh. She was on a short tour in Kolkata and dropped by unannounced to read her translation of Nikki Giovanni's poem "Women." She is usually unavailable for public functions because of a fatwa on her life by extremist mullahs in Bangladesh. The first African American poetry anthology in Bengali, *I Do Not Need My Freedom When I'm Dead*, was officially opened by Yusef Komunyakaa and Sunil Gangopadhaya.

Entry 9: *Questions and Answers on Australia and Other Subjects*

I conclude these entries on Yusef's time in India with two examples of Komunyakaa's speaking directly or indirectly to Indian audiences. The first example consists of excerpts from a question-and-answer session that followed a program at the American Consulate on the day we returned from Shantiniketan:

Audience Member: You have spent quite a bit of time in Australia. Do you think that both Aboriginal people and the Australian landscape have played a role in your writing?

Komunyakaa: I spent ten years going back and forth between the U.S.A. and Australia. It is hard not to recognize Aboriginals, and I was quite taken by their relationship to the land. For it is as if the land itself is the foundation of their existence. Take, for example, the name of an individual Aborigine. Oftentimes, his or her name refers to where he or she was conceived and born, because Aborigines were basically nomadic. They have an old, oral tradition.

Kath Walker (Oodgeroo Noonuccal) published the first book of Aboriginal poems, *We Are Going*, in 1964. The very next year, in 1965, Colin Johnson (Mudrooroo Narogin) published the first short Aboriginal novel, *Wild Cat Falling*. What is interesting about that book is that it is a composite of blues, Beckett, and the land. I was quite taken by that. I have also written poems associated with the landscape.

Audience Member: Were you influenced by the Australian national poet "Banjo Patterson"?

Komunyakaa: Not really. I read some of his poems. They are period pieces. They capture certain time periods. The language is arcane and the rhythm is borrowed from the British.

Audience Member: Do you think Blake's poem "The Black Boy" has influenced African American poetry in any way?

Komunyakaa: I like Blake's "America" poem—it is a long poem. African

American poetry started with Lucy Terry's "Bars Fight," which was published in the Deerfield newspaper in 1746. I doubt that she was influenced by Blake. The next African American poet, Phillis Wheatley, was published in 1773. She was influenced by Alexander Pope. That is why she was writing those heroic couplets. During the Harlem Renaissance period many black poets were writing what I call protest sonnets, and they were directly influenced by British and Italian literature. My own first influence came from reading Paul Laurence Dunbar's poems.

Audience Member: It seems that you do not consider any subject taboo. How do you define poetry?

Komunyakaa: I have said a number of times that there is no subject that is taboo as long as it is human experience. I define poetry as celebration and confrontation.

Entry 10: *Komunyakaa speaks to the* Statesman

In the following interview, conducted by Dhritishankar Sen, and published in the *Statesman* under the title "Readers Should Not Be Told Everything" on February 20, 2005, Komunyakaa provides some insights into his aesthetic.

Dhritishankar Sen: Racial discrimination has been one of the burning issues in your poetry. Do you feel somehow or other that Afro-American writers are largely marginalized?

Yusef Komunyakaa: Racial discrimination is not really the total substance or the direction of my work. That suggests just a minor part of the overall tapestry. However, I do recognize that there is still discrimination, but not only in the United States. A good example would be to look at the caste system here in India.

Politics usually is not on the surface of my poetry. It is inside the poem and depends on what the reader or listener brings to the poem because I demand that they not be told everything. They have to work, and that work has to be informed by a certain kind of passion and necessity.

Sen: What is the current trend in African American poetry?

Komunyakaa: I hope that there is not any particular trend. I do think that the internal quest is important because "service literature" was at one time the only map we could follow, basically, and it had to do with defining blackness and addressing racial issues.

I think within the context of the last thirty to forty years, we have moved closer to the resolution of those problems. Individuals have to recognize the fact that racism itself harms them as much as it does the individual it is aimed at. I think James Baldwin talks about this in *Notes of a Native Son* (1955) and *The Fire Next Time* (1963). He is one of my inspirations.

Sen: The historical past has played a major role in your poetry. How do you manage to coalesce the historic and poetic in your works?

Komunyakaa: History has to be used not simply as mere statement but as poetic imagery. I hope that is the way it functions within my poetry. Otherwise, it is just a statement embedded in a poem.

Sen: You have experimented with jazz and blues in your poetry—

Komunyakaa: I grew up on the blues tradition and that of spiritual and gospel music. I listened to modern jazz for the first time in my early twenties. The process of improvisation fascinated me. I asked myself how could a musician play his or her instrument and compose at the same time with passion.

So it is that surprise, the experience of surprise and its extended possibility—the possibility of everything happening within the same frame. The melody is composed, but the musician improvises. So there is a great deal of control involved, as well as a kind of expanded canvas. So I feel that although I write, I am still a jazz musician (smiles).

Sen: The Vietnam War left a deep impact on your psyche as well as on your poetry. Once again your country is engaged in war. How do you react?

Komunyakaa: It is difficult for me to make political statements. So I go back to poetry. The poem becomes problematic when politics is on the surface. One needs distance and time, but in addition it is useful to look at what happened to the poets in the United States. Most of the poets came out against that war. They demonstrate that the task of the poet is to pose serious questions that can make us more human. The poet is not what he or she knows but what he or she happens to be willing to discover. In making discoveries, the poet can establish a dialogue about war, and the dialogue is important.

Sen: In the coming years where do you see Afro-American writing going?

Komunyakaa: I think collaboration is important. I think more poets will be collaborating with musicians and visual artists. A few people in the United States have been trying to return language, as opposed to melodrama, to theater. So there is going to be a celebration of language, especially in plays. I hope poets will start writing songs, because the lyrics we are receiving are really problematic. Some are misogynistic, some rather profane.

Language must be taken more seriously, for we convey meaning through language.

Sen: Tell us about your next book. Are you planning to write anything about Kolkata?

Komunyakaa: I have already started writing two poems. However, my upcoming book perhaps will focus on love in the time of war; it will be a compilation of short quasi-sonnets. Usually I work on three projects side by side and tend to go back and forth between those. At the moment I have four different books. It is a real serious dance for me this time.

1. Bengali is the national language of Bangladesh and the state language of India's West Bengal.

2. During the past few years, I have been inviting poets, writers, and theater and film personalities from West Bengal, India, to come and spend time with me and my friends in the New York area to collaborate. My idea is to bring the local Bengali community up to date with the current culture of West Bengal and also to promote new works in the Bengali language.

3. I should add that every African American poet and organization I contacted gave me all the assistance I needed. Rita Dove was in constant touch with me. Cave Canem and Third World press helped get contact names and the phone numbers to get copyright permissions on the fast track. Nikki Giovanni and Sonia Sanchez called me to give me copyright permission, and Sanchez gave me Baraka's telephone number so that I could contact him to get his permission. This is how things went throughout the production of the anthology.

4. The line is from Langston Hughes's poem "Freedom."

5. From "Shantiniketan," (www.bengalweb.com/wbtour/wbentou5,htm).

Yusef Komunyakaa

Dan Webster/2006

From *The Spokesman-Review: Online Book Club* (20 April 2006). © 2006. Reprinted with permission of *The Spokesman-Review*. Permission is granted in the interest of public discussion and does not imply endorsement of any product, service, or organization otherwise mentioned herein.

This is how Ivar Nelson, director of the Eastern Washington University Press, describes Yusef Komunyakaa: "(T)he whole American experience is wrapped up in his lifetime."

Born in Bogalusa, Louisiana, the fifty-eight-year-old poet truly has led a varied life.

"He writes about jazz," Nelson says, "he's a black guy from the South, he writes about Vietnam and Vietnam veterans because he was in the war, he writes about the black experience, and now he's a professor at Princeton."

One of the headliners at Get Lit! 2006, Eastern Washington University Press's annual literary arts festival, Komunyakaa is one of two Pulitzer Prize winners scheduled to speak (the other being Marilynne Robinson, author of the novel *Gilead*).

Komunyakaa won his prize for his 1994 collection *Neon Vernacular*. And as Nelson indicates, Komunyakaa's topics comprise this life's experience. His most poignant poems, though, deal with his childhood and the war of his generation: Vietnam.

In a half-hour phone interview, Komunyakaa talked, among other things, about Vietnam and the literature of war, about the use of language to capture the writer's internal terrain and a number of other topics.

Dan Webster: It's a pleasure to talk to you. You and I are contemporaries. We were born in the same year, and I served in Vietnam from October of 1968 to December of 1969. So we have a few things in common, and I wanted you to know that right off.
Yusef Komunyakaa: Yes, thank you.

DW: It's hard to read your poetry collection *Dien Cai Dau*. On a Friday morning, I'm trying to read about you being at the (Vietnam) Memorial, and I can't sit here without my eyes tearing up. I have to tell you, I love the way your poetry is structured, but it's the way it hits in my heart that truly affects me. So, I guess I'd like to start by asking you about the relationship of constructing a poem on the page, the beautiful academic structuring of it, and the emotional effect. Do you see difference there, do you see a disaffect there? What is paramount to you when you sit down to write?

YK: Well, the image is so important to me. Of course, the music of the language is the thing that I listen for. . . . So there's a kind of compression in the psyche. I never planned on writing about Vietnam, for instance. I often find myself doing physical work and I'm writing at the same time. That is what happened when I began working on the poems associated with my experience in Vietnam. I was renovating this house in New Orleans. With the poems that address my childhood, I think I had to write the poems about Vietnam before I could go back in time and write about my observations and experiences in Bogalusa, Louisiana. I do think that we internalize the terrain. I know that this is true with Louisiana, and I'm thinking in terms of experience, there's a kind of internalization that even . . . at least is dealt with in my analysis about Vietnam.

DW: I know a little bit about Vietnam myself, so those poems had a particular effect on me. But the first poem of yours that I read was "Venus's-Flytraps," and I have to tell you I've been through Louisiana but never lived there. I don't know what your childhood was like, and I don't know how autobiographical the poem is. It doesn't really make any difference. That poem flat kicked my ass. I saw that little boy; I felt that little boy's life. And that line at the bottom where his mother says you basically were "my problem." My god! That is the story of every abused child in the history of the world. But it was so beautifully put on the page, as well.

YK: What's interesting about that poem is if I hadn't written "Venus's-Flytraps," I probably wouldn't have written *Magic City*, the collection. That was an image, the Venus Flytrap, an image I took around with me in my psyche, you know. That image was the image that brought me back to all the other experiences.

DW: I certainly know well enough to mix the writer up with the work . . .

YK: That's right, that's right.

DW: Because it's all blend of fiction and memory. But it seems to me that your work is so vital and so representative of life itself and of a life lived in a certain way that you have to have drawn a lot from your experiences, at least your memories of them, your feelings and your reactions to them, to give your work the power that it has.

YK: The speaker in the poem is always willing to discover something. It's not so much what the speaker knows as much as what the speaker, he or she, is willing to discover. This is what I feel.

DW: Do you find yourself really having to delve deeply into parts of yourself that you otherwise might not want to go to, to get there?

YK: I think that's part of the process, but it is not constructed in that way. It just happens. We're facing the page, and one image creates another image, and there's momentum. And this momentum defies logic and defies structure, sometimes. It has a kind of velocity that happens. And then there is the way I write. I write everything down, and then I come back to the poem to revise, to shape it as . . . as art.

DW: Can I ask you specifically about your Vietnam experience?

YK: Yes.

DW: Can you tell me a little more about where you were and who you served with?

YK: I was stationed in Chu Lai. I served with the Americal Division. At that particular time I think it was the largest division, around 24,000–25,000 troops. The first six months I was pretty much out in the field every day, and the last six months I was able to spend a little more time in the rear.

DW: What were the dates of your tour?

YK: I went there in '69 and was there until '70.

DW: So you predated Tim O'Brien (author of *The Things They Carried*) a bit? He was with the Americal, too, wasn't he?

YK: I think so. That's right.

DW: Have you ever met him?

YK: I met him just briefly. I think it was a reading or something of that sort. Maybe it was associated with the William Joiner Center for the Study of War and Social Consequences. I used to do summer workshops there for veterans, and a number of veteran writers have been involved with that workshop. Perhaps that's where I met Tim O'Brien.

DW: Did you talk about the war?

YK: No, not really (laughs).

DW: That's a question I had to ask, but I kind of knew what the answer would be. And I know your work is wide-ranging, but, given my personal experience, I'm really curious about the Vietnam poems. How well do you think that Vietnam has been written about? How honestly, maybe compared to other wars?

YK: Um . . . (pause) I think it's still going. I think it's ongoing. I would hope that it has been written about, especially by veterans, with care and understanding. Sometimes with almost shocking truth of experience. But I think in general, wars as history, as lived, experienced history, there's a constant excavation. And sometimes there's a kind of excavation that happens within the context of the psyche, because there's needful forgetting. At times.

DW: Have you read anything that's come out of the Gulf War or the war that's going on right now?

YK: You know, I really haven't. I've only read news accounts, but I haven't read the literature. I'm waiting to visit that work.

DW: I haven't seen any poetry or fiction. But I have read a fair amount of what passes for journalism or memoir. There's one particularly affecting book titled *The Last True Story I'll Ever Tell* (by John Crawford) that is a pretty amazing book. But here's the funny thing, and maybe you can relate to this, too. I got back in early December of '69, and I remember how—not that we were spit on, though I do remember being treated rudely more than once—our fathers reacted to us. My father was a World War II and Korean War veteran. They had less than full respect for us because we had a war in which we were only there a year and we had Medivac helicopters that came in right away, blah-blah-blah. And I remember thinking how I resented that. And now I find myself listening to people who had a four-day war in the Gulf and who basically do nothing more in Baghdad than police security, and I find myself being resentful. And I have to pull back and say, "Buddy, war is war."

YK: That's right. War is war. Matter of fact, it is really a composite of death and destruction. And very few beautiful moments. And what I mean by that is that if one is able to pull back from the everyday experience of war, just for a moment, just a glimpse of that which hasn't been touched by war stimulates feeling for life and beauty.

DW: I teach a class in beginning journalism, and whenever the kids here ask about war, the first thing I assign them to read is Mark Twain's "War Prayer."

YK: Yes, yes. Isn't that amazing?

DW: It is amazing, and it blows their minds every time.

YK: The fact that he didn't publish it is even more, um, devastating in a way.

DW: Absolutely. And if certain powers had their way, it would never be in print right now.

YK: Right, right.

DW: Because it just too much let's us know that there are real, live human beings on both sides. And there's not necessarily a good or bad there. At least not for the foot soldiers.

YK: That's right.

DW: I really have appreciated the chance to talk to you, and I don't want to take up a lot of your time, but I did want to ask you one last question: How much trouble have you had with people mispronouncing the title *Dien Cai Dau* (deenk-ee-dow). That's how we pronounced it. "You numba 10 G.I. deenk-ee-dow."

YK: That's right. I haven't had much problem with that. Initially, the publisher thought it would be a problem. However, most of the veterans carry that phrase around in their psyche, because they heard it so much.

DW: In fact when I saw the book and I tried to pronounce it, I had to work out the spelling with the phrase as I knew it. No one who speaks Vietnamese has come up to you and told you the proper way?

YK: No, no (laughs).

A Conversation
with Yusef Komunyakaa

Jeffrey Dodd and Jessica Moll/2006

From *Willow Springs* 59 (Spring 2007). Interview conducted April 21, 2006 and reprinted by permission of Jeffrey G. Dodd, Jessica Moll, and *Willow Springs*.

Contributing to a roundtable discussion celebrating *The American Poetry Review*'s twenty-fifth anniversary, Yusef Komunyakaa described a vision of American poetry: "Ezra Pound beside Amiri Baraka and H.D. flanking Toi Derricotte, Joy Harjo back-to-back with Frank O'Hara and Garrett Hongo alongside William Carlos Williams or Wallace Stevens—a continuum of impulses and possibilities that creates a map . . ." While modesty might prevent Komunyakaa from placing himself in this vision, abreast Mina Loy, say, or Theodore Roethke, the fact remains that his is one of the most intriguing voices in contemporary American letters.

The "impulses and possibilities" of Komunyakaa's poetry depend upon precise imagery that points toward an essential experience, while reminding us that this experience must be grounded in external context. In his recent poem "Tree Ghost," the speaker moves swiftly from a discovery of "three untouched mice dead / along the afternoon footpath" to an embrace of connection: "I can almost feel / how the owl's beauty scared the mice / to death, how the shadow of her wings / was a god passing over the grass." How many gods shadow us daily, scaring us nearly to death with their beauty?

The provocation of such questions is a major strength of Komunyakaa's work, achieved through mastery of image, rhythm, and diction marshaled on behalf of a conviction that "poetry in our complex society connects us to lyrical tension that has everything to do with discovery and the act of becoming." Poetry is not mere experimentation. That view, he says, "is a kind of selling out—to remain in that landscape of the abstract, when there's so much happening around us. Not that the politics of observation should be on the surface of the poem. But we want human voices that are believable."

178

Komunyakaa has achieved this humanity in more than a dozen collections of poetry, of which *Taboo: The Wishbone Trilogy, Part One* is the most recent. He has been honored as a Chancellor of the Academy of American Poets, and has won the Kingsley Tufts Poetry Award and the Pulitzer Prize for Poetry. He recently joined the faculty at New York University, taking the position vacated by Galway Kinnell. After giving a public reading for GetLit!, the annual literary festival sponsored by Eastern Washington University Press, Komunyakaa met with us at the Palm Court Grill in Spokane.

Jessica Moll: The slightly elongated lines in a poem you read from last night, "Requiem," allow for a flooding sensation that you can hear when the poem is read aloud. What might tip you off to a formal necessity?

Yusef Komunyakaa: For "Requiem," I think the subject matter dictated the poem's structure. I had been asked to consider writing a poem about Hurricane Katrina, and after thinking about it for a while, I said yes to the editor of *Oxford American*. I said to myself, Well, I'll write the first part for the magazine and then continue, because now I see this as a book-length poem. I knew I wanted "Requiem" to have long and short lines. I wanted movement on the page, because that happens with water, that happens with chaos. And also I remembered Richard Hugo saying that the poem needs a combination of long and short lines. Years ago when I was wrestling with this concept, it took me some time to understand what Hugo meant. But he'd also mentioned that he loved swing music, that he was influenced by swing. Long and short lines—swing music—it now made sense to me. He was talking about a kind of modulation that takes place, a movement that happens in music and language. I knew that "Requiem" was a long poem, its changes and ebbs held together by ellipses. So it's one sentence, basically, with a one-word refrain. And that one word is "already."

Jeffrey Dodd: Does the role of the refrain in your work—in a poem like "The Same Beat," for example—find its roots in the musical tradition and diction and speech patterns of where you grew up, or in a broader Western poetic tradition?

Komunyakaa: I think it is associated with storytelling. How I began hearing stories. Having grown up in rural Louisiana, I remember people telling lengthy stories, and such verbal escapades were mainly paced through repetition. One can view the refrain as a call seeking a response. But also, I use the refrain, sometimes, as part of the process in composing the poem. And then I may extract the refrain from the poem. So, in this sense, one could say that the finished poem has been driven by a false engine. Unless a refrain functions as an integral part of a poem, as an element of its natural pace and breath, it can be viewed as merely a formal gesture, as an unnecessary stroke on the emotional canvas. Of course, I'm also thinking of music. After being asked to consider reading on HBO's *Def Poetry Jam*, I wrote "The Same Beat," and it began with this: "I don't want the same beat." There's an insistence tangled in this voice, and I think it gave me permission to pursue the poem.

Moll: So the refrain was just a way to get you into the subject matter of the poem?

Komunyakaa: Yes. And, in that sense, that's what I mean by a false engine. However, it doesn't falsify. It helps us to get to a basic truth.

Moll: I suppose there are refrains in visual art, too.

Komunyakaa: That's right. Colors don't remain static on the canvas. There's movement. The images and the hues force the eye into the rhythm of reason. Colors create a dialogue. It depends on how we're willing to dance with a painting. How many places we're willing to stand and view it. I love visual art. Often I daydream about it, not necessarily about putting paint on canvas, but maybe about creating sculpture.

Dodd: In earlier interviews, you've mentioned Romare Bearden and Giacometti and a whole list of artists who push against representational images. How does that anti-representational move work in your poetry, when your images seem uniquely representational—so striking, so precise. Is there a complementary understanding between your view of visual art and written images?

Komunyakaa: I think where the abstraction exists is actually in that space between images. And that space helps to create tension in a work of art. In writing or music this space often equals silence. I suppose, what we're really talking about here is a way of thinking and seeing, a way of dreaming and embracing possibility. For instance, in thinking about Picasso, it is important to note that he started out as a representational artist. Probably because his father was a representational artist, who stopped painting after seeing early paintings by his son. Then, of course, as we know, Picasso's work takes on an abstracted dimension clearly influenced by West African sculpture. It's what we now call cubism. There's that story about Picasso and Apollinaire stealing a few small African statues from the Louvre. Supposedly, Apollinaire was arrested, but he refused to incriminate Picasso. The poet takes all the blame. That says something about Picasso, I suppose.

Moll: I'm curious about your interest in Bearden—does the idea of finding things in the world and placing them side by side to create art come into play in your writing?

Komunyakaa: Bearden studied mathematics when he attended NYU. When he uses collage technique, it seems mathematical. So many beginning paint-ers have attempted imitating Bearden, and it doesn't work. But if you look at his more impressionistic paintings, especially the ones painted in France—if you look at those paintings beside his collages, they're very different. And yet, they possess an aspect of the collage, and I think that has something to do with movement. How colors are juxtaposed against each other. He's one of my favorite American painters. Along with many others, such as Norman Lewis, an African American painting around the time of Jackson Pollock. He's rather political as well. There's a photograph of him with some other artists, protesting the lack of work by black artists exhibited at the Metro-politan Museum of Art. To get back to the heart of your question, I have to say this: I like how ideas and images fit into a single frame of reference to create tension, how things can be taken from the natural world and placed in the world of the imagination.

Moll: Listening to you read "The Same Beat" last night, some of the lines that stood out referred to people in the music industry "selling out." There was the line about a guy with a mouth full of gold—

Komunyakaa: The one already bought and sold.

Moll: Do writers confront that phenomenon at all?

Komunyakaa: Writers do confront that phenomenon. I've written about the erasure that takes place in some contemporary poetry through over-experimentation. That's a kind of selling out—to remain in that landscape of the abstract, when there's so much happening to us and around us. Not that the politics of observation should be on the surface of the poem. But we want human voices that are believable, and that's why Walt Whitman is so interesting to me. Whitman addresses everything, and is clearly influ-enced by Italian opera, so everything reaches for a crescendo—but he didn't dodge anything. He really confronts the essence of being an American. Even though there's fetishism, or, I should say, there are certain characters on his poetic canvas that become eroticized. I do think that contemporary poetry confronts a lot. If you think about the importance of someone like Gins-berg, and "Howl"—if "Howl" hadn't appeared, in 1958, I hate to think where American poetry would now be. There were some brave souls to come along and confront the Fugitives.

Dodd: Ransom and Tate?

Komunyakaa: Ransom and Tate. Was it Tate, who, at Vanderbilt, cam-paigned against Langston Hughes and his poetry? I think so. Look, we have come so far, in a way, within the last thirty or forty years. There's Tate plead-ing to academia, "Don't recognize Hughes."

These were the Agrarians, the Southern Agrarians, but this wasn't the only camp of poetic expression that was stuck in the mud in America.

Dodd: Do you think the Fugitives got "stuck in the mud" because they confused politics for art, or confused the function of politics in art? It seems they made so many statements trying to maintain their southern regionalism in the midst of the Depression, trying to make these economic arguments for which they weren't trained at all.

Komunyakaa: And also, they weren't farmers either. They were removed from the realities of farm life. But they were presenting themselves as the voice of the agrarians, though they didn't understand the machinery of economics. They did, however, understand the politics of culture and race in America, as well as the divide and conquer stratagem. The Fugitives had to know that language is political.

Dodd: They seemed to underestimate the power of capitalism, even during the Depression, when nobody had anything. They seemed to misunderstand how powerful the popular response to capitalism would be.

Komunyakaa: They didn't want to deal with a critique of the social realities of the time. And Hughes's work attempted to criticize the hierarchies of power. The Agrarians didn't want to face themselves in the mirror, basically, because they were a part of the structure that had systematically benefited from privilege. So it's interesting that we would have poets who refused to give voice to an individual because of the color of his skin, and also because of his politics, his audacity to confront the beast that hurled hardship onto the backs of his brothers and sisters.

Dodd: It seems that Robert Penn Warren was the only one who even made an effort to re-evaluate his position in that social reality, moving into the 1950s and 1960s.

Komunyakaa: Robert Penn Warren was different. I was probably nineteen or twenty when I first read *Promises*. Penn Warren seems to have had an ongoing dialogue with Ralph Ellison, and I don't know if the bulk of that has been published or recorded.

Dodd: There were a couple of interviews, one in which Ellison interviewed Warren for *The Paris Review*, and one in which Warren interviewed Ellison for Warren's 1965 book, *Who Speaks for the Negro?* But they're ambivalent interactions, as though Ellison doesn't quite trust that Warren isn't simply an unreconstructed southerner, a suspicion that he's making these efforts to rehabilitate his reputation. And it seems as though there's no way to prove the sincerity of his re-evaluation of his early views. He spent his whole life writing against his segregationist essay, "The Briar Patch."

Komunyakaa: How did he even enter that dialogue—because he's younger than Tate and Ransom. And, of course, after being beckoned to the Fugitives, he tried to distance himself from that movement and its agenda. But he'd already been implicated. He couldn't outrun "Here we take our stand," that line from "Dixie." I would've loved overhearing those discussions between Warren and Ellison.

Dodd: Last night you talked about how you see silence as part of the emotional music of Samuel Beckett's work. Does the silence in music and drama work the same way in poetry?

Komunyakaa: Maybe it works slightly differently in poetry, because the silence begs for an abbreviated meditation to take place. And I don't know if that happens, especially, in music. It definitely occurs in drama, where silence is an intricate part of the narrative. In that sense, silence is dramatic. In poetry, since the reader is sitting there with the page, and even in a reading by the poet it can take place—a silence—because of stanza breaks. So, I view silence in the poem as a moment of meditation. I think someone said that there should be space enough to fit one's heart into. That resonates with me.

Dodd: Enough space for the reader to become fully invested in the action on the page?

Komunyakaa: Poetry is an action. It relies on the image, on the music in each line. Perhaps that's why the reader usually refuses to embrace statement in poetry as readily as in prose. There's an active investment, and that's why a poem can have multiple meanings. The meaning is shaped by what an individual brings to the poem. A poem isn't an ad for an emotion.

Moll: When you're composing, and you decide how to put the words on the page visually, do you hear the silence as much as you hear the music of the words?

Komunyakaa: I hear the silence because I read everything aloud as I compose the poem. The ear is a great editor. I hear the silence in the music of language. Not exaggerated, but as a part of the natural continuity of process.

Dodd: Who was the first poet you learned that from, to hear the music as well as the silence?

Komunyakaa: I suppose when I first began to think about it, I was reading Emily Dickinson. There's so much silence in her work. But I don't believe it is a silence that erases content. In fact, in her poetry, it seems to inform content. I was interested in what wasn't being said as much as in what was being said. Her poetry always makes my mind very active, as if I'm attempting to seek a dialogue with the unknown or the unknowable. This is entirely different from Whitman, although as a poet I embrace Whitman more, with his long lines. And again, the length of the lines, the long lines, seems to beg meditation as opposed to the vertical trajectory of short lines. For the most part, I embrace the short line, and maybe that has something to do with contemporary time, the way everything seems sped up. There's a kind of vertical plunge of the poem.

Moll: How does writing plays, with its importance on setting up a dramatic scene and moving the narrative forward, inform your poetry? Are you learning new things from working in another genre?

Komunyakaa: Not really. I think maybe I'm bringing something from poetry over to drama. I realized that poetry could be an ally in my first play, *Gilgamesh*, which is an adaptation I wrote for the stage. It is primarily a verse play, with limited moments of silence. Of course, it would depend on the director, whether he or she wishes to introduce certain silences. In the play I'm working on now, called *The Deacons*, there are numerous places for silence—matter of fact, I express it there in the notes: "Pause" or "Silence." Each piece, whether poem or play, is propelled by its own language and music because the speakers are different in their unique physical and emotional landscapes.

Dodd: How does the process of collaboration enliven a project, open new doors, or ask you to look at your work in new ways?

Komunyakaa: I welcome the perspective, the energy. In that way, it's almost like an ensemble. We begin, and from the outset, we are trying to visualize where the process is going to take us. But it's always most interesting to see what happens in between, in that space where surprises occur. I trust my collaborators. Otherwise I wouldn't do it. I'm hoping that these kinds of collaborations are going to happen again and again, that poets are going to start writing for the theater, where language is going to again inform plot because the stage seems to have been adversely influenced by television and the movie industry.

Moll: By focusing on plot at the expense of the work?

Komunyakaa: And usually it's a sped-up plot: one collision after another, one mindless chase after another, one bloody scene after another.

Moll: Every time you come out with a book or project, it feels as if you've found something new. How do you keep challenging yourself?

Komunyakaa: Maybe it has to do with growing up in a small town, Bogalusa, Louisiana, where there was always an embracing of something, and in that same moment a moving away. Whatever it was—dealing with it, going through it, attempting to move past it, and then realizing that everything's connected. We humans possess this great capacity. The human brain is amazing. But it is also gluttonous. That is, it seems willing to almost embrace anything and everything. Perhaps that has a lot to do with how we have evolved and survived as a species.

Moll: That's a pretty optimistic view. A lot of people talk about the narrowing of the human mind, with TV and media.

Komunyakaa: The problem with turning on the TV is that one has too many simplified choices. A glut of ball games, comedy shows, soap operas, whatever distraction is on at the moment. The typical American city is a universe of cultivated distractions. But at the same time, there are probably a couple poetry readings in session in the vicinity. Also, maybe a few individuals are trying to write that first line of poetry, or that refrain as a false engine. And not only in America, though I do think the United States is a healthy place for poetry and other artistic pursuits.

Dodd: Has it gotten better? In your interview with Vince Gotera back in 1990, you said that the U.S. is a healthy place for poetry, but at the same time—

Komunyakaa: There is a similarity. But also there are some unique voices that pop out. However, I was thinking this morning about the phrase, "between then and now," and I wanted to place certain poets beneath that phrase. Certain voices. Tonally, each of these voices seems to exist in his or her own world, and yet there's a shared personality. They're later than the Modernists. There were a number of names floating around in my head. This thought came to me early this morning. I was thinking of W. S. Merwin, Gwendolyn Brooks, Robert Hayden, Adrienne Rich, Galway Kinnell, James Wright, Alan Dugan, Robert Bly, Allen Ginsberg, Robert Creeley, Etheridge Knight, and Donald Hall. These voices. I think this body of work forms a collective voice that's uniquely North American.

Dodd: You've written several articles about Hayden and Etheridge Knight. I don't think Knight's poetry is celebrated as much as it ought to be, and I don't know if it's the politics of his personal life or what's there on the page.

Komunyakaa: For young poets who aren't acquainted with Etheridge's poetry, it is always an engaging surprise for them. He speaks directly to their concerns, without any embellishment or facades. It's also interesting to think about some of the abovementioned poets who directly embraced Etheridge in friendship, such as Brooks, Bly, Kinnell, and Wright.

Dodd: All of whom were doing interesting things on their own.

Komunyakaa: Right. So they felt safe, I think, embracing this man, this poet whose work was different, his personal life entirely different from theirs.

They seem not to have been threatened by him. In that sense, this reflects the spirit of the Civil Rights movement, because that movement was truly an American experience accelerated mainly by blacks and whites. Of course, many from different minority groups, especially ones who arrived after those turbulent years, have benefited directly and indirectly from the movement. For many, this is a bone of contention. We only have to look at those thousands of photographs as a reminder of recent history. Just think about those eighteen- and nineteen-year-olds boarding those buses in the Midwest, heading for the Deep South on a freedom ride.

When I was teaching at Indiana University, I used to ask students to look at the photographs of those nineteen-year-olds going south. I said, "Where do you place yourself in this equation? Can you visualize yourself doing this?" Many couldn't, you know, coming from very safe situations. They couldn't see themselves stepping forward to help implement change in America. And that sense of change influenced the rest of the world, really. In Australia, I was talking with some aboriginal writers about a decade ago, and they said, "Yes, the Civil Rights movement in the 1960s and 1970s influenced the idea of change in Australia." This is true throughout the world.

And at the same time, especially during the 1980s and 1990s, there was a concerted effort to undermine what happened during the movement. That should be analyzed, our need to turn back the clock to the so-called good old days. Do we need to hold a national séance to raise the dead in order to know the meaning of the good old days? I know I don't.

But many helped to prompt some change, and we as Americans should embrace that recent moment in our history instead of agonizing about it. Because I hate to think about our situation here if the Civil Rights movement had not happened. Indeed, many of those post-Modernist poets were in the bloody mire and sway of the movement.

I remember assigning students to write about the photographs depicting those nineteen-year-olds getting on those buses, you know. Some of those protesters are still in our towns and cities. The Civil Rights monument in Birmingham is dedicated to their heroic efforts. But I think our poetry is also robust enough to embrace that moment in our history.

Dodd: Since we began by asking you about "Requiem," how do you envision New Orleans ten years from now?

Komunyakaa: I hate to think of that tragedy being parlayed into a real estate project, but given that it's in the United States, most likely the Ninth Ward is going to become a boom area for developers. However, we have to keep the horror of Katrina in our conscience, in our psyche, and we have to make decisions based on that awareness. For years, whenever I went back to New Orleans, I thought, "I'm going to move back here. I'm going to have an apartment here." That's the furthest thing from my mind at this moment, because I don't want to participate in that evil at all.

Also, let's face it, New Orleans is really a composite of cultures. Of course, that is its uniqueness. The Crescent City was where suburbanites would venture to escape from themselves and do things they wouldn't do in their own neighborhoods and hometowns. New Orleans was Saturnalia, a place of ancient rituals of harvest and feast. It was one of those places where people probably scared themselves: "My gosh, I'm alive." We can't stretch a suburban attitude like gauze over the Big Easy and expect to have the same place. Why did this happen to our most African-influenced city, our Double Scorpio?

Every Tool Became a Weapon: Talking with Yusef Komunyakaa about Race and War

Tod Marshall/2006

From *Poetry Foundation Online Journal* (21 April 2006). Reprinted by permission of the Poetry Foundation.

Tod Marshall: You're working on a series of "quasi-sonnets" called "Love in the Time of War." The title implies that the poems might directly connect to our country's present conflict.

Yusef Komunyakaa: "Love in the Time of War" is the first section of my forthcoming book, *Warhorses*. The first poem in this sequence is about weaponry, and the first phrase in it is "The jawbone of an ass," echoing the biblical history of human warfare. And, yes, our involvement in Iraq is central; that was perhaps what initially triggered the need to write *Warhorses*, but I think this collection addresses multiple dimensions of the history of war.

TM: By beginning with "the jawbone of an ass," are you implying that the capacity for violence is a fundamental aspect of what it is to be human, that we are tool-making and weapon-making animals?

YK: I believe that, especially when considering the evolution of the species, almost every tool became a weapon. In that sense, our capacity for violence is perhaps biological or chemical. I believe that the torture chambers in Europe advanced the continent's acute attention to mechanical devices. Not merely the rack and drawing and quartering, but other acts of imagined violence. But we humans are also blessed with a mechanism for disarming an aspect of that hair-trigger, instinctual violence. We do possess the powers of reasoning and reflection, and we're also creatures capable of negotiation and diplomacy.

TM: Do you think that poets have a keener responsibility during times of war to speak against violence?

YK: I feel that the artist or poet—more than the politician or professional soldier—is condemned to connect to what he or she observes and experiences. One thinks about Walt Whitman's visceral Civil War poems; of Siegfried Sassoon and Georg Trakl and Wilfred Owen responding to the horrors of World War I; of Anna Akhmatova's "Requiem" and Osip Mandelstam's "The Stalin Epigram" giving voice to an outcry against the repression in the Soviet Union; of Aleksander Wat and Wislawa Szymborska and Zbigniew Herbert calling out from Eastern Europe; of Yehuda Amichai and Mahmoud Darwish in the Middle East; of Federico García Lorca and Miguel Hernandez challenging the silence during the Spanish Civil War; of Max Jacob and Bertolt Brecht and Alan Dugan attempting to depict the ugliness of World War II; and the long list goes on and on. Plato was aware of the poet's obligation as witness. If one is totally connected to his or her feelings, then one sees and hears and witnesses—fully engaged—and one will have to address what one has seen and heard and dreamt. We address the internal and external, and perhaps speaking of both terrains can almost make us whole.

TM: The impulse to address internal and external forces is certainly an important part of your poem "Requiem," which is addressed to the victims and survivors of Katrina. It explores the devastation of a place that was home for you, but also articulates emotions about the aftermath of that destruction.

YK: "Requiem" is written to acknowledge those individuals who died and those who lived through Hurricane Katrina. Victims and survivors. Also, I wanted to recall the history of the Crescent City, the cultural and social histories, to underline the watery fire that has been pulsing underneath the place since the Spanish and French arrived, and even before, when Native Americans inhabited this swampy landscape. History helps us to understand what happened during Katrina; it helps us to decipher the psychological lethargy there in the Big Easy. I think "Requiem" speaks for itself. Here is the poem's beginning:

[Text of poem follows.]

In New Orleans, in the Deep South in the 1960s and 1970s, there was great consternation surrounding the civil rights movement. Members of the White Citizens' Council were reactionary and violent. This is recent history, and the evidence is at our fingertips. The Katrina situation underlined a problem that we Americans attempt to deny or erase with silence. We talk about race and Du Bois's infamous color line, but seldom do we discuss problems of class in America. I always felt that at least blacks and whites in the South live in close proximity to each other. I think of James Baldwin saying that "in the South, the Black man is always the topic of discussion, but in the North, never. Exaggerated in one sense, and denied in the other sense." This dichotomy has facilitated an unhealthy suspicion between the various ethnic groups—especially blacks and whites, because they seem more culturally and socially connected through the history.

Certain blacks and whites during the 1960s and 1970s went into the streets and forced change here in the United States. We must accept this: numerous oppressive laws wouldn't have changed in this country if some progressive-thinking people hadn't put their lives on the line in the name of freedom and change. That's recent history. I do know, however, that positive changes have happened within the last thirty or forty years in this country—really, in the world. Consequently, it seems as if the soul of America has been given a second chance. The civil rights movement was the beginning of change—surface changes through the changes of existing laws and ordinances.

For each protester during the civil rights movement, there were hundreds—thousands—resisting change, still embracing the status quo. Thus, until our country's psyche, until its heart, has been really changed, we'll always have slow, clumsy responses to disasters that involve so-called minorities—descendants of slaves. Even with civil right laws in place, there are individuals and institutions that violate those laws daily. And I'm not merely talking about the extreme, about some rednecks dragging a black man behind a pickup truck in Jasper, Texas.

TM: You said that "Requiem" was a work in progress. What other issues will the poem explore?

YK: I wish I knew. I hope that "Requiem" embraces a multiplicity of moments in the overall history of New Orleans. For instance, it is important for me to address the social realities of the Native American in that region. Let's face it: It's embarrassing to walk upon the soil and not realize that this is stolen property. I'm always interested in what the poem can risk discovering. The writing helps me to get to what I need to say. Perhaps I still write to surprise myself. At least, I hope so.

TM: Can you discuss your vision of the audience for poetry? To whom do you hope to speak?

YK: I would hope my audience includes anyone who cares about language and humanity. If I thought about demographics when writing a poem or play, I wouldn't write anything. If the imagery and music of a poem surprise me, it has my attention, and that's all it takes to speak to others. No topic is taboo, as long as a system of aesthetics informs the poem or play. Anything that triggers a meaningful dialogue. The ideal reader responds to the poem, whereby an internal dialogue exists in the reader. That is, at least, how I like to read poetry. When I get to the ending of a poem that truly moves me, I'm automatically propelled back to its beginning. I like to read poems again and again, because I view each successful poem as something more than an ad for a momentary emotion. Discovery is important to me.

TM: What's the first poem that led to such a moment of discovery for you?

YK: Robert Hayden's "The Whipping" is a poem that forced me to discover how love and self-hatred can couple to form brutality. I felt that the grandmother in that short poem is striking herself each time she strikes the boy, as she struggles not to kneel beneath the weight of a heart attack. She's also striking at the boy's mother, at some unsayable curse or sin. That poem pointed me to Hayden's "Those Winter Sundays." I admire how this poem is stripped down, how it presents such austerity, and at the same time how it engaged me, beckoned to me. At first, I didn't know what it was that drew me to "Those Winter Sundays," but finally I realized that the immense silence beckoned me again and again to the poem. It was a moment of beautiful insinuation. What wasn't said underlined everything, and that realization taught me a lot about writing, how silence is always an integral part of music.

TM: In response to a discussion of rap music, you said that "Pain is the last possession that a person has." Those poems that you mention by Hayden are both emotionally powerful, and yet your phrase suggests to me that it's important to keep that emotion from becoming co-opted, especially through the commoditization of rap music.

YK: Yes. I think so. Pain is often a place that centers us and connects us to a larger world. When I said that, I was responding to the fact that for many contemporary—I won't say artists—entertainers, pain becomes a commodity. I don't have to give names and dates, because most of us know that rap and hip-hop dominate the streets of certain communities. I can't say that there's been a conspiracy against the inroads that the civil rights movement spearheaded, that entertainment has been used as a psychological weapon against black Americans, but it is troublesome to realize that numerous buyers of rap and hip-hop are young white males.

Most of us are aware how stereotypes were used to create and maintain a system of racism in this country. Also, internationally, black Americans possessed an immense moral currency during the heyday of the civil rights movement. Much of that moral presence has been undermined. I do see much of rap and hip-hop as troubling in other aspects as well, such as the misogyny, the abusive language. I think that there are phrases that dehumanize the individual who expresses them and the individual who hears them—not just the N-word.

Index

www.ingramcontent.com/pod-product-compliance
Lightning Source LLC
Chambersburg PA
CBHW020655030726
47498CB00002B/515